MIDNIGHT DONKEY

Paul McCloskey

Superfluous nod of thanks

I would just like to say a tremendously huge thank you to The Big Bang for creating this crazy existence. Otherwise, none of this would have happened.

About Midnight Donkey

Three unlikely housemates take a late summer trip to the wonderous Greek islands; intent on ferry hopping their way around as many places as they can in sixteen days; while engaging in as much fun and relaxation as time and fate will allow. But like the decision to go itself, things don't quite go to plan when they get there. For one thing, one of them has a drink problem and can't manage his money, or his mood swings. Another is on his first proper holiday in over twenty years; new to Greece and health concious. And the third can't stop goading the first about his many failings, whenever the opportunity arises.

Yet somehow, the intrepid trio make it through airport security with only the confiscation of a corkscrew and knife. Survive the inevitable first and last night emotional breakdowns, without throwing a punch. Suffer, the early loss of an all important debit card, several items of overpriced clothing and accessories; the lure of Blackpool upon Greece, a malicious mosquito attack, drunken excess, a night on a remote beach stalked by a wild beast of uncertain origin; an overly superstitious taxi driver, two attempted drownings, one man's sanity, sex in public; a Greek wedding reception, an American temptress, and, the beautiful allure of a siren called Greece.

Throughout, the whole delicate balance of the journey is thrown into jeopardy, by one of the party constantly losing his marbles and getting lost; especially within the narrow winding paths of Lindos. Forcing the other two into the imagined establishment of a late night homing taxi service - the ever so slightly fabled Midnight Donkey.

Reviews

"Laugh? I almost fell off the donkey!" **Matt Cross**

"Couldn't possibly have happened, nobody's that stupid." **Charles Chrichton**

"Pack my bags and book my ticket, I'm on my way." **An impressed reader**

"She'll be coming round the winding path when she comes."
Old Donkey Tenders Song (Trad.)

"The worst travel book I have ever read; a mite engaging but trite none the less. Why is it called Midnight Donkey? Morning Ass would be more appropriate."
Critic of great standing.

"One of them should be dead, another in a sanitorium." **Graham Hill**

"Hilarious; too funny. Laugh out loud; side splitting; humour beyond humour."
Anon. 1

"Poignant; carefully observed; touching; heartfelt." **Anon. 2**

"Existential critique of the Greek myths." **Anon. 3**

"A donkey! My bedroom for a donkey!" **Mark Anderson.**

Slight Word of Apology

To those who may think that they recognize themselves in the following events and are easily offended by my description of both; sorry.

Midnight Donkey

Contents

Well, here goes...

You Got the Notion...

The idea of going on a two week holiday in September had taken root back in April of that particular year, when I determined to go on a proper summer vacation for once in my errant life. The plan at that stage was to go alone to Spain, to some unknown place, a notch or two above the dubious delights of a Costa Blackpool. To an imagined resort, where the warm character of the surrounds and the people welcomed and relaxed you, yet the night life was fast and exciting. A destination above all, one fervently hoped, with available women; friendly and like minded in their pursuit of sexual fun.

As things unfolded I found all that I was looking for and more. Not in Spain as envisaged but by fateful circumstance in the ancient and mythical lands of Greece. A country that has held sway over me since. Herein lies an Homeric tale worth relating. Though I cannot promise it will last the test of time. Your's included.

Like Minded Souls...

Greece reared its beautiful head in conversation with my flat mate Roger, who had already spent two weeks there in June with his Dad. I told Roger after he had just got back, that I was going to take a Mediterranean holiday in September myself when it would be cheaper, less crowded, less hot and my current building job would be finished.

'Where?' He asked.

'Spain.'

'Have you been there before?'

'Only to Barcelona, which was great.'

'In September?'

'Yes.'

'Are you going alone or can I come as well?' He queried.

His question threw me slightly for being a confirmed bachelor I normally like going on my own when traveling as it's usually less hassle more personal and you can do things without argument or delay. Easier all round really. But I thought why not? Roger was single and liked women, great. He also liked to have a really good time, great. At times he drank like a fish and smoked like a trooper, maybe not so great, but that was his business and besides so did I at one distant time so who was I to judge? Anyway he was good company and two might make for more fun; and that was priority one this time around not the cultural sightseeing.

'Yes, if you want. More the merrier.'

'Are you set on Spain?'

'No, but I'd like to go there.'

'Why?'

'I've always fancied going to one of the resorts there.' Was the honest reply.

Roger tried to pin me down on exactly where in Spain, but I'm a sort of winds-of-fortune idiot who wants a bit of serendipity to come into play; which it had just done. I left it vague.

'Somewhere in the Costa Del Sol. Leave it to the last moment.

Roger seemed fine with that, but intrigued I asked him about Greece.

'It's different, I prefer it to Spain.'

'You've been to Spain?'

'A few times. Marbella, Ibiza, places like that.'

'Greece is better?'

'I think so, it's more interesting.'

'Is it expensive?'

'No, it can be cheap, depends.'

For all of Roger's promotion of Greece it didn't sound likely then, it was just a thought. I had a preference for the well advertised delights of Spain and that's where I thought I was headed, or rather we. In the event nothing was decided destination wise, until two weeks previous to our leaving. All we knew up to then, was that we were going on "Hol's" in September. Oh, and that two had become three. Serendipity for you.

The Somewhat Good...

Roger was seventeen years younger than myself but I got on well with him since we met in March, at the flat where we lived. He held down a high powered financial job at Canary Wharf, risking millions in the pursuit of vast company profits and now he wanted to go on holiday with me, a forty something going on twenty one. Is there anything worse? But then again he had just gone on holiday with his Dad, perhaps he wanted to repeat the experience.

You could say I have described Roger as a bit jack-the-lad, though he would prefer alpha male, of which both are true to an extent, but this is also a man who can whiz through a Times cryptic crossword with no bother and take refuge in a book or two, or three. Inject savvy cutting wit into most situations and sometimes come across as the most arrogant son of a bitch, you ever had the misfortune to meet. It's just a natural fault of his though and God knows we all have those, though in his case I think its just an over abundance of confidence. In my book Roger is a great bloke, he just takes a little getting use to at first, for those who don't know him.

So who am I to talk so freely of others? Well I'm no more or less than any other regular person. Honest at the very least, generally perceptive; try to be nobody's fool; impatient at worse. That's all I'm saying because in the course of relaying this tale, you the reader, will glean everything about me and draw your own conclusions. Just don't be too hard on me, I'm really not that bad. Talking of which.

The Rather Bad...

The third person entering into this trip of a lifetime, if I can call it that, was our then landlord and my long standing pal of twenty odd years, Mark. The title and much of this sorry tale is attributed to him, for reasons I will relate. Mark is a former near successful actor, who has been on the slippery slope for some time now; willfully committing slow suicide with a drink called cider. A large can of it is what starts his day and as many pints as he can afford is what ends it. This would all be very well if he had a job and paid his bills, particularly the mortgage; but his sense of responsibility and setting aside for the priorities, the electricity and gas for prime example, have long diminished and he is fast running out of options for his well being. "Dead man walking." Roger calls him and I sadly confer, because no matter the amount of talking good sense to him, it has absolutely no effect. He psychopathically refuses to do something about his sorry life before it's too late.

For reasons of friendship I have felt somewhat responsible for him, especially in light of the fact that his drunken misdemeanours have lost him the sympathy and liking of many former friends, associates and lovers; a wife included sadly. Some people actively disliked him, finding it hard to understand his woeful descent or unable to forgive his transgressions. Truth is, witnessing a once gregarious, intelligent, funny, life-of-the-party man, descend into obstructive behaviour and willful patheticism, is no fun let me tell you, it can get quite wearing in fact.

The determined fool needed a miracle or barring that a holiday abroad, far from the stuck-in-the-mud life he'd been leading. Perhaps that would jolt him into changing course. As naive a notion as that was, maybe that's just what he was thinking too, while the three of us were basking in the sun on the back patio one hot July day. The subject of our planned yet unplanned holiday came up and from way out of the blue, Mark expressed an interest in coming along.

'Nobody has asked me yet if I want to go.' He blurted.

Slightly taken aback by his sense of exclusion I answered,

'Fine, if you can make it, come with us.'

But for obvious reasons I didn't take it seriously. Where for one thing was he going to get the money from? He certainly couldn't save for it, the rent money evaporated in his hands.

'You do know it costs money.' Said Roger.

'How much money?'

'Couple of grand.' I said.

'Much more than you've got.' Stated Roger remorsefully.

'How do you know?' Replied Mark with some bravado.

'It's obvious isn't it?'

'There's the rent money.'

'The rent money?'

'It could.'

'Could it fuck, be serious.'

'Why couldn't it? If I started saving now I-'

'You've already got an advance on next month's rent.'

'So?'

'And there's two weeks of July left.' I interjected.

'So?'

'Did you do maths at school?' Asked Roger.

'Yes.'

'Were you any good at them?'

'Yes, very.'

'So how come you're always in debt?'

'I don't know.'

'How's this as a simple sum, you spend more than you get.'

'Sometimes.'

'Sometimes? No, all of the time. That's why you scrounge.'

'For what?

'For rent money.'

'When?'

'Most mornings, when I have to go to work.'

'I don't.'

'What do you call that skulking around in the kitchen then?'

'I can't help it if I happen to be up.'

'Don't make me laugh. Face it, you can't afford it.'

'I can.'

Roger began to laugh. Irritated, Mark began to physically twitch. Time to step in I thought, before it all got silly.

'Roger's right mate, the rent won't do it. Besides, that should be paying the mortgage.'

His stone face nodded acceptance of the undeniable.

'You'll need to get a job to pay for a thing like this.'

Internally he was recoiling in horror at the suggestion. I was after all talking about mixing oil and water. It was clear he badly needed a break from his nowhere existence though. I empathized and reiterated he would be welcome if he could manage it, knowing full well he couldn't in his current parlous condition. Yet, in the back of my mind I prepared for the possibility. What if he really did come? How would that work out? Imagine it, a dysfunctional alcoholic on tour, loathe to bad mood swings and impetuous behaviour. And that's just for starters.

How for instance would he look after any money? Given his habitual careless spending, anything he had would all be gone in a few days and Roger and I would be left carrying his sorry self for the rest of the journey. What a thought; no, what a potential bloody nightmare.

On the other side of the coin if he didn't come how could we deal with the jealousy and resentment that was evidently underway? Being a friend and possibly the only one that gave a damn about him in the last two years I'd be left feeling if not guilty then certainly sorry for him, and that wasn't part of the master plan. I wanted a care free holiday with no strings attached, and to return refueled and refreshed from all the hard work I had been doing over the last few months. Better he was encouraged I concluded, so he wouldn't feel that badly when the reality hit home and we'd escape major fall out. Was I being scheming? Overly analytical? Self-protective? Possibly.

Thing was, against all my normal certitudes, instincts, predictions, call them what you like, I badly underestimated Mark's resolve in this matter. He needed this trip and if it meant borrowing against what was left of his flat's diminishing equity, then by hook or by crook he was going too; and so he did. He called his "Advisor", a shady character who projected the airs and graces of a cultured, concerned friend. He came over all Harrods while being all Soho, having the wiles of a petty crook. Sober minded persons could pierce the disguise but to an impressionable alcoholic with desperate financial problems, he must have appeared on that first meet, at whatever drinking hole, like a Guardian Angel. He had already wangled Mark three remortgages on the flat, thereby solving the dire financial lapses before the knock on the door arrived; while of course filling his pockets with a sizable fee. All of which further served to increase the amount owed and to simply delay the inevitable. To Mark's appeal, he promised to secure the sum of fifteen hundred pounds when the time came, just enough to make the trip. What the payoff was is not known, five hundred probably. This same phony had already scammed Mark out of twenty thousand pounds, borrowed against the flat, for a directorship in his book publishing company. A venture that had only two published titles to it's name; one on repetitive action injuries in the work place and the other, on the colours used in horse racing. Quite what an alcoholic ex-actor wanted with such an exalted position at a mere twenty thou' was beyond me. His name in print, instead of lights? Or the chance of shared liability perhaps?

A little dumbfounded at first by the news and bracing myself for the inevitable "events" ahead, I then thought otherwise, "Good Mark, well done." I told myself. I was pleased he'd achieved something positive for himself. So there was life in the old dog yet. He'd have a fun holiday and it might help to change his ways. Then someone asked me down the pub what Roger thought of the idea of Mark coming, I didn't know that yet, but I ominously replied that you needed two to carry a stretcher.

Now I don't wish to give the impression that the trip evolved from me wanting a fun time, into having to put up with Mark tagging along or more importantly, of helping Mark out of his situation; that was a forlorn hope of course. I would be a liar though, if I did not carry the notion with me as things unfolded, because that's the sort of hopeful person I can be. No, first and foremost I wanted a good time, all other thoughts about the nature of the holiday attached themselves later. When it was all far too late.

The Comparatively Ugly...

For reasons soon to come I should say something about our other flat mate at the time, Greg; a mad Australian with a penchant for fighting and drinking, at which he was bad at both. Best that I give an account of our first encounter if only for the virtue that it's somewhat related to the tale but more importantly worth telling. I first met him in the living room which also doubled up as Mark's bedroom at most times of the day. Mark seemed anxious when I walked in one Sunday afternoon in May.

'I've got this bloke here, he's moved in.'

'Really, what's he like?'

'Don't know, he's asleep.'

'Where?'

'In my old bedroom.'

'This is Roger's mate?'

'Yeah, I got back and he was already here.'

'Where's Rog?'

'No idea.'

'And you haven't met him?'

'No.'

Whereupon, the bedroom door opened in the hallway and we listened to the sound of our new yet-to-meet flat mate stumble into the adjacent bathroom, coughing and spluttering, before suddenly spewing and retching over and over like a beached seal.

'Don't let it be the sink.' Pleaded Mark.

'Sounded like the toilet.'

'You think?'

As if to confirm it the toilet was flushed.

'Thank God.'

Then Mark's voice went down a level or two.

'I'm really not sure about this.'

He made it sound as if he was an offended stranger to such awful behaviour.

'It's money isn't it?' I reminded him.

'Yes.'

'Money you haven't got.'

'Well, yes.'

'How much you charging?'

'A hundred a week, cash.'

'So what's the problem?'

Then the door swung open and in wobbled a tall shirtless gangly bloke, with a mop of black tussled hair. It wasn't what I first noticed though, no, it was the two massive black eyes and a puffed up nose cocked to one side, he was sporting. It caused a slightly awed pause, until our new flat mate broke the stunned silence.

'Allo', Greg's the name.'

'Paul, nice to meet you.'

'Likewise.'

We shook hands. He turned to Mark who smiled weakly, attempting without much success to not notice the obvious.

'Are you Mark?'

'Yes.'

'I've got sum'thin' for y'er.'

He reached into his pocket and pulled out a pile of crumpled twenty pound notes, and handed them to a near flinching Mark.

'A hundred right?'

'Erm..'

'What Rog' said.'

'That's fine.' Said Ali Baba, with his new found riches.

'Is that the latest look from Australia?'

I boldly asked, unable to contain myself.

'Nah, told some bloke down the Northcote his team were shit.'

'Chelsea fan?'

'Nah, Arsenal.'

'Hard luck.'

I said it with sympathy, for their fans are not known for their aggression.

'He was a prick.'

'Are you a football fan?'

'Nah, soccer's shit. Aussie Rules mate.'

'Thought as much.'

Flushed with money and a'shake with alcohol withdrawal, Mark stood up and announced he was going to the shop and shot out the room. I was now alone with the not-so-sure-about Antipodean, he of the worrying black eyes, broken nose and sickly skin.

'Did you get him?'

'Nah, he walked back in after I'd slagged him off and hit me when I wasn't looking. Fuckin' nearly knocked me out.'

'Jeezuz, what are Arsenal fans coming to?' I said rather cheekily; resisting the temptation to say hard luck again, with any great sympathy this time.

'Well, your eyes look like two oil spills.'

'Seen 'em; he got me good. Broke me bloody nose too.'

'Looks a little cock eyed.' I proffered.

'I'll fix that.'

Whereupon he grabbed his nose, felt along it, then with both hands gave a quick hard tug and pulled the nose straight again, without a hint of pain.

'You've done that before, I can tell.'

'Yeah; you Mark's mate?'

'That's right.'

'I hear he's an arsehole.'

'No, he's just got a bad problem with drink. If you just ignore the bollocks he's alright.' I believed it but thousands didn't.

'Here check this out.'

In a selfless act of male bonding, Greg pulled out his mobile phone and after a few clicks on the buttons handed it to me; whereupon a video played. It showcased a lovely naked girl with spectacular breasts, excitedly screaming at the top of her voice, while some over musculared man, with an enormous penis, pistoned in and out of her rear orifice. Greg cracked a large smile and insisted on showing me more examples of unadulterated high grade porn, until Mark came back with a large carrier bag of cider and beer. Then Roger showed up some minutes later with some bottles of wine and the evening went a long way into morning from there. Sensibly, I opted out around 2am and left them to it. Something which didn't appeal to Greg's sense of manhood.

'Are you a puss or what?'

'Yes, I have to go to work in the morning.'

'So do I, so does Rog'. So does Mark.'

'Mark doesn't work.' Said Roger.

'What?' He looked at Mark in disbelief.

'You don't work?'

'That's why he's rented his bedroom to you and is sleeping in the living room.' I added, departing.

Spag' Bol'...

First week of September duly arrived and decisions had to be made. I was running behind on the job and stressing a bit, though I had made it clear to the client I would be taking a holiday come what may and he appeared fine with that; though as it turned out later on he wasn't. Roger had been trawling the Internet to see if there was any good deals to Spain and also as a tempting prompt, to Greece. I had run my eye over the print outs but done little else. Mark was definitely coming, his money was ready for him anytime he wanted. I was concerned he'd get it early and spend half of it but to his credit he seemed aware of that likelihood and was holding fast.

Thursday I ran into Roger in Somerfields supermarket, he like me was trying to get a meal sorted out for the evening.

'Fancy eating spag' bol'?' He asked.

'Absolutely.' I replied, glad for the chance to escape the chore of deciding on what to eat for a change.

'Greg's cooking, I'm buying the ingredients.'

'I'll get the bread then.' Said I, cheap as ever.

'What about the holiday? We need to make plans soon.'

'Yeah I know, let's do it tonight hey?'

'Fancy a drink to discuss it? Pitcher&Piano?'

'Sure, we can decide there.'

'I'll drop the food to Greg and meet you.'

While waiting for Roger outside the P&P I changed my mind about doing the Spanish resort thing. I don't know why, I just did. A decision in fact that changed my life. Perhaps on reflection Roger's promotion of Greece appeared more unpredictable, hence more appealing to those of a carefree nature. Besides as I explained to Roger when he showed.

'Greece; I've never been so let's go there.'

'Package or Island hopping?' Asked Roger uncontesting.

'Hmmm, don't know, what do you think?

'Island hopping.'

'Really?'

'Yeah, that way you get to pick and choose what to do.'

I weighed it up for all of two seconds, the freedom to move around at our leisure was all me.

'That's what we'll do then.'

'When?' Said Roger.

'Two weeks time, leave say on the Saturday.'

'How about Friday?'

'I don't mind, though Saturday would give me more time to get things together.'

'You planning on taking a suitcase then?'

'No, just a bag.' I said, slow on the sarcasm.

'If we were to leave Friday night, we'd get to Athens early morning, catch the ferry to Paros and be there by lunchtime.'

'Is that what you did last time?'

'Yes, if we come back on a Sunday evening then that gives us sixteen days and be back to work Monday morning.'

'You've convinced me, let's do it.'

'I checked some flights already, we can catch Olympus out on Friday around eleven from Heathrow and fly back Sleazyjet on the Sunday evening.'

'How much are we talking?'

'Olympus is one hundred and ten pounds, sleazy is sixty nine. That's one hundred and eighty including taxes.'

It sounded perfect and incredibly cheap. Too cheap to refuse.

'Can you book them tomorrow?'

'I'll do it first thing at work. What about Mark?'

'What about him?'

'Is he still coming? He hasn't spent all his money yet?'

'He's coming, for better or worse.'

'Just checking.' He said with a telling grin.

I was feeling fantastically good and an easy smile lit up my face. "Nice one Rog'." I thought. If it had been left to me or I'd been traveling alone, I'm afraid it would have been a Thompsons package deal secured on the upcoming Saturday. That would have worked of course but I liked the way things had fallen nicely into place; and you know? At various times in life they just have a great way of doing that.

Roger got a phone call, it was Greg. 'Just having a drink with Paul. Who are? Oh, okay; no not long be back after this one, later.' Finished, he looked at me like someone with bad news.

'Mark and Pedra (Greg's girlfriend) are on their way.'

Now that presented a small problem because Mark was barred from the P&P after being in one of his drunken moods and no doubt being a twat. However the Manageress who barred him wasn't there. Mark and Pedra duly arrived, and Mark being sober and concious of his status, stood outside of the front patio wall tentative to join in, like an underage child.

'Mark, do you want a pint?' I asked him joyfully.

'Yes, but you know they won't serve me here.'

'I'll get you one, don't worry. And for fuck's sake join us. Stop acting like you've got the plague.'

'I'll just sit on the wall.'

So he sat on the wall, as if he was half in and half out of the place, not really drinking but drinking there.

'You'll be alright, I'll talk to the barman.'

I didn't need to as he was standing behind me.

'I don't mind, wasn't me that barred him.' Said he.

The holiday vibe was clearly creating good karma. I got the drinks and relayed to Mark what had been decided. If we had told him we were rowing to Greece from the pebbled shores of Dungeness, on the remains of the fabled Kon-Tiki with one broken oar, it wouldn't have mattered a jot.

'I'm just going along with you guys. Where you go, I go; just don't leave me on my own.'

He said it with a deep worrying note of insecurity. I didn't like the sound of that, for I wasn't prepared to take on a puppy dog. There was something more though, I could tell he was concerned about my friendship with Roger for one thing, which harked back to that July day of "Nobody asked me..." He didn't want to be left out of any fun we might have, even if he couldn't afford it. But at that happy point I pushed it aside, what will be will be, was my motto. Little did I know quite how the evening would change my view in that regard. Mention of the spag' bol' was made, I asked Mark if he was going to eat that as well.

'No, I'm gonna' get a kebab instead.'

He looked forlornly over at the fish and chip shop, which weirdly enough sold kebabs, but then again nothing's sacred anymore. Not thinking anymore of it, Roger, Pedra and I finished up and went back to the house. Greg was getting things ready in the kitchen, and about forty minutes and two bottles of red plonk later, had cooked up a tasty and plentiful meal for four. I was half-way through mine when Mark entered the living room somewhat agitated.

'How was the kebab?' I asked innocently.

'Didn't bloody get one.'

'Why not?' Perplexed by his terse reply.

'I wasn't hungry!'

The penny suddenly dropped, he felt excluded from the meal. A silence came over the room. He glared at Greg.

'Course it would have been nice if someone had asked me if I wanted to eat!'

'It wasn't up to me, I only cooked it.' Said Greg.

'This is my fucking house. I'm the fucking landlord and you fuckers didn't ask me!' He exclaimed belligerently.

Greg fought back.

'Fuck you.'

Mark stared at him like magma was about to explode from the top of his bald, volcanic looking head.

'I'm not fucking having it! You cunts can all leave!'

And on that high note he stormed out, leaving us a bit bewildered yet not surprised. Pedra spoke up.

'See I told you. I knew he'd be like that.'

'Fuck him and his kebab.' Said Greg.

'Got any more parmesan cheese?' Asked Roger.

Mark's fit of pique had made me angry though. A set of circumstances had led to this and as typical he wasn't seeing sense. He was fortunate Greg hadn't got up and hit him. Hell, he was damn lucky I hadn't got up and hit him. I'd been on a high since Somerfields and now Bozo the Clown had ruined the whole mood. It didn't bode well for the holiday.

'I'll go talk to him.' I said

'It won't do any good Paul. It's Mark, you know what he's like. It's the attention, that's what he wants.'

Replied Pedra with an understanding of the actor in him.

'Oh I'll give him some attention.' Said I.

I went outside to the back patio and found him sitting at the table, resentment burning him up, defiant in his misplaced emotions. I laid into him.

'What the fuck is the matter with you Mark? Are you going to be a prick all your life?'

He looked away from me staring into space.

'You just listen to me, this is a good friend talking. You are in the wrong over this.'

I explained how I came to be invited to dinner, how he'd got the wrong end of the stick and had managed to ruin the evening with his selfish attitude. That all he ever did was act like a prat when it suited him. It was a scene out of Eastenders. And all the time he just looked away, constantly drawing on a cigarette.

'Tell you what Mark, you act like this on holiday and you
might as well not come, because it won't be any fucking fun.'
'Then I won't.' He finally reacted.

The dummy had been thrown from the pram except this time I wasn't prepared to pick it up.

'Good, don't.' He got the message and I left him to brood.

Bloody typical, the next day when I saw Mark he had forgotten about the whole episode and was sweetness and light; enthused about the trip and telling everybody about it. I'm no expert on alcoholism but I've never been sure if this is a constant put on, or he genuinely forgets about such tantrums and other emotional fits that have pervaded his sorry life in the last few years. To this day I cannot make my mind up. The amount of times I have tried to help pick him up and see the error of his ways are numerous. Does it do any good? Does it fuck. The very next day it's all forgotten about in the circle of self ruinous habit. I must admit it's hard to keep liking a person who persists in such ways. It's enough to slowly put you off them.

What was Roger's reaction to all of this meantime? Not just the spag' bol' incident but the whole issue of Mark wanting to come and finding a way to do it? At first he was like me dubious that it would happen but unlike me, horrified if it came to be. Now it was going to happen he adjusted accordingly, assured in the prediction that, 'He'll last two days and then we'll be waving him goodbye.' Chances were he'd be right.

Waiting for the Day...

Mark collected his fifteen hundred pounds from the Shady Character, on the Monday before leaving. I got the one hundred and eighty off him quickly, to give to Roger for the tickets, and pleaded with him to give me the rest to look after, but to no avail. Sure enough, flushed with money he predictably went on a bender with a dubious mate of his who lived over in Streatham. On one such occasion before, the inebriated mate had fallen and badly hurt himself and Mark had called an ambulance. When the Medics got there such was Mark's command of the situation, they actually believed that he was a doctor who had stumbled upon the scene and were following his lead. Their belief was dispelled only by the despairing mate imploring,

'Don't listen to him! He's not a doctor, he's a fucking actor.'

For two days Mark was nowhere to be seen, holed up in stuporland burning a large hole in his holiday money. Finally, he showed up Wednesday evening and entreated with me to look after what he had got left of the cash, eight hundred and fifty pounds. At first I said no, explaining that he had taken responsibility to get it so he should take care to look after it himself; but I was just pissed off he hadn't listened to my sound advice. Eventually swayed by his piteous plea, I made him promise in a hope-to-die fashion, that from hereon I looked after his money all the way through the holiday, budgeting him daily. Sensibly, for once, he agreed. Mind you it wasn't that difficult given the disheveled state he was in.

It meant that even given the excellent exchange rate he was already down to about eighty euros a day. Take away a forecasted twenty for accommodation a day and he was left with sixty euros for spending per diem, plus he still had to pay for the cost of any ferries we took. I was going on the basis of a hundred euros a day spending money, excluding ferries, Roger's was likely more. Already there was a disparity between Mark's ability to have a good time and ours. Friday couldn't come soon enough.

Early Friday morning there was a loud repeating knock on my caravan door. I was in fact living in a caravan at the end of Mark's paved over garden; that we had somehow managed to squeeze in through the gates to the street, with a can opener, a pry bar and a large vat of grease; so tight was the opening. It was a cosy little number, which I had bought off a very dodgy creature in Dartford, whose middle name was likely "Shifty". On meeting, it took an age for him to answer his door, and when he did he avoided facial contact and looked right pass me and a helping friend to survey the street beyond, before convincing himself things were kosher. Somewhere in our conversation he revealed that he had just been "Inside." What for, he didn't enlighten us, but it didn't really come as any surprise, especially as the caravan door showed clear signs of breaking and entering. He wanted three hundred and I gave him two, due to it's dubious provenance and it's filthy outside state; which soon scrubbed up nicely with soap and water, later on. Inside needed a little work but was in fantastic condition considering. A week later and it was done up ready for a colour supplement article.

Fortunately, it's location in the paved garden was covered by an existing car port, which I had trellised on three sides, to help keep the prying eyes of the neighbours off the fact that I was living in it; which as a rule I kept very low-key. As far as I could tell it had worked perfectly, there had been no warning notices from the Council or the Freeholder, or any complaints made. So it didn't help that someone was currently trying to destroy the illusion, and get the entire vicinity's attention fixed on the caravan.

'Who is it?' I asked with some uncertainty; sounding like some bloke called Shifty, from Dartford.

'Mark; listen mate can I have some money?'

I should have known who it would be and for what for.

'At this time of the morning?'

'I had to catch you before you went to work.' He had a point.

'What from your holiday money?' I stated blandly.

'Yes.'

'What for?'

'I need to get some things for the trip.'

'What sort of things?'

'Toothpaste, shampoo, things like that.'

'But Mark you're taking hand luggage.'

'So?'

'You can't take any large sized liquids with you.'

'Why not?'

'Because of the security measures. We talked about this.'

'Well, I still need some things.'

'Like what?'

'Like some shorts.'

'You were going to borrow a pair of mine.'

'No, I want to get my own.'

'How much you need?'

'Forty.'

'Forty?'

'Twenty then.'

Shorts indeed. I knew what he really wanted the money for; his usual daily fare: a four pack of cider, a packet of fags, and a microwaveable ready-to-eat burger; one of the foulest creations known to man, in case you haven't tried one. The spare change to be used down the pub at lunchtime of course. I was inclined to say no but like so much with Mark, I relented and gave him twenty.

'That leaves you with eight hundred and thirty, and we

haven't even got there yet.' I admonished.

'I know; but It's my money.' He piqued back.

'Well go easy.'

'What time are you back from work?'

'Hopefully four o'clock.' He nodded and went to go hot footed to Raj's shop.

'And Mark.'

'Yeah?'

'Don't get pissed up today before we leave, please.'

'I won't.'

He sounded annoyed by my distrust as if privately saying, "God, what does he take me for? An alcoholic?"

Work went well and I got back to the flat around four thirty and found Mark in the living room, watching his umpteenth episode of Friends; his favourite TV show. Transfixed by the screen, I couldn't tell if he was sober or half cut.

'Hey, okay?'

'Fine, waiting to go.'

Thankfully he sounded and looked in good shape. Perhaps he did buy a pair of shorts. He got up to go to the toilet and I checked down the side of the couch to see how many ciders were left. Three, that meant he'd only had one since this morning. He'd been circumspect, hat's off to him I thought.

'Are you packed?' I shouted.

'Since ten o'clock this morning.'

'No big liquids or sharp metal objects? I hope.'

'I'm not that stupid.'

'Just checking.'

It was time for me to head to the caravan and pack myself. I spent an hour deciding what to take and tidying up after me; carefully hiding my laptop computer and discarding my wallet of cards I didn't need with me; like my Somerfields discount card, my Wandsworth library card and my ten-visits-the-last-one-free Spearmint Rhino card (no, not really). It was a good feeling, like a special preparation or ritual for the holiday. I took one last look around my very presentable abode. 'Well, here goes.' I said to an imaginary entity and exited locking the door behind me. Went back to the living room, looked at Mark.

'Ready?'

'God, since lunchtime.'

He bounded up from the sofa ready to grab his nearby bag.

'Hang on Deputy Dawg, got to wait for Rog' yet.'

He crumpled back down on the sofa in disappointment.

'Do me a favour Paul.'

'What?'

'Look after my passport 'til we get to the airport.'

'Why? Can't you look after it?'

'I keep forgetting where it is.'

'Jesus, Mark.' But he had that useless look on his face.

'Alright, hand it here.'

As if to prove the point, he couldn't find it easily in his bag. After finally locating and handing it to me, Mark, now comforted, grabbed a tin of cider and opened it, his hand tremulous with alcohol withdrawal. He offered me a tin but seeing what it had done to him, I declined.

Suddenly Roger came in, looking cool, calm and collected.

'Boys.'

'A'ha, thought you'd be ages yet.' Said I.

'Boss left early. Won't be long, just got to change.'

'Have you packed?'

'No.'

'Well how long is that going to take?'

'Ten minutes.'

'Ten minutes? Are you sure?'

'Yeah, I'm only taking two shirts.'

He wasn't joking either. In less than ten minutes he walked back in changed and ready to leave, with a small travel bag over his shoulder. Mark even had to hurry up his cider, spilling some of it down his nice clean shirt, ironed especially for the occasion.

'Fuck! Why does that always happen?' He implored.

'Because you're an idiot?' Said Roger.

'Takes one to know one.'

'Not in your case.'

'What gives you the right to be so high and mighty?'

'I have a job? I work for a living?'

'So do I.'

Roger and I looked at each other with some bemusement.

'Oh, you do? And what's that?'

'I'm a landlord. I help look after you two.'

'Mark the only thing you help look after is the company that brews your cider and Raj's shop where you buy it from.' I said, with a strong note of truth.

'So what? If I didn't provide a roof over your head, what would you do then?'

'Find somewhere else to live maybe.' Said Roger.

'What, round here?'

'Are you the only landlord then?'

'I could be.'

'Alright, when we get back I'll find someplace near here.'

'You just try.'

'I will. That way I might get regular hot water.'

'What's wrong with the hot water?'

'Nothing, apart from all the cold water in between.'

'Don't mess with the boiler then.'

'It's broken, how can I?'

'It's not, it's just temperamental.'

'Hey, what's going to happen to the cats while we're away?' I said changing the subject, but not without a note of real interest.

'They'll be fine.'

'Really?'

'Both bowls are full. I've left them water.'

I wasn't sure I'd heard Mark wrong, it sounded to me like he had left four days sustenance for sixteen days away. He caught my facial concern.

'They know how to look after themselves.'

'How?

'There's plenty of mice around.'

'What about Tripod?'

'What about her?'

'She's only got three legs.'

'She's very clever.'

'How about leaving them in the street?' Said Roger.

'So they can get run over by a car.'

'No you idiots, Greg is going to keep an eye on them.'

'But Greg hates cats.'

'Pedra then.'

'Have you asked her?'

'No, but she'll know. Greg will feed them.'

'Yeah, the day we head back.' I stated, factually.

We left the flat and went out the side gate, each of us with one hold-all bag; the start of our big adventure. Spontaneously, Mark and I broke into singing that well worn number from our childhood:

"We're all going on a, summer's holiday...".

Cliff Richard would have walked the other way but not Roger, who walked on briskly ahead, distancing himself from the two forty something mad men.

'Got to get some cigarettes from Raj's.' He cried, as we carried on entertaining the street.

"We're going where the sun is shining, we're going where the
sea is blue...".

Terrified pets were scrambling for cover and concerned mothers were rushing to haul their frightened children inside. Oncoming cars were pulling up and reversing back down the road. Okay, so I exaggerate a bit.

Re-gathered outside Raj's shop, we walked along the Northcote Road towards Clapham Junction and destiny. But on nearing the P&P, Roger asked the eternal question. 'Fancy a quick one?' Unable to break a long standing tradition we popped in.

The after work Friday crowd littered the place and with our jaunty air and bags, we soon became the center of attention for friends and foes alike; those who reveled in our good fortune and those who were peeved by it. It's funny how in such moments of impending departure, you, the about to be holiday goer, have a feint whiff of fame, exoticism even about you. The fact that you are setting off abroad to somewhere warm and bright and fun, and the people observing you are not, invokes a lot of various feeling. Naturally we were also enjoying our about to happen journey with some relish. We drank a quick one, took the well wishes and the not so well wishes and set off for real this time, Greece here we come.

Easy on the Jet...

From the gateway to the world, Clapham Junction, we railed it to Feltham. The train was packed with commuters leaving the city and as per normal in England everybody was a stranger to themselves, and we rode in uncomfortable silence; separated from each other in both senses of the term. Faced with such a normal abnormal situation, Mark stood there with a silly grin on his face at first, but then started to get uncontrollable suppressed giggles. Roger and I were at pains to know what was so damn funny, thankfully we soon reached Feltham and got off.

'What were you laughing at?' I asked him.

'It was too funny.'

'What was?'

'The train, everybody ignored everybody.'

'That's not funny, that's downright sad.'

'I like it myself.' Said Roger.

'What, uncomfortableness?'

'No minding your own business.'

'If I had to travel like that everyday I'd end up topping myself with the sheer terrible weight of it.'

Unfortunately, this comment got Roger thinking.

'If you had to commit suicide Mark how would you do it?'

'Drink myself to death.'

'But you're doing that already.' I corrected.

'It doesn't count, too slow. Come on what would you use?'

'I don't know.'

'How about slitting your wrists with a razor blade?'

'Why would I want to do that?'

'It's cheaper and quicker than booze?'

'Very funny Roger.'

'Well wouldn't it be?'

'Can't we talk about something else?'

'How about you Paul?'

'Overdose I guess. Less mess.'

'Guys, we're going on holiday and you're talking suicide.'

Implored a less-than-understanding Mark.

'I can lend you one if you want.'

'Lend me what?'

'A razor blade.'

'Fuck off.'

'Just trying to help. Speed up matters.'

From Feltham we took the bus to Heathrow and while riding pass the airport's perimeter fence, witnessed the impressive sight of a jet plane coming into land from our right, just a few feet above us. It's roaring engines shaking the air and it's shiny metallic undercarriage glinting the low evening sun into our faces. It flew over us to set down onto the runway; the smoking impact of it's tyres upon meeting the concrete and the loud immediacy of the engines in reverse, forcing back the powerful momentum. Roger and I smiled in mutual admiration but Mark looked like he'd seen a ghost.

Terminal 2 was surprisingly quiet, this was the terminal I used to fly out from, to go to the Middle East during the nineteen seventies and eighties and it was never less than busy, but it had been a good twenty years since I'd been in the place. It didn't look that much different, though a bit past it's heyday. Maybe that's why it was scheduled for demolition. It held some good memories for me, a good omen for the trip I felt. We breezed through check-in and with time to linger, ignored the departure area and headed for the nearest bar two levels up.

Both Roger and Mark could drink like fish but not me, the previous fifteen years of living in California had made me fit. Swimming a mile almost every day for the last seven, and keeping my drinking to a minimum. Since moving back to the UK the swimming had reduced and the drinking had increased, but even so, I wasn't use to the drinking culture they were use to. Compared to their three pints at the bar, I had one. Roger called me "Captain Sensible", after Top Gear's James May, not the venerated punk rock bassist. I told him that since the moniker was already in use I should be termed "Doctor Reason" instead. Fortunately it never stuck. Problem is when your body is not used to drinking copious amounts of alcohol it gets out of practice, it stops absorbing the poison and lets you know about it instead, doing you in for up to three days. There was a time when I could drink for England like the boys and win gold medals in the process. I enjoyed it and it was part of my life. If I had never moved to California I'd have become an overweight, pot bellied, unfit forty something, who still enjoyed a good drink and occupied a pub at all available times.

One of the things I wasn't looking forward to on this trip was being in the presence of two piss heads, who would be expecting me to drink as much as them, like some return to a bygone era. Far as I was concerned that wasn't going to happen; so I was going to have to take the incoming wearing a steel helmet. But Roger had a point, with all my youthful appearance, aged experience had made me boringly sensible.

Other than us commenting on the lovely Russian barmaid who served us, there wasn't much to talk about, but then Roger decided to liven things up by playing his favourite game of getting under Mark's skin. A game in which Mark always rose to the bait. Usually it started with a contradiction of what Mark had said (an obvious lie normally) and ran from there, but on this auspicious occasion he happened to notice that Mark was wearing a new watch, something I hadn't.

'Got a new watch?'

'Yes.'

'What happened to the old one?'

'It, erm, stopped working.'

The "erm" aroused immediate suspicion.

'I bet you lost it in Streatham.'

'I haven't been in Streatham.'

'Yes you have.'

'When?'

'This week, getting rat-arsed with your mate.' I injected.

'Oh yeah.'

'So you did lose it there?'

'No.'

'Bet you did.'

'No, I didn't.'

'Alright, if you say so.'

'Did you?' I asked, knowing Mark had a hard time lying to me.

'Did I what?

'Lose it?.'

'Erm, yes; but not in Streatham.'

'Where then?'

'Can't remember.'

'Streatham then.'

'Probably.'

'How much did it cost you?' Asked Roger.

'What?'

'The watch.'

'Thirty quid.'

'Thirty? For that?'

'It's Swiss Army, the best.'

'Let me see.'

'No, piss off.' Shouted Mark.

'Come on.'

Mark fended off Roger's attempts to grab his arm and see the watch. This carried on for awhile and I had to check we weren't in school uniform.

'I just want to look, I'm not going to hurt you.'

'Yeah, you just try.' Said Mark, mock heroically.

'Watch out, grown children are present.' I weighed in.

'Come on Mark.' Pleaded Roger.

'No touching it.' Mark put out his arm for Roger to see.

'See, I knew it.'

'What?'

'Swiss phoney.'

'Bollocks is it. I bought it off a copper in the pub.'

'Was it a bent copper?'

'No, he wasn't.'

'Why would a policeman sell you a watch in a pub?' I asked, sensibly.

'I don't know, I never asked him.'

Mark lifted the watch to his ear and listened to it like an expert horologist.

'That's definitely Swiss Army.'

'By way of Swiss Family ROBinson.'

'Piss off Roger. It's a Swiss!'

Roger and I started to laugh as it almost sounded like he'd said "Swizz".

'Fuck the both of you. Who's round is it anyway?'

Roger then started on his other favourite sitting around game, the 'which, would, why, what if?' assortment. This one went along the lines of, "If you were going to be one of history's evil bastards, who would you pick and why?". How could one resist such a tempting proposition? Not me anyway. Mark answered first after much deliberation.

'Hitler.'

'Why.'

'Because he was evil.'

'Yeah we know that, but why would you want to be him?'

'I wouldn't. He wasn't very nice, was he?'

Mark wasn't getting the hang of it really.

'Paul?'

'Henry the bleedin' Eigth.'

'How was he evil?'

'He was a rampant, egotistical, tyrannical, vain murdering bastard; whose base desires and fit's of pique, destroyed two wives, an established religion, numerous ancient communities, and he tortured and executed those who would oppose his will.

Oh, and he also stole a wealth of treasure that didn't belong to him. Basically rode roughshod over the rights of Englishmen. That's an evil bastard to me.'

'Good; so why?'

'For all his undoubted faults, he told the Pope to get stuffed and helped create a better suited religion, thereby sowing the seeds of a robust and wholly independent nation. Arguably, the most influential the world has ever known. Plus, there was all that hunting to do and screw the best looking bird in the manor or palace after.'

I can't remember what Roger's selection was.

Intellectually challenged and suitably quenched, we said our fond farewells to the Russian barmaid and went to security where, like check-in, there was no wait. We put our bags through the all seeing machine to scan for explosives and high velocity weapons. It's not something I personally pack on a trip but you never know about other persons. As the bags were making their progress, a red light went on and the Observer called over a Security Man. The bags came out and the Security Man lifted one up and asked, 'Who does this belong to?'. I knew it was Mark's but he didn't seem to recognize it, as he was still busy checking the credentials of his admired watch.

'That's your bag isn't it Mark?' Nudging him.

Mark answered that it was his and the Security Man asked him to go to a table with him.

'I haven't done anything.' He said with concern.

'Over here Sir. Just need to check the bag.'

Mark followed as if to the Headmaster's office.

'Bet he brought a knife with him.' Roger lent over, saying.

'He can't have, I told him time and again, nothing sharp or tool like, he knows. He's not that stupid.'

'Want to bet?'

'No.' I said, after careful consideration.

The Security Man carefully checked the bag, removing some clothes first, then he felt around and pulled out a folding corkscrew with knife, and waggled it in front of Mark with a look of disdain; before throwing it into a nearby clear plastic bin, which was full of prohibited items of varying incredulity; among which I noticed, was a small fire extinguisher. Mark was given his bag back and let through. Coming over to us he looked vexed.

'It was only a corkscrew. It's for opening a bottle of wine for

God's sake; what's wrong with that?'

I rolled my eyes and shook my head and we moved on through to the comforts of the departure area, with an hour to go until take-off.

Due to a delay, the Athens flight was now the last plane of the night, which meant that everything was closing up and the floor sweepers were moving in. The remaining passengers were hogging acres of space, awaiting the command to head for the gate. Meanwhile, in the impressively low priced Wetherspoons, bar the three of us and no more than a handful of others, held fort. Roger was goading Mark about how many plane journeys he'd made in comparison to him, when not to be outdone by something Roger had said, countered by claiming he had flown on the very first Jumbo Jet out of Heathrow in 1970. Which as tall as it sounded was likely, as his Dad did work quite high up in BA or BOAC then, so it had legs. Long enough to keep Roger at bay while he digested it's veracity.

There was no stopping Mark though, keen as mustard he suddenly stated that he'd been to Greece, to Paros even; which was news to us, as he hadn't mentioned it before.

'When?' Asked a revived Roger, smelling blood.

'Mid-eighties.'

'Who'd you go with.'

'Paul Furie. I think.'

'You don't know who you went with?'

'No, it was Furie; we were stoned a lot.'

'Which airline did you take?'

'Didn't, went by Magic Bus.'

'Magic Bus!? More like magic carpet.'

'No Rog;' I interjected.

'Magic Bus was a cheap way of getting to places like Greece back then, it was kind of a hippy thing. You caught this bus from central London and two days later you ended up in Greece somewhere.'

'And it was called Magic Bus?'

"Yes." Mark and I uttered together, dispelling Roger's look of dubiousness.

'So where did it take you, this Magic Bus?'

'I'm sure it took us to Paros, I remember the name.'

'You can't remember you were in Streatham this week.'

'I can!'

'What's Paros look like then?'

'Well, like an island.'

'Is it north, south, west or east of the main land?'

'I don't fucking know. It was the first island you got to when you left bloody Athens.'

'Piraeus.'

'What?'

'It's Piraeus you leave from.'

'What's Piraeus?'

'It's a port.'

'We didn't leave from a port.'

'You have too, unless you fly it's the only way to get there. Or did you go by Magic Boat?'

'Fuck off, you prick.'

Detecting an air of anger I determined to cool down the conversation.

'So where did you end up in Paros?'

'We drove to this beach, and the bus driver was as stoned as us; he couldn't stop in time and drove into the sea, and we got stuck.'

Roger started to laugh heartily, convinced Mark was telling big porkies.

'What and you had to get out and help push the bus?'

'Don't be silly. We fucked off, left the driver to it.'

'So what happened to the bus?' I asked.

'It got left there.'

It was my turn to laugh this time, seeing the image all too vividly.

'Can you remember the name of the beach?" Posed Roger.

'Yes.' Answered Mark.

We both waited for an answer, and Mark's air of seriousness turned into an inability not to try and laugh.

'You don't know.' Taunted Roger.

'Golden beach, it was Golden Beach.' He blurted, correctly.

Roger and I knew there was a Golden Beach on Paros, a famous beach that had it's notoriety in the Seventies, when travelers would live on it all summer long, taking whatever high was freely available. Well, so the story goes and who you believe. Either Mark was telling the truth, and you never were sure about his tales, or he'd sneaked a look at my travel guide book to Greece; or heard us mention it in conversation.

'So if we go to Golden Beach, your bus will still be there, in the water?' Dangled Roger.

'Maybe.' Smiled Mark.

'I don't believe you.'

'Don't have too.'

Before we could dig further into this Greek tragedy, our flight was called and we were instructed to go the gate asap, because the selected gate was the furthest from the departure area. They weren't kidding either, we must have walked a mile and a half to the place; through long deserted corridors, passing numerous darkened gate lounges. At one point in the trek we diverted to check out the intriguingly sign posted, Prayer Lounge; which really should have read, Bare Surround Lounge; as it consisted of vinyl floor, flat painted walls, fibre paneled ceiling and strip lighting. Not an iota of spiritualness anywhere; like a sterilized hospital unit in fact. It was clearly designed by an atheist, though it did have a pointer for Mecca. You wouldn't want to be saying your last prayers in here I thought.

Finally making the gate, we remains of the day eagerly awaited boarding. So too, the waiting vacuum laden cleaners, who were desperate to get in after us and go home. Looking around at my fellow fliers it struck me that most were Greek. I had expected a good portion of my own countrymen to be making the trip, though I did get the impression that most there lived and worked in England; London most likely.

It wasn't long before we boarded the plane. Air traffic control must have been in a hurry to get home also, because as soon as the plane door closed we taxied hurriedly out to the runway, barely pausing to line up for the invigorating take off. During which, I noticed Mark was sitting bolt upright, gripping the arm rests and likely contemplating the prayer lounge. "Too late to stop now." Sang Van the Man. This was it, we were truly on our way. What lay ahead for the three amigos I hadn't a clue. It was all in the lap of the Gods. Greek of course.

Port of Call...

The plane's intercom roused me from my patchy slumber, announcing our imminent landing. Roger was on his third or was it fourth? Plane sized bottle of wine. Which given the five or six pints of beer he'd drank at Heathrow, wasn't bad going, considering there was nothing drunk and disorderly about him. To all intents and purposes, the alcohol had little effect on the man. So much for all that testing in laboratories. No, he was just keen to land and have a smoke as soon as humanly possible. Same with Mark, though he did look rather subdued by flying so high up off terra firma.

The plane banked and we could clearly see the multiple dotted lights of Athens and it's boroughs, stretching far inland and along the coast line. Spectacularly resolute from the air, not a cloud in sight. Not before long, we landed and Mark breathed a big sigh of relief.

'Alright?'

'Yes, glad that's over, I'm dying for a smoke. '

'You sleep at all?'

'Fuck no.'

'Are you scared of flying Mark?' Asked Roger.

'No, why are you?'

'Were you, when you flew the first Jumbo Jet
out of Heathrow?'

'No, why would I've been?'

'Just wondered.'

Mark looked to me. 'What's he on about?'

'The way you grip the armrests.'

'You're supposed to do that when taking off and landing.'

'Are you? Mean I've been doing it wrong all these years?'

'It's what I was taught.'

I tried to imagine under what trying circumstances he had been taught to do such a thing. The Millfield Jet Cadet Club perhaps?

'Well you can let go of them now, we've landed.'

'Not until we come to a complete stop.'

I looked at him carefully to see if he was taking the piss but he wasn't.

We passed muster with passport control and whizzed through the redundant customs hall of Diagoras airport; a sparkling new showpiece built for the 2004 Olympics, and located outside arrivals to await the 4:30am bus to Piraeus, smoking tabs to our hearts content or ill-tent as the medical case shows. It was four in the morning and I thought of the same titled song by Farren Young, a chart hit when I was fourteen and stupid. Only I've grown older and still can't help recalling that song. The air was nicely warm and comforting. Roger had gone to the little shop inside the airport and procured some cans of beer. 'Want one?' He asked. Being healthy and fit and reasoned, I declined, but Mark didn't. I was beginning to realize that Roger was as big an alcoholic as Mark, the only difference being he was a functioning one and he bloody well enjoyed it; alcohol was fuel to his engine. Besides, he was on holiday.

Piraeus is the major sea port from the Greek mainland to the Aegean islands, and elsewhere in the Mediterranean and beyond. It lies south of

Athens, but such has been urban sprawl since the 1950's it's really a continuous part of it nowadays, though still a separate city of long distinction. It's role as a prime social, political and economic link to the numerous and outstretched islands, dates back to antiquity. Hence anyone using the port, is in some large respect following in the footsteps of long departed persons of various civilizations, from before and beyond the classical age; including the relatively recent and not so beloved German occupiers of WWII. It puts a young transportation hub upstart like Clapham Junction, in it's place anyhow.

The bus came and we clambered aboard; the journey time to Piraeus was roughly fifty minutes. It was a long bendy type, two carriages held together by a rotating metal floor disc and concertinared rubber sleeves, sides and top. However it was made, like all bus rides you've never been on before, it would be interesting to see where it took us.

We sat apart from each other on the bench seats, mostly in silence; Mark and Roger seemingly resting. Not me, I was eager to savour this country, and sat witnessing as much of everything that passed me by. A new motorway had been built to service the airport. As we sped along it, I witnessed the brave new world of IKEA and Toys 'R' Us super stores constructed along side. Familiar symbols of the creeping monoculture across the world. There were newly built suburbs close by too, ready made customers in effect. It could have been Southern California. That soon changed though, when we came off the motorway after five miles or so and onto an older two lane road. Patchy, scrubby land lay either side of it, and for three miles or so, the only buildings were those of established construction and material yards and light industrial units, spaced distances apart. Further on there were a few modern showrooms built here and there, mostly selling German cars and high end furniture, appealing to the wealthier middle class. Five minutes later and we encountered shops, flats and houses, built in the last four decades. Many of the street side businesses had rolled down metal shutters in place. While outdoor furniture sellers occupied most road junctions, with their wares just sitting there; secured only by the flimsiest of means; and not just any old furniture, this looked modern and exciting. See how long that stuff would last unmolested in the UK. For a Saturday morning everything looked incredibly quiet, there were a small number of food outlets and little tobacco stands open but not much else. Cars were few and far between. What did I expect? An all-night revelry of activity? Well strangely enough I did.

The bus took a right hand turn at a T junction and it appeared to be an extension of the town we had been riding through, with buildings either side, but not long after things began to change, and the line of premises to our left disappeared. I could see that we were passing by the sea and were now traveling along the famed 'Riviera', east of Athens, along the southern coast line. This was where Athenians came to relax and enjoy the beach. I knew this because I had just read about it in the in-flight Olympus magazine. No wonder writers use coincidence as a device all the time.

Along it, were landscaped beach areas, some clearly public others with private clubs attached. At one point a large marina loaded with luxury boats was in view. To our right bigger and bigger apartment blocks became the norm, packed close together and endlessly filling the inland as far as a side street would allow you to see. Smaller, older structures squeezed the spaces in-between and even though it was devoid of human activity, you could feel how extraordinarily busy it all was. Then we passed by some huge nightclubs, with crowds of revelers teeming out of them, proving the city was truly alive; but really all I was doing was catching a glimpse of a dense slumbering metropolis.

The bus arrived at the port of Piraeaus, it was still dark and the streets looked deserted and run down. I got the feeling it wasn't that safe and I became very conscious of my wallet, residing in the back pocket of my jeans. This was enhanced by the appearance of a few unfortunates who emerged from the shadows, but who in fact never bothered us. Following Roger into the port area, we came upon a clump of storied buildings, with a number of competing cafes and ferry ticket offices at ground level; it was fairly busy considering the surrounding area. We quickly booked our tickets for the morning ferry to Paros and then sat at an outside table at one of the cafes, and had some breakfast. I ordered an omelette; on delivery it was like no ham and egg dish I had encountered before, but I sensibly drank Coca Cola with it to disguise the taste. By now the dawn was emerging and the tables were beginning to fill with a steady trickle of travelers and local workers. The boat was scheduled to leave at 7:30am, we still had about an hour and there was very little banter between us, other than Roger prodding Mark about the Magic Bus saga.

'Recognize the place?'

'No, I've not been here before have I?'

'What, not even on the Magic Bus?'

'Maybe I was asleep at the time. I probably was.'

'Definitely, I'd say.' Said I.

'Did you have a job back then?' Prodded Roger.

'Yes; no, I was at acting school.'

'What do actors do at school?'

'Learn to play cunts like you.'

'One nil.' Said I.

Roger then asked the inevitable.

'Got the time Mark?

'It's...' Hesitated Mark, as he checked his watch.

'I bet it's broken already.'

'It's not.'

'Well then, what's the time?'

'Give me a minute, I haven't changed it yet.'

'Greece is two hours ahead.' I informed him.

'Ahead or behind?' He queried.

'Ahead.'

'Not behind?'

'Anything east of GMT is ahead.'

'No, that's not right; behind isn't it?'

'Ahead, you berk.'

He shook his watch wrist, then held the watch to his ear and announced.

'The battery is gone.'

Roger looked at me with a large satisfied grin on his face.

'Good those Swiss Army watches aren't they?'

'It was working fine before I got here.'

'Are you saying Greece is bad for your watch?'

He thought about it.

'Quality time pieces are known to be sensitive to changes in...'

'In what?'

'I don't fucking know, do I? But they are.'

I got up leaving the two boys to work out their differences and took a little wander around the island of buildings. Aside from the immense ships that were docked eastwards and mostly hidden by a tall fence, I didn't see much to impress.

Getting back, Roger said we should make a move to the ferry so we could get a good seat on the open decks. From what I could see around us, we weren't about to have too much trouble in that respect; but by the time we had gone half a block, I had to change my tune. We were now in another part of the port, with three massive ferries backed up to a long wide quay. Perimeter railings separated it from the main road, now filling with morning traffic, and the facing apartment and office blocks standing silent witness. Across the road lay the rail station, which could be reached by a newly built glass and steel footbridge.

On the ground, everything about the quay was one hundred percent fascination, incredibly alive and real. There were long trailing lines of trucks, vans, cars and cycles filing onto their respective ferries. Streams of backpackers, tourists, and local Greeks, weaving paths towards the boats and queuing up to get aboard. Numerous friends, family, girlfriends and boyfriends on hand, to give their well wishes, farewells and embraces. A number of Police personnel were keeping a semblance of order. Dressed combat style, in blue-grey fatigues with matching baseball hats and making liberal use of their piercing metal whistles, seemingly glued to their mouths. A sharp form of communication, which every nationality understood. Smartly dressed boat crew, were assisting boarding and overseeing maritime operations; de rigueur in crisp, white, short sleeved shirts and gold braid on black lapels. Seemingly, the gaps in-between were filled by general public with no particular place to go, just observing the scene. While to a person, smoking a cigarette. Where on earth had they all come from? It was another world from where we had just been. Hell, it just is another world. It's a form of hustle and bustle travel like no other. Way older than trains, planes and automobiles; with that long, deep connection to the past.

Roger led us to our ferry, the Blue Star line Naxos, liveried in white and blue. Queuing with the many others steadily going aboard, I watched the large electronic screen above the back entrance, print out the boat's destinations, first in Greek then in English - Paros, Naxos, Amorgos, Santorini, Ios, Piraeus. A feast of interesting sounding places. It would take the boat a day to complete the round trip, but in four to five hours we'd be disembarking at Paros and for me at least, a first proper taste of Greek living. Hopefully it would be better than what I had just eaten.

Entering the boat, our tickets were checked and stubbed and we moved to the upper levels by means of an escalator. Soundly aboard we made for the upper open deck, led by the experienced Roger. He quickly located a table to sit at near the back railing; good job too, as before long every available seat was taken up. We had a grandstand view of the quay and the increasingly busy road, and the nearby buildings; which by now were bathed in the warm sunlight, that still failed to disguise their dour appearance. For the next half hour we watched things unfold, while passing the odd comment. We admired the big trucks skillfully back onto the ferry with their huge loads. We oversaw the sudden, short lived shouting matches, that occurred between frustrated drivers and police or crew. And we took particular note of the attractive women that walked by, remarking as you do. Overall it was a parade of interacting characters and machines, more than Cecil B. De Mille could imagine. This paltry description doesn't do it justice, the whole dramatic effect was mesmerizing.

All aboard, the ferry was ready to go. The massive engines increased their power and the water between the stern and the quay, began to whirl and foam violently. Two dockers waited for the boat to reverse ever-so to the quay wall, then lifted and released the two thick holding ropes from the stubby metal ground moorings, allowing the boat to engage forward thrust and motor away. The ropes were then power winched aboard, and the back vehicle ramp was slowly raised hydraulically and locked into position. The entire manoeuvre monitored and commanded by a team of the ship's officers, engineers and general hands.

As we progressed out of port, I noted the many other revealed facilities and docks that cared for a variety of moored ocean liners, passenger ships and luxury boats. Many more ferries were loading up, taking passengers and goods to distant Greek islands like Crete and Lesbos, and other countries like Italy and Albania, but not with the same hurried populous mayhem of our departing quay. Curiously, the design and build of the boats were somewhat different from each other, and the assortment of operators surprising. From what I could see, Piraeus was essentially an extensive transportation hub for passengers and trucked commercial goods, not a container port. Near the mouth of the port, covered passenger platforms stretched up from the shore and outwards, across part of the water. Concrete in construction and from another era, either they served the then sea liners or they were used by the Germans to transport their soldiers in WWII.

As we left Piraeus, it's surrounds began to take center stage. What seemed like never ending masses of apartment blocks, stretched along the eastern coast, far inland, up and down the rises. Closer to the port, large industrial sites and power plants, occupied the nearby western shore and lowland. It was a sight to behold, and I kenned that very likely I was in the cradle of seafaring. No wonder Greek shipping magnates had once been famous.

Open Deck passages...

The Naxos made it's steady spectacular way east, across the Aegean sea towards the island of Paros, how long we planned to stay there and where to after, was up for discussion. For now we were just content to get this show on the road, or sea as the case was. It was a beautiful sunny warm morning, and the day would clearly get hotter, but for the moment the sun was in front and we were sitting on the open deck shaded by a canopy; facing aft, watching the two churned foam trails of the ship's engines, stretch far back to the horizon, monitoring our speed and progress. This was further assisted by whenever we passed a small island, or we passed or were passed, by a slower or faster boat. I imagine that being on a large body of water with nothing to physically reference, other than an horizon and the sun's movement, would give a sense of going nowhere even though you are.

The bar opened and before long Roger got beers for him and Mark. I opted out, even though severely reprimanded by both of them. Content to sip water and take in our situation, dreamingly thinking, "What a lovely place to be and a great way to travel". The truce over, Roger started up again on goading Mark about the discrepancies in his life stories. Unable to give as good as he got, Mark was always on a loser and would variously get annoyed, irate, or simply befuddled by it all. To involve me in fun and games, Roger came up with another of those "If" scenarios, i.e. "If you were to be any general in history who would it be and why?". Succeeded after much useless debate by, "If you could shag any super model who would it be and why?" I'm not sure which got more consideration, though one was treated more seriously than the other. Eventually worn down by the traveling, Roger's engaging questions and Mark's forgetfulness, I sought refuge in one of the interior lounge rooms, found an empty seat and promptly fell asleep.

Coming to, I noticed Mark noisily asleep on the seat next to me, I left him there in snooze land and went out on deck again. Roger was happily reading a book, ciggie in hand, a beer on hand. The sun was by now almost directly above us and he was stripped to the waist, not wasting a moment of tanning opportunity.

'Get any sleep?' He asked.

'Couple of hours I think.'

'See Mark?'

'Yeah, I woke up to him snoring next to me.'

'Nice.'

'Paros?'

'Won't be long now.'

My watch read 11:30am. 'An hour yet.'

'Should be able to see it up ahead.'

'Really?'

I was highly intrigued, so carefully avoiding the table and it's collection of empty beer bottles, I made my way to the front section of the deck and looked at the distant view of Paros. It was too far away to make anything out in detail, so for the moment it was just a landmass, with other landmasses to the left and right of it. Nevertheless I felt a tinge of excitement at my first sighting, and the nearing of our destination. I went back and joined Roger.

'You said Paros isn't a very happening place?'

'Not really, it's more of a jumping off stop, and then you move
on and catch another ferry.'

'Did you come here in June?'

'Spent a couple of nights, that's all you need really.'

'But it's worth spending time there is it?'

'Oh yeah, it's a nice place and it's got a couple of good bars.
Met some Canadian bird last time, that was fun.'

'Do you think we'll be okay for accommodation?'

'Shouldn't be a problem this time of the year. We'll check
with the fishermen.'

'The fishermen?'

'Yeah, we'll get hooked when we get there.'

I was a little perplexed by this but let it be, even though I wanted to clarify what on earth Roger was talking about, but being English I didn't bother.

'Any thoughts on where to go after Paros?' Roger asked.

Funny enough I did, I had loaned out from my local library the Lonely Planet guide to Greece, and had been reading over and over to see the best plan of attack within the time we had. I bought it out and waved it in front of Roger like a manifesto.

'I was thinking we could do one of two things; we could go to
Santorini and Ios and then somewhere else after.
Or we go to Rhodes, then Kos; then somewhere.'

'Where's Rhodes?'

'The Dodecanese island group.'

I was informed to say, and I showed him on the map.

'That's over to the east, near Turkey. Could take a whole travel day, two because we got to get back.'

'Can we fly?'

'Not really, it's not that easy or cheap.'

'Have you been to Santorini and Ios?'

'Yes, both. Santorini is a must see but full of Americans and over priced. Don't want to spend long there. Day at most.'

I was surprised by Roger's take, given that it is regarded as Greece's most spectacular island. Mind you the thought of a place full of Americans didn't thrill me exactly.

'And Ios?' I asked.

'Party central. Full of students getting fucked up.'

It sounded great, even if I was a forty something.

'Let's go there then.'

'It might be a little late in the season.'

'Still, could be worth a trip.'

'Well I'll go again, no problem. We should go to Naxos too, it's got some good beaches.'

So it looked like Paros for a night or two and then onto Ios. Santorini also, but just for a day, then Naxos. Trip sorted for a few days. But whereto, if there was time, after that? Rhodes had a strong pull on me though, I liked the sound it made. Like it was telling you to come visit.

Mark appeared, looking rather sheepish and forlorn.

'Aren't we there yet?' He pleaded.

'No, soon though.'

He slumped down in his chair and lit a cigarette.

'Thank God we're not coming back this way.' He stated.

Roger and I looked in disbelief at each other.

"What?" We said almost simultaneously.

'No Mark we are, in two weeks time.' I said.

It was Mark's turn to look baffled.

'I thought we were flying back.'

'We are, but we go back to Athens for that, remember?'

'Thought we were leaving from where we are going?'

'We're not sure where to go. We're planning on island hopping, remember?'

'We're not staying in Paris then?'

'Paros, you mean.'

'Just a couple of nights, then we move on.' Added Roger.

'Thought you knew that, we've been talking about it for the last two weeks.'

Classic Mark I thought, bemusing but slightly worrying too. All that cider had made Swiss cheese of his memory.

'So hang on, we're going to stay in Paris-'

'Paros.'

'Right; for two nights and then go somewhere else?'

'That's right.'

'Why?'

'Because that's the plan.'

'Nobody told me.'

'Bollocks, we've told you time and again.'

'When?'

'Mark I told you, you've known all along what we decided.'

'I don't remember you saying anything about this hopping.'

'I did, we're island hopping and that's that.'

'Well I might stay on Paris. Paras; whatever it's called.'

'Fine, I'll give you your money and you can stay.'

He thought about it long and hard, giving the impression that he was in the right to begin with. Finally answering.

'It would have been nice to have been asked first is all.'

He got up and went to the bar, still none the wiser.

'Bugger me his memory is shit.'

Roger lent over as if imparting a close secret.

'Look I've been meaning to say this, any trouble like the other week with Mark and I'm off, he's not fucking up my holiday. I just want you to know that Paul, he's your mate.'

'He'll be okay, don't worry.'

Though as ever I had my doubts.

Tranquility Base...

Paros was upon us, and before it were the smaller islands of Anti-Paros; sparsely populated stretches of land, that disallowed the motor car. In comparison, the approach to Paros was dominated by a large table mountain, that rose along the north western coastline. A large monastery had been built someway up it, while small white painted buildings dotted the lower slopes and filled the coastal shores.

Our boat was heading just a bit northwards for an opening in the shoreline, before it lay some rocks that jutted from out the sea. One a small reef and further on, two curious vertical lumps, pillars almost; as if the ruins of some grand entrance way but clearly not, for they were naturally eroded features that acted as markers. The boat came nearby to turn into the opening, and I viewed them with a strong sense of history and a fabulous notion that they were ancient sentinels guarding a special place. Did the mythical Greek gods, turn to stone two favoured mortals who displeased them, sentencing them to an eternal watch? No, of course not, too fantastic; but it's a fanciable enough idea.

Leaving the rocks quickly behind, the boat entered into a large natural bay and harbour, along which lay the port and main town of Parakia, radiating in the mid-day sunlight. It's many bright white buildings stretching inland and along the southern shore for a mile or two, against the backdrop of the mountain. It was a lovely sight, the type of first encounter that leaves an indelible impression. "What a great place." I immediately thought. I went back to join Roger and Mark and we sat watching the two shores of the bay either side of the ferry. One sparse, arid and hilly, the other showcasing the town and the elevated land mass.

The boat began to signal it's arrival by blaring it's horn and announcements were made in Greek and English to the effect of, "We are here and for those wishing to be here, you had better get ready to leave the boat; sharpish." The three of us were of course, but something about the mood of the place made you feel quite relaxed, so we took it in our stride, with no big effort to be the first off the boat, even though I was worried about getting accommodation for some reason.

Being aft gave us a great sight of docking at the concrete quay that stuck out from the shore, firstly though, the boat swung around so it's stern was facing the quay, then it quickly moved towards it, directed by the back end crew using walkie-talkies. The rear ramp swiftly lowered and with some yards to go, the engines dramatically slowed the boat and it got to within five feet of the quay side, whereupon thin lines, end weighted with a small sack and tied to the mooring ropes, were thrown to waiting shore hands, who drew the ropes and looped them over the mooring cleats. Skillfully holding position at five or so feet, the ramp came down onto the quay with a bit of a crash. We'd landed. All hell then broke loose. Hordes of foot passengers began to stream off, followed by every pent up, petrol driven vehicle known to man.

We quickly moved to join the fleeing throng and before you knew it we were once more on dry land, staring ahead at the tumult, the town, the mountain, and the covered terminal area; that separated the quay from the main road, where an old run down windmill stood forming a roundabout. Two thirds of the very basic terminal was full of foot passengers awaiting to fill our place on the boat. The other third was seemingly full of crazy people waving placards around in the air. For a moment I thought a protest was going on. What in the hell was it about?

As we got closer I could make out the signs, they were advertising the names of accommodation like Jimmy's Apartments, Hotel Livadia, Costas Rooms, and Paros Studios. Now I knew who the "Fishermen" were. One ran up to us. 'You want room?' He frantically asked.

'How much?' Queried Roger.

'How many you want?' He asked.

'We need three rooms for two nights.'

'Sixty euros each.'

'What you think?' I asked Roger.

'We'll get it cheaper.'

'Fifty euros each.' Countered the man.

'We'll ask around first.'

He gave up and left us for another catch, but we were soon fished again. Two were showing us their abodes on picture boards for around fifty each, when another came up and slyly asked how many nights we were staying. His offer was forty euros each for separate rooms including breakfast, plus he would do any washing we had for free.

It was an offer we could not refuse, especially for Roger, as the two shirts he'd brought had been pulled from his dirty laundry pile. And so we followed our enterprising hotelier to his minivan, piled aboard and went about half a mile from the harbour towards Livadia beach, turned right then right again, and stopped outside the man's two star hotel and went inside, to be shown three very comfortable rooms on the second floor.

What more could you ask? Well, I asked if you could smoke in the room, and he instantly produced a packet of cigarettes and offered me one, saying, 'In Greece, everybody smokes.' Well, you just had to like a place like that, didn't you?

The three of us took our time acquainting ourselves to our temporary residences. Each clean and tidy room included en-suite shower room, two comfy beds, a/c, refrigerator, television, and best of all, an ultra violet bug zapper. All for an incredible twenty euros a night. Ensconced, we changed out of our jeans into shorts, apart from Mark who didn't see the point. Then met up to take a quick walk into town to get the lay of the land and more importantly, to find a hole in the wall to get some cash out. Roger had recommended using cash machines rather than bringing the usual wad of cash or travelers cheques. I agreed, as like him my bank didn't charge for using my debit card abroad at the right link, and I got a good up to date exchange rate every transaction. It was taking a risk, there could always be a major system failure or a constant run on the machines, or a revolution, but it was less worry than storing money for the entire trip. We found a bank on the wide pavement leading from near the old windmill, to the main church and it's plaza.

I put my debit card in and withdrew mine and Mark's daily budget amount. The great thing about using the card was, with each receipt I could pretend to be in control of what I was spending everyday, even if I wasn't. I gave Mark sixty euros.

'Sixty? You said eighty a day.'

'You owe twenty euros for the room tonight, remember?'

'Don't I have to pay that?'

I could tell his mind was working on some debt ridden scheme to get the full eighty in his hands every day, I countered quickly to nip the idea in the bud..

'It would be better if I paid it Mark, that way there is
no problem is there?'

'No, but it is my money.' He sounded, all out of joint.

"Oh, oh, here we go" I thought, problems rearing their ugly head already.

Roger came to the rescue.

'Best if Paul deals with it Mark, seriously.'

He accepted the fact, though his grudging inner mind was still trying to compute eighty into sixty, but he kept it to himself for now.

We walked back to the hotel and prepared for the beach. This time, Mark changed into a pair of fetching black football shorts. His long thin legs and white pallid skin vividly contrasted. We sauntered down the road towards Livadia beach, which formed the eastern shore of the bay. On the first corner of the shore road we encountered a fish restaurant, which displayed some freshly caught squid on a high rack. They were well attended by some fifty flies, who were somewhat attracted to the pungent, fleshy suckered, long tentacled monsters.

Mark and Roger were all for going in there and eating one or two immediately, but I persuaded them to wait until after the beach, when perhaps the flies had all gone home sated. Further along was a pool hall with a lived-in bar and it had real American tables, proper pool. The kind of pool I had grown up on as a teenager in the Middle East. Squid or not, we'd be back here for a game later for sure.

We passed some scooter rental places and I took note of their cheap advertised prices; ten euro a day sounded too good to pass by. It had been ten years since I had ridden one but it would be a great way to see the island. Just before an end of shops, we sought out a mini-market and Roger and I stocked up on some beach essentials - crisps, nuts, chocolate, cigarettes and bottled water. We were served by a very attractive Greek girl who Roger engaged in conversation, or as much as you can engage a Greek girl in conversation.

'She was nice,' I said on walking out.

'Lovely.' Said Roger. 'And she talked to me, that was a rare thing for a Greek girl. Maybe she wasn't.'

I was puzzled.

'What, don't they normally?'

'No, it's the distance.'

'The distance?'

'Yeah, Greek women generally keep a distance between themselves and tourists; men like us.'

'Why?'

'Something to do with their culture I think.'

'Or maybe they know not to trust us?' I said offering good reason.

'Greek men aren't any better, especially with our women.'

'Shame, from what I've seen already some of them are gorgeous looking.'

'Yeah, some.'

'Sounds like a challenge to me, it can't be that bad.'

'Wait and see, you'll find out what I mean.'

While we had been talking about the finer points of life, Mark had been side tracked by a rack of sunglasses at a tourist trap shop next door, he caught up to us wearing a teardrop number with mirror lenses.

'What d'yer think? Cool hey?'

I had to admit they were, if a little early Seventy's looking.

'How much they cost you?' Asked Roger.

'Ten euro, and I got these too.'

He pointed down at some flash surfer sandals he was wearing, to replace the rather grotty plimsols he'd bought with him. Without doubt he suddenly looked the part, stringy white legs excluded.

'How much?' retorted Roger.

'Twenty euros, not bad hey?'

Roger and I looked at each other in amazement. In one fell swoop, Mark had managed to cut his budget for that day by fifty percent and we hadn't even gone out to play yet. At this rate Roger was going to be asked, nay pleaded with, to pay next month's rent earlier than planned.

Guided by Roger we found an ideal spot on the beach, secured three sun beds at a cost of three euros each and settled in. Behind us, beyond a low wall and dirt road, was a cool looking restaurant bar with a large part-shaded patio. It operated the beach beds and a waiter service, more importantly it had a toilet. In front us was the full sweep of the bay, where we witnessed the comings and goings of the ferry boats, every forty to fifty minutes it seemed. Nearby to our right were anchored a few private boats and yachts, some of which were presumably island hopping in their own unique way. A private beach club with it's own small landing pier filled the tail end of the beach To our left was the most impressive view of the mountain yet, a towering yet calming overseer.

It was a Saturday so the beach was reasonably busy, some beautiful bikinied women of a suitable age were on display, most appeared Greek, a few, tourists. We ordered three beers from the waiter and while Roger tucked into a book and the sun, Mark sat in the shade, reading a bin retrieved English newspaper, his pale legs covered by a towel. I went for a swim. Given how lovely and warm the air was, the water was surprisingly cool but once in it soon adjusted nicely. I swam on average four miles a week but I was now inclined to take a break from my usual routine and relax for a change, so I went a few metres one way and a few metres back, and floated on the surface a lot, absorbing the wonderful views and the fabulous atmosphere of Paros. I had only been there for three hours but I was already taken by the place. How great a feeling that moment in time was, barring dementia I won't forget it.

Suitably sunned, bathed, and relaxed by an afternoon on the beach we made our way back to the hotel. Roger and Mark as intended, called into the fish restaurant to try the squid, I declined and went back to my room for a well deserved sleep. We arranged to meet at the pool hall at eight.

Bad Scenes Outside the Storm Front...

I woke around seven fifteen and had a warmish shower, and changed into T-shirt, shorts and flip-flops - the undoubted uniform of warm climates. Curious, I checked out the TV to see what was available. It was seven or eight Greek speaking stations, with the odd lousy American film showing in English. I watched some current affairs show for awhile, followed by a game show, and then what was either a soap opera or a serious modern drama. In each case, a beautiful well dressed woman with overly styled hair, paired off against a middle aged be-suited man of no appeal. It was like three different versions of Mr and Mrs, except there was no challenge test, and one represented beauty and brains, and the other age and experience; either that or I was reading far too much into the coincidence.

Waylaid by my sudden interest in Greek programming and it's significance, I got to the pool hall late. Mark and Roger were already playing and two beers in. It was an ideal starting place for the night, especially as the beer was a euro fifty a bottle. We stayed about an hour racking up a few games, with me teaching both compadres the American way of playing pool, i.e. free and easy, no stupid scratch rules, no bloody snookers and no spotting the cue ball in a stupid D.

Mark did a fair imitation of Paul Newman in The Hustler, constantly changing the cue after a bad shot and over applying the chalk with hurried enthusiasm, which resulted in more powder on the baize than the tip. He was a fair player though, almost as good as me, even to the point of giving it the big show off; like you do when playing well.

'Is this what you do all the time at The Gardeners when you're not working?'

Asked an impressed Roger.

'Sometimes. What else am I supposed to do?'

'Get a job maybe.'

'That's easy for you to say.'

'Have you thought about playing professionally?'

'Think I'm good enough?'

'No.'

'I can beat anybody in The Gardeners.'

'That's not saying much.'

'It is; some top players there.'

'Like who?'

'Zipper, Speedball, Quickhand.'

'These are real people are they?'

'Yes, you'd know if you went there.'

'And you can beat them?'

'Yes.'

'What's your nickname then?'

'My nickname?'

'Well they've got monikers, so should you.'

'Haven't got one. Don't need one do I?'

'Is that because you're that good?'

'We could give him one Rog', how about Morechalk?'

'Morechalk?' Pained Mark reactively.

'How about Sponger?'

'Or Scrounger?'

'Or Cadger?'

'Or Moocher?'

'Very funny, you two. Piss off.'

'Well you need a name don't you?'

So far, everything was going really well but then again the evening was just underway. Leaving the pool hall, we took Roger's lead again and he took us to visit the old town for the first time. Along the way the shore road and it's pavements were largely deserted, and we passed mostly empty restaurants, clearly the season was winding down.

The old town consisted of narrow winding streets running this way and that. Underfoot, the irregular pieces of mortared togethered stone shined with wear. It's quaint two storied buildings were tightly packed together. Some with balconies, a lucky few with courtyards; the majority with businesses at ground level. Most had simple upper windows whose divided frames opened inwards and, along with much of the wood work in Paros, were painted Greek blue as decreed.

Roger took us to see the Frankish fort, which had been constructed from the remains of destroyed ancient buildings. Conically shaped and sat atop a high point overlooking the bay, it was interesting to see within it's outer wall the use of former carved columns, marble blocks, reliefs and stone needles. How we got there I don't know, for the old town initially appeared like a maze, and as Roger explained that was the whole idea, for in times gone by it helped to defend the place from sea marauders and invaders, who were unfamiliar with the layout and therefore could get easily confused and be prey to defeat by the town's defenders. Clearly in the case of the Franks that didn't work, they even scavenged the town's architectural legacy to state just who was King of the Castle for awhile. Joking aside, I for one was fascinated by it all.

We moved on down another winding path and ended up God knows where, but Roger knew, so we happily followed until encountering a bar that divided two paths. It was the Jazz Bar, a watering hole of note in the Lonely Planet guide. So we had a beer there and admired it's sunken floor, it's compact live music stage, it's well stocked bar and it's well established traditional feel; but it didn't do much for us on this occasion and we moved on to savour more immediate delights.

We came out of the old town onto the shore road again, but this time on the busy part, a stretch of mostly bars and restaurants vying for the evening crowd. We called in at two of the bars Roger knew and had a drink in each, but they were not exactly humming with night life, though some of the restaurants were busy. More worrying though, Mark was doing his famous party trick of going from Jekyl to Hyde in three easy drinks. Aside from the momentary lapses of reason, so far he had been pretty good but after leaving the Jazz Bar something began to take over.

The time was now nearing ten thirty and if I didn't eat soon I was going to resemble an active member of the infamous Donnor Party. I relayed my concern to the other two and Roger said he'd join me as he was hungry again. 'Fine, let's go look for a restaurant.' I said. Mark said nothing, instead he made a drunken point of reaching into his pocket and counting the small amount of change he had. "Guess who's not coming to dinner?" I thought. Even if he had the money, he'd reached that drunken point of no return, saying silly things to the waitress, laughing at things of his own witnessing, making gestures and arm movements to nobody in particular, only his own troubled mind. He was in short, making a spectacle of himself and becoming a bit of an embarrassment. No, I stand corrected, he was rapidly becoming an arsehole.

'How much money have you got left? I asked, trying to engage him back into the real world. He looked at me and shook his head, as if he had not heard me.

'Mark?' I barked and he stared at me.

'I said, how much money have you got left?'

'Nothing, I've got nothing; you've got it all.' He said pointedly.

I should have ignored the rebuke, but mistakingly I tried reasoning with him.

'Mark we discussed this, if I give you more money now then you'll have less for tomorrow and so on'.

'I don't care.'

'No, I know you don't, that's the problem with you. Besides you've had enough to drink already. You need to go home, sleep it off and wake up for a good day tomorrow.'

He stared blankly at me as if I was some kind of nut. Roger meanwhile stayed resolutely quiet but clearly not enjoying the situation one little bit.

'I'm not giving you anymore so you might as well go home. Roger and I have been buying the last few rounds and the night has a long way to go yet.'

'You're not going to buy me a drink?' He said accusingly.

'Not all night long, no. You shouldn't have bought the sunglasses and sandals should you?

'I needed them. I'm on holiday remember?'

'Well maybe you shouldn't have gone to Streatham on Monday and Tuesday, and blown four hundred and fifty quid of your holiday money, hey?'

As if on dramatic cue, a spectacular lightning storm started up at that moment. 'Wow, look at that.' I added in awed response. But Mark was in that world called boreish sullenness and couldn't even understand what I was talking about, even though his prompt for enacting the tribulations of King Lear had begun.

'You ready?' I asked Roger

'Yes.' He stated firmly.

We paid the bar bill, got up and walked out, leaving Mark sitting there. I turned back to him.

'Mark, what are you doing?'.

'I guess I'm going home.'

He stood up and followed us, but hung back. Soon Roger and I came across a restaurant we liked the look of, a traditional Greek taverna.

'Mark, Roger and I are going in here to eat, we'll see you in the morning yes?'

He made no verbal reply but gestured to say so what?.

'You've got your key to the room?'

The Marcel Marceau impressions kept coming, as he fumbled around in his pockets and eventually produced the room key.

'Good;' I said. 'See you in the morning.'

Roger and I went into the open style restaurant and sat down.

Mark stayed outside, took out a cigarette and tried lighting it but kept dropping it on the ground; then he came into the restaurant. "Fuck's sake." I thought. He stretched out the bent cigarette towards me.

'Light this will y'er?' He slurred.

'Sure.'

And so I lit the deformed cigarette and handed it back. He examined it and happy he slowly left, turning round at one point to utter, 'Enjoy your evening.' He moved on out of sight, in the general direction of the hotel and we began to relax slightly.

'Maybe we should have walked him back to the hotel first?' Said Roger surprisingly.

'No 'effing way, he's got to learn.'

And just then it started to rain somewhat, and along with Roger's words I began to feel a tad guilty; but only a tad.

The Owner came over from sitting down with the rest of his family, who were eating their evening meal before closing the place. A nicer man you could not wish to meet. We ordered two beef stifados and a half litre of house white. As the Owner came back with the metal jug of wine, Mark reappeared looking somewhat wet.

'I can't find the FUCKING HOTEL!' He exclaimed loudly.

'I can't get back to the SODDING room, understand?'.

'Mark, keep your voice down.' I told him.

'Don't tell me what the FUCK to do!.'

The concerned Owner looked at Mark and then at us, and couldn't see the connection. "Do you actually know this madman?" he appeared to be saying. I tried to calm the situation.

'Mark don't be a child, try again.'

'How can I?'

'You just follow the shore road until you get to the fish restaurant and turn up there, you know where it is.'

'I don't know where it fucking is! You need to help me!' He shouted.

I was beginning to feel uncomfortable, not so much for me but for the Owner and his family, especially the kids.

'Mark you are being obnoxious, there are women and children here; now shut it and leave!'

'Fuck you!'

'Leave now Mark, before I get mad.'

'Go away Mark.' Added Roger for effect.

Mark stood staring at us with unconcealed rage, while we chose to ignore him. He then turned and stormed off.

'You WANKERS!' He exclaimed super loudly.

'Absolute fucking WANKERS!'

Not soon after, it began to rain even harder, as more spectacular flashes of lightning lit the sky, accompanied by the ominous heavy rumble of thunder. Providing the perfect theatrical atmosphere to Mark's tawdry Lear.

'He'll get soaked.' Said Roger.

'Good; may he get struck by lightning too.' I said piteously.

When the Owner came back with our food, myself and Roger apologized profusely, he took it with no hard feelings though the same couldn't be said about Roger.

'That was bad Paul, really bad.'

'I know it was. I had a feeling the first day could be trouble but not like this. He was fine for ages though. I don't know what happens to him, he suddenly changes. Did he drink much at the fish restaurant?'

'Not really, same as me.'

Well that wasn't a good indicator I thought, and wasn't sure what it meant given Roger's capacity for drink.

'And he went for a kip afterwards?'

'Far as I know.'

'He must have some booze in his room.'

'If he does that again tomorrow then I'm definitely off, I'm not going to put up with him.'

'Let's see hey? He's out of his safety zone. He freaked.'

'I mean it, he does that again I'm going.'

What could I say? I was in complete agreement.

'Me too.'

'You'd leave him here?'

'Yes, it's my holiday to enjoy also.'

Mark was on the verge of ruining the trip, and if it meant cutting him loose as a stray then so be it, we'd leave and pick him up on our return to Paros. Presumably from the gutter or the jail, or Golden Beach. How could I possibly do that though? He was a mate after all and he couldn't survive one day out here without one of us being around. Well, it didn't seem that difficult a decision at the time, let's put it that way.

Roger and I finished our good food and wine, and paid up, thanking the Owner for his understanding and patience; though his family didn't warrant the dire performance.

'Where to now?' I asked Roger.

'There's Tree Tops, fancy going there?'

'Sure, where is it?'

'Back where we were but higher up.'

'Let's go.'

We walked back towards the previous bar, strolling past until we came to a section where the buildings stopped and a high retaining wall was in place for a hundred yards or so. Halfway along, Roger pointed up above the wall.

'It's up there.' He said.

I peered up to see a singular two storied building built on the last of two terraces on the rocky hill side, with a stairway leading to an open door, above which was a sign obscured by a bright light. The place was somewhat masked by four tall palm trees that grew from the first terrace above the wall. Stone steps stood at the far end of the wall, where the next set of buildings began. With a twist here and a turn there, they led to the upper terrace and on up into the old town.

The terrace was narrowly spacious and to the right, a stone bench had been formed from the hill leading along to the building. Left, a low wall marked the boundary of slope and level, and was nicely lined with chairs and tables which all lay unoccupied. We climbed the stairway to the upper door and entered into a different but instantly likable world. The first thing that struck me was the trippy, cool music that was being played. I was not familiar with any of it, but it was new and exciting, and music to my ears, it matched the warm languid feel exuded by Paros.

The other immediacy, aside from the physical dimensions of the place, was the low key lighting. Candles on the tables and bar area as per course, but strung along and hung down low over the bar at varying heights, were a number of spherical glass lamps; swirled in colours of red, orange, blue and yellow, and just like the music they were quite hypnotic and soothing. The rectangular room was about four meters by nine meters, with the long bar taking up about a third of the space. There must have been twenty people in there, locals mostly, with two barmen and a DJ behind the bar. One of the barmen recognized Roger from his June trip and gave us a warm welcome.

'You come back.' He said to Roger.

'Yes, couldn't keep away.'

Roger introduced me and he poured us two large draught beers on order and a minute later, he further handed us two free shots of Sambuca as a welcome and we toasted with him. Me, somewhat reluctantly, as I wasn't a shot type person, in fact I secretly looked upon it with all the enthusiasm of drinking thick bleach.

'Yamas!' He cried.

'Yamas!' We replied.

As he collected the empty glasses and moved away I quickly asked Roger,

'What in the hell did we just say?'

'Yamas; that's the Greek way of saying cheers, but it's more encompassing.'

That one magical word goes a long way to explaining the heart and soul of Greek culture. It speaks of welcome, of hospitality, of warmth, of good times, of health and cheer, of thankfulness. And of saying, "Welcome to Greece Paul."

Two hours went by, we drank plenty more beer and under goading from Roger had a couple more shots, though they didn't go down any easier for me than the first one. Enthused, relaxed and friendly, we talked to some people including a lovely girl or two, though as Roger had said, the Greek girls definitely kept their distance. The place got busier, close to packed and the DJ played better and better music, artfully altering the style and mood along the way. We met some Australian guy who had just come from hopping the Cyclades. He told us that Ios was closed down and not worth visiting now, and that everywhere else was getting quiet; which rather took some wind out of our sails. Then, as I was looking out one of the small windows either side of the door, I saw something I will never forget. It was the sight of a fast moving ferry boat, lit up like a huge chandelier, coming in to dock; and the perspective from Tree Tops high position, appeared to magnify it's presence. It was something to behold, floating larger than life across a darkened sea. It had a real absorbing power, a fantastic sight to encounter. Either that or I'd had way too much to drink.

A Slip of the Card...

The next morning, the Sunday, I arose at a ridiculously early hour considering what I'd drank not too many hours previous. I was keen to discover what Mark's state of mind was, so I listened in on his room door but couldn't hear a thing, so satisfied he was asleep I went into town to go to the bank and then look into renting a scooter. Along the way I got to thinking that maybe he didn't make it back last night, that he could be just waking on the beach still no wiser as to where the hotel was, and clueless as to why his clothes were damp. Come what may, if I got the scooter I determined to take him on a ride straight away and make him feel involved in events, before things deteriorated further.

The town was busy, many locals out and about congregating outside the main church, or indulging in coffee, pastries, and the odd ouzo at the busy pavement cafes. Numerous tourists and travelers thronged around the windmill and terminal area, preparing for departure and the arrival of their respective ferries due in. I went to the same bank from the previous day; waited in line for the cash machine and come my turn, I pulled out my wallet, went to extract my debit card from it's regular place, and to my shock and dismay discovered it was missing. I checked my wallet thoroughly, then my pockets, but there was neither hide nor hair of it. "Shit." I reasoned. I had a few euros on me, so I went to a nearby cafe and ordered a strong coffee, then worked my memory overtime to establish what had happened to my valued card.

One thing I knew, was I used it often in my day to day life and always in the same way and manner. So the fact it was suddenly missing didn't make much sense, it was like losing a trusted and dependable friend. I questioned and answered myself, hoping to arrive at a possible explanation.

Q. "Think, when did I last remember using it?"

A. "Yesterday at the same cash machine."

Q. "Did you use it later? At the restaurant say?

A. "No, the cash machine was the last place. Hmmm."

The caffeine began to whir the slow moving gears of my brain into sync. I ran through the memory of processing the machine. "Let's see I put the card in. It asked me for Greek or English, then my pin number which was accepted, then how much I wanted, two hundred, yes...ahhh." The least conscious part of my recall clicked into place and I had a eureka moment, which being in Greece was very appropriate. I got the money before the card! Therein lay the solution. I felt rather proud of myself.

"I say Holmes, well done."

"It was nothing my dear Watson. Truly nothing."

"And all before breakfast too."

In the UK I always took my card back before the money was dispensed, and it made a convenient alert noise requiring you to do so. Here, I had extracted the money first, thereby assuming that in the normal scheme of things, I had already taken my card and put it back in my wallet, which I hadn't. A moment or two after taking the money, I'd turned away from the machine which then inquired if I wished to finish using the bank's services, and receiving no answer determined I did and returned my card from the slot in a slow juddering manner; without an informing high pitched whistle or bell, or merry tune. What a dimwit! Me of course, not the machine, that was just doing it's job. I was on auto-response.

There was my problem in a nutshell, I had left it in the bloody machine without a hint of realizing it. Other than me who could I blame? Mark! He was there and desperate for his money, so I had that on my mind at the time. It was definitely his fault. But on a more practical level just what was I going to do now? Being a Sunday, the Bank was closed all day, if someone had handed the card in then I wouldn't be able to get a hold of it until Monday morning. Roger would be able to sub me until then, but what if someone had my card and had figured out a way of using it? I had to call my bank and tell them I'd lost the damn thing. What a bloody mess. How was I going to do that? The number to call was on the card. I'd passed an internet cafe on the way to town, I could get on line there and find the number to call HSBC. So I did, and I also purchased a phone card, in order to call from a phone box outside the Post Office.

After pushing in more numbers than was healthy for my index finger, I managed, incredibly, to get through first time (typically, I've found such situations a bit like trying to thread a needle with a shaky hand.) and in a bit of a stressed state explained the predicament. Rather more incredibly, they knew everything already. Firstly, they had confirmation that my card had been handed into the bank so it hadn't been stolen or misused; unfortunately, it was the bank's policy to destroy the card three hours of keeping it.

"What?!" I shrieked in my head. Immediately I'm thinking, I'll have to ask Roger for a major loan and pay him back when we get home; when the very helpful service rep pointed out that I had an HSBC credit card.

'Yes, that's right I do.'

'Do you have it with you?' She asked.

'Yes, but it only has a limit of five hundred pounds.'

Chicken feed for this holiday, I'm thinking.

'Not a problem, with your authorization we can transfer
money from your current account to your credit card.'

And with those few accommodating words, hey presto, accessing my money for the holiday problem solved. Well not quite, because of course I couldn't for the life of me remember my security password, so I had to be passed over to a manager who had to be convinced that I was who I said I was, which proved difficult, because apart from my address and birth date, I couldn't give the right response to any of the security answers I had given upon registration of the card. Simple, easy to answer questions like, "What is your favourite colour?" I got wrong. In the end I think the authentic timbre of my general concerned state convinced him I was Paul McCloskey.

We then had to re-set all the security information and the like; at the end of which the money was transferred to my credit card and I could exhale a big sigh of relief. Hereon, I had to make sure that I understood how Greek ATM's operated and to double check for the rest of the holiday, that whenever I used the machines I had my card back safe where it belonged. Got it? Got it. I cannot remember the re-set security password though.

I lavishly thanked the people on the phone who had helped me through the minor trauma of feeling cut off from the world; their fantastic service and manner was second to none, they even wished me a great holiday. Whoever you were thanks a million, you were truly amazing. Happy, I strolled down the road towards the scooter rental place; feeling good, a renewed swagger in my step.

The Great Escapade...

There were a number of scooters to choose from, different makes and cc's, Italian made mostly. I was checking them out, when I heard a voice from some steps that led from the street to an office fifty feet up on the hillside.

'Do you want a bike? Twelve euros a day. My best price.'

I looked up at a Greek lady in her forties, with a strong attractive face.

'You want?'.

'Maybe.'

'How many days you need?'

'Two maybe three.'

'I give you the 80cc for twenty euros, two days.'

'How much for the 125cc?'

'Is more expensive. Thirty euro.'

'For two days?'

'Yes, for two days.'

'Okay, I'll take it.'

She came down to street level and ran the rule over me.

'You ride a scooter before?'

'Yes a 125cc for three years, ten years ago.'

'Because you know I have many people who ride not so good and have accident. Somebody similar to you just recently. A Canadian, I have his license and he owes me money.'

'Don't worry, I do know how to ride these things; safely.'

I added, to comfort her obvious concern.

'I have a 125cc here.' She pointed to a new looking bike.

'It looks good'

'Brand new from May, very nice.'

'It has oil?' She checked out the level.

'Maybe it needs some more. Where are you going?'

'Around the island.'

'Let's go to the office. I need a driving license, you have?

'Yes, I have this.'

I gave her my California license with a less than flattering photo attached. I half expected her to say, "Who is this?" But she didn't.

'This is American. But you are not American, no?'

'No, I lived there for many years, but I live in London now.'

We got to the office and did the straight forward paperwork. She took and kept my license as security and I paid her thirty euros cash. She gave me the copy of the hire agreement and a tourist map of the island, pointing out the good spots to go if I was so inclined. She was a bright intelligent lady, who operated the business with her husband, who also had an internet business on the go. They had two grown children and like a lot of Greek islanders, spent the winter months living and working in Athens. In conversation I told her how much I liked Paros and that this was my first time to Greece, and where we might be going. I mentioned the small possibility of going to Rhodes.

'Rhodes? The ferry is tomorrow night.'

'Really?' I perked up.

'Yes but you must get it in Syros.'

'Syros?' I said with a note of disappointment.

'Yes, but it is easy, many ferries go to Syros.'

'Oh, okay, that could work.'

'I have helmet, do you want?' I didn't, but thought of Mark.

'Yes, I'll take one for my friend.'

She gave me a one size fit's all number, which made you look super uncool. Even better for Mark I thought.

'Careful hey? This Canadian he still in hospital in Athens.'

Her reminder about the poor unfortunate Canuck was unwarranted though understandable, perhaps I came across as reckless; who knows how people view you from their side of things?

'I'll be fine don't worry, I will be extra careful for you.'

Placated, she picked up a bottle of oil and we went to the bike and she showed me the basics; how to start it being the most important. She topped up the oil then checked the petrol tank.

'You must go straight to the station for petrol.'

'How much is there?'

She looked once again, sloshing the tank.

'Enough to go to the station.' What an answer I thought.

She showed me on the map where it was, then I straddled the seat and familiarized myself with the functions - indicators, horn etc; and shoved the bike forward to move it off it's stand, held it's weight and started the engine. No doubt I'd have a bit of rust to shake off but I already felt comfortable. There were a few things I had to remember, the most important being, always read and anticipate the situation ahead. Which essentially meant keeping a beady eye out for cars suddenly pulling out or car doors opening. Another was, don't be shy to use the horn anytime you need to let 'em know you're there.

Checking the road first, I twisted the throttle and went off slowly, tried a couple of quick emergency brake procedures to make sure I shifted hand controls; as in emergencies, novice riders can all too often forget to shift grip, and accelerate, rather than brake. After a few hundred yards I began to ride more freely, opening her up and running through the pattern of throttle and brake. Now I was really recalling how to ride, using my body to move with the bike, especially around corners and swerves. I tore along the road, passing Tree Tops and the long line of shore front businesses. At the far end, I followed the road steeply up to a bluff, where a large hotel dominated. Passing it, the road wound and twisted and I encountered two dilapidated windmills. Soon the road junctioned with a main road back in to town, and I took the left and went in search of the petrol station, before it was too late.

Riding in the warm air without a helmet I had the feeling of being totally free, in response I went faster, as there was little traffic ahead. I wasn't being cocky or stupid just calculated, assured, experienced. Even though it had been ten years or so since I had ridden the streets of Santa Barbara, California on a scooter, it had taken less than five minutes to ease back into form. Elephants may never forget and nor do humans generally. I found the station with no bother and filled the tank for five euros. From there I rode north on the road to Naoussa, a fishing village four to five miles away, but I only went two miles and turned back. It was time to gather up Mark, there was no telling what the response would be, but hopefully he'd come; it would be good therapy after that disastrous evening. Getting back to the hotel, I knocked on his door.

'Yes?' I heard him say a little sheepishly.

'Morning matey. Listen, I've hired a scooter and I'm going on a ride around the island, want to come?'.

He opened the door already dressed for the beach, seemingly fine; oblivious to the shenanigans of the previous evening.

'Will it take long?'

'An hour I guess, I've never been around it before.'

'I need some breakfast first.'

I wasn't sure if that meant a drink or food, or if in Mark's mind they are one and the same. Problem was, if we took breakfast first I knew he wouldn't come on the ride. I thought quickly, averting the chances of another repeat performance.

'Tell you what, let's get on the bike and we'll stop in this place called Naoussa and have breakfast. It's only two miles away, and we can go on from there.' I lied the distance.

Mark thought about it; as he did I further added,

'I'm buying.' Said with a salesman's touch.

'Do I need to take anything?'

'Bring a top and some sunscreen.' He went and gathered both.

'Money, I haven't got any money.' As if I didn't know.

'I'll get some out in Naoussa.'

Assured, he pocketed his cigarettes and lighter.

'Don't forget your sunglasses, you'll need those.'

'I can't find them.'

'You can't find them? Here let's have a look.'

I helped search for them but they were nowhere to be seen.

'When was the last time you remember seeing them?'

I asked with a severe case of deja vu or something like it.

'Don't remember.'

'So you've lost them?'

'Think so.'

Now there was a surprise. This was a man who could lose anything, including a house.

'Come on then let's go.'

'Have you got a helmet for me?'

'Yes, top of the range.'

'Because the last time I was on a scooter there was a crash.'

I must admit, by now the portents were not sounding good. First the scooter lady and now Mark relaying the accident theme big time.

'Mark trust me I'm a good rider, nothing will happen.'

I was officially tempting fate. I went and knocked on Roger's door.

'Huh?'

'Listen mate I'm taking Mark for a scooter ride. We'll be back in a couple of hours. You going down the beach later?'

'Yuh.'

'Okay, we'll see you there hey? Same spot.'

'Yuh.'

'By the way, Mark has lost his sun glasses already.'

'Guuud.'

Mark and I exited the hotel and I pointed out the scooter.

'Is that it?'

'Yes, why?'

'I thought you meant like a motorbike.'

'No I told you, a scooter.'

'You'd better go on your own then, I'll stay here.'

'Why?'

'How's it going to carry the two of us?'

'No you idiot it will get us around, don't worry.'

'Are you sure? It looks too small.'

'It's a 125cc, plenty enough power for two. Come on.'

I got on and pushed it off the stand, and shifted further down in the seat. I pointed out the two foot pedals for his feet and warned him not to touch the exhaust pipe with his bare legs or toes. He got on and immediately put his arms around me. At seventeen or so I probably wouldn't have thought much about it but not now, it looked decidedly gay and besides, who wanted a friend like Mark clinging onto your mid-drift for two hours or so? I quickly implored:

'Don't hold on to me mate. It's not safe that way. Grab hold of
the handles at each side of the seat.'

'I thought I had to wrap my arms around you?'

'Only if you're a beautiful girl with big tits.'

'But I thought it made the bike go faster.'

'Well I'm not worried about that am I? We're not going to be
racing Valentino Rossi.'

'Who?'

'Never you mind.'

I waited patiently while he found the proper handles to hold and to position himself comfortably, in a fashion. After which I remembered the helmet.

'Hold on, forgot the bloody helmet.'

'Are you wearing one?'

'Hell no.'

'But what about your head, didn't you fracture your skull a few years ago?'

'Yes, but I'm not bloody wearing a helmet.'

'I don't want to wear one.'

'You sure?'

'Yeah.'

'Better wear some sunscreen on your head then.'

'I'll be alright.'

'Sure?' Pointedly staring at his mostly hairless head.

'Sure.'

'Okay, your decision.'

We took off, knowing in either one of my nostrils he wouldn't be.

Taking the back streets by the hotel, I weaved our way up to the main road to Naoussa, essentially the same road that would lead us around the island. It was clear sky and wonderfully sunny, just what you needed on a bald pate with no sunscreen. I decided to go steady on the bike, having two people on it made it a more difficult ride, though when the opportunity arose I'd open her up.

Leaving Parakia behind, we quickly encountered lovely wild countryside, sparsely populated by roadside buildings and the odd small farmhouse or residence. About two miles in we climbed a hill and coming over it, stared down into a fabulous view of prominences either side. The sea ahead, rolling open land between, and the road stretched out in front. It caught our attention, and we shouted about it over the noise of the engine and the sound of the wind. There was hardly any other traffic, it was like having the place to ourselves. Ten minutes later a sign told us Naoussa was a kilometer ahead, and the road curved to the right and began to wind in to some bends, which the bike easily glided at a constant speed. We were now skirting a big bay, deep blue in colour and devoid of any boats and human activity; presumably because it was whipped up by an ever present wind.

Rising up the eastern bluff of the bay, passing a series of apartments that looked out to the sea, we came into Naoussa. We followed the road around and down to the main area, where the small harbour lay, and easily parked the bike. Mark got off first, seemingly a new man.

'That was great, can we do it again?'.

'Got the rest of the island yet.'

'Fantastic.'

'Let's check it out shall we?'

Appropriately, we did a quick stroll around Naoussa's pretty harbour which was packed tight with restaurants, cafes, and retail business. A number of fishing boats lined the quay and they were variously, offloading the day's catch or cleaning up after them, or preparing to go out when the time came. Small ferry boats were plying passengers back and forth to Naxos or spots of interest close by. An old fort protected the harbour's east side; small and compact it now acted as less a deterrent to attack, than as a barrier from the elements.

The buildings and streets were much like Parakia's yet different. Incorporating the scenic harbour and less numerous, they held you more in thrall by their simplicity; and in places by their sheer picture postcard aesthetic. For example, some of the main harbour restaurants backed on to a small wharf type area, which faced and defined an inlet marina filled with small traditional boats. Brightly coloured and all displaying the striking blue and white Greek flag, with it's cross in the top left hand corner. Plain wooden dining chairs and tables, filled much of the ground space and it all looked so quaint and magical.

Tour done, we settled at a cafe facing the fishing boats and a very attractive Greek lady in her thirties served us. We ordered some eggs, toast and coffee, and I got a nice smile from her. I asked Mark if he wanted a drink, but to his credit he said he'd wait for later. That was a positive sign, presumably the exhilarating ride here had helped blow the cobwebs away. While enjoying breakfast, our server and Naoussa, Mark and I talked; but I left mention of the previous night's events strictly off the menu. I felt it was no good upsetting him again and besides I knew that he would claim to have no recollection of it. But from hereon, everything had to start going well as he was on shaky ground, but I didn't tell him that. Instead we discussed the bike.

'I can't believe it takes the two of us!'

The ride to Naoussa.

'How did you learn to ride that well?'

And,

'Those cows we saw weren't they amazing. Wasn't expecting
to see real cows amongst all that scenery, were you?'

No, I wasn't, they rather caught me by surprise too. More amazingly
he had the gall to say,

'I'm so glad I came on this trip with you and Rog', I'm having
such a great time already.'

Hey? Followed by.

'I'm in Greece! I'm on me holidays, yeah.' He said smiling and
laughing.

Chalk and cheese? More like salt and sugar.

Hallowed be thy Sands...

Breakfast, Naoussa and chequered memories successfully done, we got back on the bike; quickly consulted the map and took off to conquer the circumnavigation of Paros. It would take at least an hour but if you are going to spend an hour doing anything, you might as well do this particular trip once in your life, as I discovered. Turning left out of Naoussa, we went a short distance and met with the main east road and took a right to head south. Soon we were steadily bombing along, re-invigorating the senses and taking in the land. Progressively, a spectacular open vista across the channel to the sister island of Naxos, opened up.

'Look at that would you?' I said, awed.

We fell into stunned silence for the next ten minutes, as we balanced the view ahead of us, the view to the right of us and the incredible view to left of us. The only problem was, the wind was getting much stronger and we were now facing it. Not only was the buffering hard going, the wind chill factor was too, even though it was a warm sunny day. I had to pull over for a minute and we put on our light jackets which we had sensibly taken along for such an occasion. I felt justified and superior in bringing mine. There is nothing worse than taking something with you on holiday which you never use, and therefore is just dead weight and taking up valuable space in your bag.

We piled back on the bike and for the next few kilometers imagined that Easy Rider had nothing on us, as we wheeled south picking up speed; passing by the villages, the small holdings, the abandoned old builds, the abandoned new builds (seemingly a regular and distressing sight in Greece. All formed cement and protruding re-bar.), the holiday apartments, the dilapidated windmills, and the many topographical features. One in particular, a huge round hill with a monastery on the top, defied any understanding of how it came to be there. As idiots do, we conjectured that Aliens had built it and half way believed ourselves.

Thankfully by then, the frontal wind was easing or rather our direction was changing to it, as we now rode along the southern part of Paros heading west. Lo and behold, we turned a bend and came upon a faded sign that read: Golden Beach 500 meters.

'Did you see that?' I shouted back at Mark.

'No, what?'

'Just passed a sign that said Golden Beach.'

'No, never.'

'You want to go check it out?'

'Yeah.'

'We'll go see if the Magic Bus is still there, hey?'

'The what?'

'The bus.'

'What bus?'

'Your Magic Bus.'

'Oh that.'

Two minutes later, another less than obvious sign for the fabled beach appeared and indicated for us to take a narrow dirt path to our left, which we did.

The bike's suspension had to work overtime as we slowly made our way down the inclining route, just wide enough for the width of a car and pot holed to hell. After a half mile bumpy slow ride down, we met with the proper road coming from a different direction, which was tarmacked and two cars wide! Riding it to it's end, a few houses, apartments, hotels and two restaurants marked the location of Golden Beach.

A hell of a wind was blowing across the sea or more precisely the straight, as an uninhabited island lay directly off the coast, with the tail end of Naxos lying to the east. Clearly it was a favoured spot for windsurfers, as absolutely dozens of them were in the water, whipping along on their boards utilizing their sails to full effect. Some appeared to go faster than a speed boat, while others where flying way up into the air as they took off on a crest. More surprises, I thought.

Eventually I got around to checking out the actual beach, which after all the fabled nonsense wasn't very appealing. Aside from the wind surfers who were mostly at sea, it was essentially empty. The beach itself was sandy, it was light coloured but it wasn't much longer than seven hundred meters in length, perhaps less. It's name definitely did not live up to it's actuality; though I did read later that the type of sand here produced a sparkle effect during bright sunlight, but not on that day. I must confess I was expecting some idyllic spot and I was also expecting to see, the rusting hulk of a Magic Bus sunk into the beach and sea. So was Mark.

'Ahhh, it's not there.'

'What isn't?'

'The bus.'

'They wouldn't have left it there would they?'

For all the world sounding like I truly believed in Mark's tale.

'Suppose not.'

'Fancy a beer?' I asked, knowing the answer.

Sitting, digesting a nice cold Greek lager beer at the nearest restaurant, I tried to make sense of why a windswept beach of no real beauty became so wrapped up in the folk lore of the Sixties and Seventies counter culture, and was now one of the best locations in the world for wind surfing? Well easy really; back in the day if you were a dope smoking, sexually liberal tourist of roughly 16-24 years of age and you wished to escape the attentions of your elders, moral society, the authorities, and you lacked money for shelter and food, well you came to the sumptuously named Golden Beach; because nobody outside of what you desired or had did. It was completely out of the way of prying eyes, and that meant you could live on there for the entire summer for free, in the open. Nights were warm and dreams were easy, as Bob Seger sang. You got stoned on somebody else's hash; got drunk on incredibly cheap bottles of ouzo, raki, Metaxa and whatever else; survived on low cost calamari, sardines, feta cheese, olives, and bread; listened to people playing acoustic guitar and bongos, and if you were one of the chosen few, got laid a lot with numerous partners. And it was all done in the spirit of sharing; diseases included. It was breaking the rules and somewhat illegal, so very liberating and great fun as a result.

Would I have done it back then if I had been of an age? Absolutely not, they had no sunscreen to talk of! I would have been a pale freckled ginger haired idiot, with a stupid laugh and no sex appeal, hiding in the shade. Overly concerned about money, meeting women, and going mad if I smoked too much hash. On the other hand how could you not have enjoyed it? It was a time and a place like no other and never likely to be again.

Suitably refreshed Mark and I got back on the bike, trundled back up the same route we came for some illogical reason (given it's direction we assumed it would be quicker, but upon reaching the top we naturally found that the proper road was only a few yards away.), with Mark having to get off once or twice so the bike would make it, and got back on the main road for the last part of the trek. Again we were treated to some wonderous sights and views, all taken in with a great relaxed air. The islands of Anti-Paros were a sight to behold and we passed the sign posted quarry where the marble used for the Venus De Milo was taken from, that fact alone made my day.

Some twenty five minutes later and we were back in Parakia pulling up outside our hotel. Aching in the nether regions and wearied by the adventure, and now contemplating going down the beach to meet with Roger. Mark wasn't quite ready to face the daunting challenge of going straight to the beach and said he'd meet us there. I still had not got him any money yet, so I wasn't concerned he'd go off and get blottoed, but I did make him promise me that he would meet us in an hour. 'Yes, yes, I'll be there.' He ratified.

I think he just needed a little snooze, for that matter so did I; something about riding a scooter around takes it out of you, especially after an hour and a half in the warm sun, with the wind buffeting you at times and all that first time sight seeing. Bloody exhausting, let me tell you. Anyway, I reasoned I could sleep on the beach and kill two birds etc.

I left Mark to his happy trails and went to the bank first, taking out two hundred euros and positively ensuring that I had my card back. Of course I still couldn't be absolutely sure, that what they said they were going to do had actually not happened for some reason, and I wouldn't find out for another two days at the rate of withdrawal. The things I worry about.

Tammy Hurtfinger...

Passing the scooter place, I saw the lady owner outside with a customer and beeped the horn and waved, she smiled back. I was hoping the gesture would help secure her the rental. I reached the spot by the beach and parked up to the low wall. I could see Roger sunning it, already on to another book, beer and cigarette close to hand.

'You already finished the other one?'

'Just now. How did it go?'

'Great, fantastic island. That view over to Naxos on the east coast is amazing.'

'What was Naoussa like?'

'Lovely place, smaller than here, quainter. We should go for a meal there tonight.'

'Could do. How was Mark?'

'Surprisingly good. 'Course nothing was mentioned about last night's performance.'

'So he's alright is he?'

'At present yes. At least he's laughing and smiling.'

'What do you think?'

'Well, we're not going to get an apology are we? So let's just tag along and see how he does the rest of the day hey?'

'Think he'll behave?'

'I think the first day was always going to be difficult for him. I'm hoping that it's all over with and he's had his tantrum, and we can all get on with having a good time from hereon, but do me a favour mate, just for today.'

'What?'

'Don't provoke him too much. I mean taking the piss has done him some good but not today; know what I mean?'

'No, I know what your saying, I won't.'

'Oh by the way, he's burnt the top of his head.'

Roger looked at me with a knowing smirk.

'Oh and we went to Golden beach.'

'And?'

'It wasn't there.'

'Do you believe that story?'

'No, of course not. I had to check it out though.'

I settled onto the sun bed for all of two minutes.

'Do you want a beer? I'm going to get one.'

I went to the bar and got two beers, admiring the rather lovely form of the waitress who was lithe, tanned and blonde, and who warmly smiled back at me. Back in England I would have likely got a scowl. I re-joined Roger and told him all about the missing card episode, and described the scooter journey in more detail. We then had a swim out to where some boats were anchored and trod water for awhile, looking back at the beach,

'Any birds around?' I asked.

'Some, not by us though.'

'Is that a volleyball net I saw further up the beach?'

'Yes, looks like it.'

'Can we play on it do you think?'

'Think so.'

'I'll go and buy a ball then.'

We made our way back to the sun beds to dry down.

'You had any more thoughts on where to go after this?' Roger asked.

'Well funny enough, the lady I rented the scooter from told me there was a ferry to Rhodes tomorrow night.'

'So you don't want to go to Ios?'

'Well if that Aussie guy said it's closed down, it hardly seems worth going does it?'

'What time does it leave?'

'I don't know, just tomorrow night and we have to go somewhere first to meet it. I can't remember where.'

'Mykonos?'

'No I don't think so.'

'What y'er reckon?'

'I'm up for it.'

'What about Mark?'

'He's got no bloody choice in the matter. Besides, who knows? After tonight he might be staying here.'

'So you want to eat in Naoussa later?'

'Yeah, I think it will be good; and you ought to see the place if you've never been.'

'Maybe we should stay there when we come back.'

'Maybe.'

Suddenly, we were interrupted by a familiar voice.

'There you bloody are! I've been up and down this fucking

beach trying to find you.'

Mark looked hot, sweaty and flustered. His balding head was bright red from the copious amount of sun it had been, and was still receiving.

'Well, you knew where we were.'

'I didn't. I didn't have a fucking clue.'

'But this is the same place we were yesterday.'

'No, we were down there somewhere.'

He said, pointing in some general misguided direction.

'Mind you, we have just been in for a long swim.'

'Ah well, how d'yer expect me to find you then?'

'Tell you what, I'll plant a flag tomorrow, the skull and cross bones; that way you'll find us.'

'You bloody would too, just for me.' He laughed.

'It'll be like a homing beacon. Even in your worse state, you'll be able to make it out in the blur of the alcohol.'

'Ah go on, get one. Can we get one?' Excited by the idea.

'Probably not, but how about a Greek flag?'

It held his excitement in check.

'Anyway I found you finally, damn near killed me. I was all the way down past those huts looking for you.'

'But it's nowhere near the bar.' Remarked Roger.

'The bar? What bar?'

In unison we both turned, pointed and said, "That bar!"

'Remember it? We had a beer and sandwich there yesterday.'

'They all look the same to me.'

'Not this one, it's the only one by the beach.'

'Very witty Rog' and for that I'll have to buy you a beer.'

He looked at me and lowering his voice in case any of the neighbouring sun worshipers heard, implored.

'Have you got any money for me?'

And I replied, quite loudly;

'Yes I have your money for the day, would you like it all now?'

He suppressed laughing by chewing his mouth around. Of course he hadn't minded them hearing those swear words, which often offend decent society in public, but never mind.

'Tell you what, how about we get on the bike and go to the shop. I'm going to buy a volleyball, and we can get a shed load of beer for half the price we pay at the bar.'

'Do we have to get back on the bike?'

'No, but it's easier that way.'

'Alright then.' He said forlornly.

'Why what's the matter with the bike?'

'My arse hurts from sitting on it all that time.'

'Well so does mine.'

He then perked up, as if receiving a vital jolt in the recesses.

'I can get some sunglasses!' Oh, oh.

'Yes, you can.' I said, with trepidation.

We went to the shop Mark and I, instinctively still trying to grab me around the mid-rift on take-off. We got some beer and a beach volley ball and Mark liked the look of some paddles with a small ball, so I got those too and paid for the whole lot, and gave him his sixty euros.

'Go easy on it mate, that's all I'm saying. I'm not your Dad

I know that, but we're going to Nassau tonight for dinner,

so just take it easy.'

'I will.' He replied with some indignity.

I went to the bike and waited awhile for Mark to reappear.

He came out wearing sunglasses and a baseball cap.

'Looks good, how much?'

'It was only twenty euros. Good hey?' Referring to the look, not the

cost.

'Ray-Bans, see?' He showed me the maker's mark.

'And the hat?'

'Timmy Hillsberger.'

'You mean Tommy Hilfilger.'

'Is it?' He took it off to check. 'You're right'.

Well I usually was. I didn't have the heart to tell him that he had just

paid way over the odds for some fake merchandise, but if it made him feel

good, great, let it be.

We joined Roger back at the beach. He looked at Mark,

'Got a hat too.'

'Yeah, needed it just in case my head got burnt.'

We both laughed hard.

'Okay, what's the bloody joke.'

'It already is Mark.'

'Only a little bit.'

We laughed again.

'Oh fuck off now. The both of you!'

'What's the badge say?' Asked Roger.

'I don't know; why can't you read?'

'I just want to know is all, sorry for asking.'

'Who is it again Paul?'

'Tammy Hurtfinger.' I replied; not given to the truth.

'There you are, Tammy Hurtfinger. Top designer.'

By this time I had collapsed on the sun bed in hysterics. So much for my warning Roger not to tease the boy today.

Mark took the hat off to check the name.

'You're a cunt McCloskey. An unmitigated cunt!'

Lucky for me and Roger, Mark saw the funny side of it. I grabbed my beer and reached up with it.

'Cheers to that.'

We laughed and toasted together in a real mood of bonhomie, what a contrast from the previous evening. Roger picked up the ball.

'Come on let's go play volleyball.'

We walked the distance to the play area and started to knock the ball around, roughly exhibiting equal ability; though Mark was encumbered somewhat by a lack of exercise over the last few years, so his dexterity was a little stiff, plus he was negotiating a lit cigarette at the same time, so consequently kept trying to get the ball to you one handed which often sent it in various directions. After awhile Roger had to pipe up.

'So Mark have you played this game before?'

'Who me? Used to play it all the time at Millfield.'

That was his alma mater, latin for boarding school in other words.

'What beach volleyball or ordinary volleyball?'

'Both.'

The lie detector sounded loudly, beach volleyball in the UK was off the radar back then. Still is.

'Were you any good?' Asked Roger.

'Too right, I was house captain.'

'Is that like team captain?' I piled in.

'No, house.' He said, in a tone that asked if I had misunderstood it's significance. He picked up the ball, put the cigarette in his mouth.

'Let me try this with two hands.'

He did, it wasn't a vast improvement but it was better.

'That's it.'

'I told you both hands were the way to do it, unless you're spiking or serving.'

'Spiking? Spiking? What's that?'

'You know when you get to the net.'

'Oh, you mean volleying.'

'You have played this game before then?'

'Fuck off.'

To play a game we needed to co-opt some more players, so Roger approached some young tourists nearby, who couldn't wait to be asked and they quickly joined us. Five came over, two blokes from Norway and three lovely girls from Canada, of whom one was particularly gorgeous looking and at times made you forget all about volleyball. The two nations had met on a ferry from Piraeus and like us were doing the Greek island hopping thing, except they were at the tail end of their two weeks and were heading home in a day or two. Surprisingly none of them had been to Ios, so they couldn't tell us anything and none of them had been to Kos or Rhodes either.

We all played for about an hour; Mark was the star of course. Had us all laughing with his determined efforts, which can only be described as a mix of acrobat and slapstick comedian. He looked a sight with his perilously white body, farmer's tan (red arms, neck and head.), sunglasses and "Tammy Hurtfinger" hat.

I'm not saying he didn't look the part, but if somebody had taken a publicity photo he'd have been airbrushed out of the shot to avoid hogging all the attention. Mind you, I didn't look that much better I suppose, after all I insisted on wearing Speedos, which I use to pool swim in but is a dated look on the beach; some would say even a "gay" look, but I didn't give a shit they were what I wanted to wear, so bollocks to the fashionista (surfers, you've got a lot to answer for.); besides, as I said to Roger, 'Shorts are for pubescent boys who want to hide their sudden erections.' Which is true and do you know how stupid a "short tan" looks? Damn stupid.

We finished up, said goodbye to our new found friends and never saw them again. Mark was a new man and thoroughly enjoying himself, he insisted on playing with the paddles, knocking the ball back and forth in the sea! Sometimes miracles do happen. Him and Roger played for quite sometime, while I watched on from the sun bed trying to get my own relatively pale skin to go a deeper shade of pink. It was hilarious to watch the both of them, Mark trying to be spectacular with his jumps and dives, like a top goalkeeper. Roger purposely sending the ball wide and high of him to get him to keep doing it. When finished, Mark came over and collapsed onto his sun bed laughing.

'I'm buggered. I'm not used to all this.'

'Exercise?' I said.

'Yes. I haven't done any since...'

'Since you last played football.'

'Yes, and that was..let me see...'

'Ten years ago.'

'Probably, you know you're right it was. How did you know
that McCloskey?'

'A lucky guess.' I lied; the subject matter was overly familiar.

'Last game for The Ship pub, SPB remember?'

'Yeah, good days.'

'Tich, Crilly, Gypo, Rob the Yob, O'Beckanbauer,
remember O'Beckenbauer?'

'Of course, great bloke.'

'And what about Clive Alive? Good player.'

'Yeah he was.'

'I hate to say it, but you were a good player. He was Rog',
one of the best I've ever played with. But fuck me, he could be
a stroppy cunt. Couldn't you?'

It's not always good to be reminded of who you were at times I
thought.

'Did you play in that game when I scored from sixty yards?'

I hadn't, but having heard it related so many times by Mark, I felt I
had. So much so, that I could swear at times that the ball whistled past my
head.

'I think I was in America then, you played a lot longer for

The Ship than I did remember?'

'Rob the Yob made me captain.'

'Maybe he wanted someone he could easily deal with.

A simpleton maybe.'

'Piss off! I was a good captain.'

'Was that before or after you became an alcoholic?' Roger asked mischievously.

'Long before, nah I was good in those days. I remember...'

Roger and I quickly dropped the subject of glory days and we all spent the last hour snoozing, reading and just watching the stupendous view. Hello London? Tranquility base here.

Tricky Tree Tops...

Finished at the beach, we went to the patio bar and had a drink and discussed plans of going to Rhodes, which we all agreed upon depending on ferry times and return journey. We decided to head into town and seek out information about the ferry to Rhodes and availability of tickets. A travel office close to the windmill, confirmed that a boat was departing from Syros the following night at eleven pm; that we could catch a ferry to Syros at six pm and that tickets were not a problem, but we had better buy them now if we wanted to make sure of a place on board. The journey time from Syros to Rhodes would be ten hours. Roger asked when the return ferry was, the answer being the coming Saturday or the Thursday after.

'What do you think?' I asked Roger.

'Sounds okay, Saturday is a good time to come back, the good thing is they are all night journeys so we don't really lose a day traveling.'

'Point; let's do it. Shall we buy the tickets for Saturday too?'

'No let's wait.'

In light of events that followed, Roger's answer was well judged.

Having secured our tickets for the next stage of the adventure, we went and found a bar to celebrate and watch the sunset; which in Parakia is a sight to behold, for the sun sets directly down the middle of the entrance to the bay. The resolution gets turned up high, and everything landside gets densely orange and red and purple, in slow degrees of shift, before "magic hour" takes over and divides the day from night. Nowhere was too busy and we found this cool looking place, which we nicknamed the "Tennis Club", as the owner was a big fan of the game and he was promoting the Paros Open tournament, with posters dotted around the bar. We sat outside and absorbed the whole atmosphere of the bar, the location and the stunning sunset. We could have stayed there for ages but we did the sensible thing and headed back to the hotel, and all three of us crashed out in preparation for the evening to come.

Around nine o'clock we took a taxi to Naoussa. Getting there we showed Roger around and then decided on a place to eat. Being quiet the quaint area was devoid of diners, so we picked out a place on the harbour front and had a meal. We talked about the great day at the beach, the ride around the island and the trip to Rhodes, and what we would do when we got back from there on the Sunday. In all of this, Mark seemed to be very aware and involved in the scheme of things, including the fact that we would first need to take a ferry to Syros and then catch a connecting ferry soon after to Rhodes, which would take ten hours to complete. "What are we going to do for ten hours?" I distinctly recall him saying.

Not seeing much else to do in Naoussa after the meal, we got into a taxi to take us back to Parakia and some night life, which we were charged up for. The taxi driver said he was taking his girlfriend back with him as she'd just finished work, which was a bit of a liberty, as the three of us crammed into the back seat; not only that, he seemed to fancy himself as a F1 driver on the imagined race back to town. Mark got a little upset about it, but I told him to consider it as a fun part of the holiday. Besides, the way the bloke drove it wasn't long before we were getting out the car and looking for our first bar.

We went to the Tennis Club first and bantered with the friendly owner a bit, then moved on to the Cote d'Or where a group of young American girls were partying. I considered them too young but it didn't bother Roger and Mark who chatted and danced with them, and were having a better time of it than me at that stage. Just when Roger and Mark thought they were charming the pants off them, they all left and the place went quiet.

'But I was getting on really well with the one I was talking to.' Said Mark.

'And then they left!'

'You were getting on really well with them because their American, they tend to be over friendly.' I replied.

His balloon burst, we moved on to the only place really worth going to, Tree Tops. When we got there Mark pointed at the sign above the door.

'But that says Evino's, how come you call it Tree Tops?'

I pointed to the large tops of the Palm trees from the first terrace, that stood near to the level of the staircase.

'Because of those.'

'Ah, I see.'

Stepping in, the place was busy but we got an immediate warm reaction from the bar guys and the DJ, and felt at home. Like me, Mark was taken by the place straight away.

'Wow, this place is great. I can see why you like it so much.'

He suddenly saw what I had witnessed the previous night through the window, he turned to us pointing,

'Look at that! Fucking hell that's amazing!'

We gave him a been-there-and-seen-it look. Mind you it was as captivating a scene as before. Roger got three beers in, plus he ordered three shots of Sambuca and we toasted the night. Much to my surprise I was getting use to shots and it wasn't long before more arrived for consumption. The cool DJ started playing classic Britrock in our honour and being in the mood, we ended up singing along and dancing. The place was already my favourite bar of all time, our personalities were tailor made for it. As time passed things got busier, we got drunker, and at some point in the general revelry Mark decided it would be best if he left, as he was drunk enough and tired. Unsurprisingly, we didn't even try to keep him there, though like a good friend I did try to ensure he'd be okay.

'Bye mate, safe journey back. See you in the morning. You know how to get home don't you? Got your key? Good; yes mate, great day, it was fun, go easy. Watch your step down the staircase hey?'

'Is there a staircase? Where?'

'Just there as you walk out.'

'Oh yeah.'

'And there's steps to the street don't forget.'

'There is?'

'If you get lost, just find the fish restaurant and you'll know where you are.'

'Which fish restaurant?'

'The one on the corner. Where you and Roger ate yesterday.'

'Did we?'

'Yes; now when you get to the street, which way are you turning to get back to the room?'

'Left.'

'No, your turning right.'

'I am?'

'Yes for God sake.'

'If I get lost, I'll come back. Make sure you're still here.'

'Alright, see you later; or sooner.'

He got to the door and turned to the bar and put both arms up high and wide, his hands showing two peace signs a la Richard Nixon, and shouted 'YAMAS!' And then left, much to the amusement of everybody there.

'Think he'll make it back?' Asked Roger.

'Oh yeah, should be fine.'

As another free shot of something came from the bar, I raised my glass.

'This is a toast to Mark. Who way beyond expectation was the star of the day. To Mark.'

'To Mark.' Agreed Roger, raising his glass.

'How the fuck does he do it?' Said I.

'What?'

'Change our whole perspective of him in one day.'

An hour later with the bar closing for the night, Roger and I said our good byes to the staff, and told them we were off to Rhodes and we'd be back Sunday night to renew acquaintances. On that news they insisted we had one more shot to celebrate, and by now I was beginning to think that I too could be an alcoholic by the end of this trip. Stumbling and laughing along the shore road towards the hotel, from God knows where, Mark appeared.

'Fuck, there you are. I couldn't find the hotel.'

Oh vey, as if I hadn't had enough fun for the day.

Factor Me Fifty...

Amazingly I was up at around ten in the morning, relatively hangover free again. We had to vacate our rooms by twelve, so I tidied and repacked my bag. Roger and Mark were snoring their heads off so I took the scooter into town. Did the daily cash run at the bank, then found a cafe near the main church and had some coffee with a croissant, and watched the Monday morning activity. At that moment I was so enamoured by Paros, I could have quite happily stayed there for the whole vacation.

I returned to the hotel, knocked loudly on the boys' doors informing them that they had thirty-five minutes left to vacate, that I was off for another bike ride and I would see them at the beach; neither of them sounded particularly bothered or interested. I took my bag and left it with the concierge, well, a private living room on the ground floor actually. The owner had offered to look after our bags until we took the ferry to Syros. I handed it to the unknown woman there with a certain wariness, what if nobody was there at five o'clock? What if we couldn't get the bags and we missed the ferry? At one time in my life I would never have worried about stuff like that, but here I was worrying about stuff like that.

I cast my concerns to providence by leaving the bag behind and got on the scooter, this time to ride around the island on my own but in the opposite direction, and what a ride it was. I started off at a steady relaxing speed for the first few miles south, taking in the air and the scenery, making a few investigative diversions here and there; but by the time I neared Golden Beach I was going as fast as the bike and the changing road would allow. Again I encountered very little traffic. Not having an extra rider and a day's familiarity with the bike and the strong wind now on my back, I was feeling really confident with how I rode the bike and how it performed. Having suffered a fractured skull not so many years before and now failing to wear a helmet, I was mindful of an accident, of tempting fate. But when you throw caution to the wind, especially in the assured feel of that moment, suddenly you're seventeen again; faithful, hopeful and willing. You're Steve McQueen riding that bike to the Swiss border is what you become, except you're going to jump that bloody wire fence.

One long section of high visible road offered the best ride, gently curved with some dips. I rode it full pelt and came out exhilarated. I eased down after that, content to just ride the bike well with a little panache; unable to suppress that terrible egotistical urge to impress, which has afflicted me since I was very young and very impressionable.

I made one stop the entire ride and that was at Naoussa, when I stopped to drink a bottle of Coke and to check out that lovely lady server again. By the time I reached Livadia beach and met up with the boys', ninety minutes had elapsed.

'How was the ride?' Roger asked,

'Fucking brilliant; stupendous.'

'That good hey?'

'Better than good; I'm ready to conquer the world now.

Did you drop your bags off?'

'Yes.'

'Think it will be open when we go to get them?'

'Better be.'

Mark suddenly sat up all concerned.

'What aren't they going to be open?'

'Well they should be, but you never know.'

'Rog' have you got his mobile number?'

'No, don't you?'

'No, I thought you did.'

We looked at each other with a is-it-worth-worrying-about-at-this-time?

'Ah fuck it, we'll be alright. Worry about it if it happens.'

'Where is it we're going anyway?' Said Mark.

The stupefying question irked me for some reason.

'Syros, we're going to Syros on the six o'clock ferry!'

'Well I didn't know.'

'What do you mean you didn't know? We must have told you six times since yesterday. Don't you remember we sat over there agreeing to it?'

'No, when was that?'

'After the beach, yesterday. We went into town afterwards and bought the tickets, you were there. Besides don't forget we're actually going to the island of Rhodes.'

'Not Syros?'

'We go to Syros first for fucks sake, and then catch another ferry two hours later.'

'Fine, I'm just following you guys.'

I looked at Mark with curiosity, something was different about him. Had an alien come and taken over his body? Did he have a doppelganger that was switching alternate days with him?

No, it was because he wasn't wearing his sunglasses or hat.

'Where's your Hurtfinger hat?

'My what?'

'Your hat.'

'Oh, I lost it.'

'Already?'

'Yes.'

'Where? When?'

'Haven't got a clue.'

'And the sunglasses?'

'Sunglasses?'

'The sunglasses you bought yesterday to replace the ones you bought the day before?'

'Something happened to them.'

'Enlighten me.'

'This.' He pulled out a broken-in-half pair of sunglasses.

'Mark, you've been here two days and you've gone through two sets of sunglasses and a sun hat.'

'So?'

'Don't buy anymore, it's a waste of money. You're fucking hopeless at keeping hold of them!'

The broad smile he had been trying to suppress lit up his face and he threw the sunglasses aside.

'You're right.'

'Too right I'm right. Tell you what, show me you're new
sandals. I want to make sure you've still got those.'

'Their here.'

He reached underneath the sun bed for them and for a moment he
could only find the one.

'You've lost one.'

'No.' He found the other and threw it at me.

'See.'

'Thank goodness. Are you ready for a game of paddle ball?'

'Not now.'

'Why not?'

'I'm sore from yesterday, I can barely move.'

'Then the quicker you get up and play, the easier it will be.
Won't it?'

'I haven't got a hat.'

'What do you need a hat for?'

'I'll get burnt.'

'Just stick some sunscreen on, that's what it's for.'

'I suppose.'

'Suppose nothing, come on let's have some fun, we're
leaving today.'

Reluctantly, he slowly raised himself off the bed and grabbed a bottle
of sunscreen from the table.

'What factor have you got?'

'Fifty.'

'Fifty? No wonder you're not getting a tan.'

'Fifty?' Roger weighed in.

'I don't want to get burnt.'

'Fuck mate, with your skin type you just need fifteen for your
head and eight for the rest. Look at your face and arms,
they've gone nice and brown.'

'No I'm putting the fifty on, I don't care about getting brown.'

I was, he still looked white as the cliffs of Dover. If we were going to
a beach or pool anywhere on this trip with lots of available women around,
I didn't want him putting them off, even if I was wearing Speedos.

We played paddle ball awhile but Mark's sore muscles could barely
move and Roger was into his book, so taking a cue from some kids
nearby, I went and bought a cheap diving mask and snorkel set and such
was their appeal we all had a go, checking out the wonders of the deep -
some rusting anchors, empty beer bottles, rocks and a few small fish.
Hardly worth the effort really, though Mark's inclination to imitate Jacque
Cousteau during his turn, was great value for money,

'And so the intrepid explorers, lured by the impenetrable
mysteries of the deep, pretend to be like the fishes that they
so envy. Meanwhile aboard the Calypso, Pascale the chef
awaits the fruits of their hunting..'.

Four thirty and we packed up to head to the hotel. Roger and I were
all for leaving our beach toys by the sun beds but Mark was convinced we
should take them with us to Rhodes.

'They cost good money. I'll carry them.'

He rescued two plastic bags from the road side bin to carry them in, such was his determination to be parsimonious.

'If he'd fussed this much over his sunglasses and hat,

he'd still have them.' I told Roger.

I went ahead and dropped off the scooter at the rental place and told the lady I'd be back Sunday or Monday to rent again, she looked delighted.

'You like?' She said. I wasn't too sure what she meant.

'If you like, I give you same when you come back.'

'Oh, the bike. Yeah, okay.'

'Paros is good?'

'Paros is beautiful.' I said with genuine affection.

Long Sea Journey Into Night...

Meeting back at the hotel, sure enough the door to the room holding our bags was locked and nobody appeared to be around.

'Shit, see I had a feeling this would happen.'

'Was it in your bones?' Roger asked.

'Yes and the tips of me hairs.' I quipped back.

'Somebody must be here. It's a hotel.' Said Mark, disgustedly.

'Only sort of.' Said Roger, correctly.

'Well go have a look.' Said I.

'Where?'

'Upstairs, out the back.'

'We are out the back, aren't we?'

'Possibly.'

'Hang on what's this notice board over here, maybe it's got a number on it to call the bloke.'

We didn't have to bother, the hotel minivan screeched to a halt outside and out got our man, offering us another cigarette. As if in a million moons we ever could have doubted him.

'Thought you'd forgotten us.' Said Roger contrary.

'Ah, I take some people to Lefkes, it's not long huh?

Come, I give ride also.'

So we rescued our bags, got in the van and he whisked us near to the windmill, told him we'd probably see him Sunday and said our "Yassoo's".

The ferry wasn't there yet, so we sat down at an outside cafe facing the jetty and had a beer in readiness.

'Here's to being on the road again.' I proposed and we clinked our bottles together. As we waited the port got increasingly lively with people and vehicles.

'Looks like a full boat to Syros.' Said Roger.

'Have I got time to get some cigarettes?' Asked Mark.

'Yeah, just don't get lost.' I said parentally.

'Don't leave without me.'

'We will if you're not back in time.' Said Roger.

'Watch my bag.'

'Why? There's nothing worth stealing.' Which was true.

'Oi!'

'What?'

'Where's the beach stuff you were going to carry?'

'Left them in the van.'

'Intentionally?'

'Yes.'

'Why?'

'Too much hassle.'

I shook my head in dismay and shouted after him.

'I'd have preferred it if you'd lost them.'

'He won't get lost will he?' Roger said hopefully.

'There's always a good chance.' I replied, less hopefully.

'If he did? Would you wait for him and miss the ferry?'

A typical Roger question I thought.

'How could I leave the poor bastard? I've got all his money,
I'd have to stay wouldn't I?'

A horn sounded, a ferry boat was coming in to the bay; our ferry boat, ready to take us somewhere new and different. I started to get that tingly feeling of expectation that comes with traveling, especially when you're just about to set off from somewhere or arriving. Tomorrow morning we'd be in Rhodes, in pastures new. Hopefully it would be like Paros but with more night life and hordes of lovely women around.

Mark managed to make it back, seemingly unaware that the ferry was here and in the process of backing up to the jetty.

'Come on, grab your bag it's here.'

'Fuck that was quick.'

'They don't mess around you know.'

We went over to the foot passenger area and waited to be let through. After a time of questioning when we were going to be let onto the boat and why nobody seemed to be that bothered, it became apparent that the majority of people there were actually awaiting another ferry, so we had to force our way to the front and rush to the boat which was preparing to leave.

Less than twenty persons got on the tub, which had definitely seen better days and more passengers. It was at least forty years old and distinctly reminded me of the cross channel ferries between Britain and the continent when I was a boy. Perhaps it had, the many original sign plates were in English only. We found an empty table easy enough in what looked like the bar area. Strangely, nothing in there was soft apart from

Mark's brain. Everything was made of hard materials, the floor, the walls, the benches, the chairs, the tables.

With the boat under way we went out on deck and watched our grand departure from marvelous Paros until we passed the 'Sentinels'. I felt rather sad about leaving, the place had captured my liking.

Being an old boat it soon became clear that she was going to rock and roll a bit with the sea. After half an hour of pitching around, Mark began to look ashen. I got to thinking that perhaps the reason for all the hard surfacing, was because it was easier to hose down the entire lounge of vomit at journey's end. The sea didn't become any worse for the crossing though, and Roger and I were okay and Mark's look did improve, but I noticed he was a bit shaky even though he was drinking plenty of beer. An hour later and we were coming into Syros's main port and capitol, Ermoupoli.

A Case of Statues...

Syros has been important over time because of it's position, and though not much bigger than Paros, it is the main administrative center for the Cyclades, a spiral chain of islands that includes among others: Paros, Naxos, Santorini, Ios, and Mykonos. Hence Ermoupoli was very different from the gentle nature of Parakia, being densely urbanized and industrialized. With shipyards and warehouses underlining it's significance. The style and scale of architecture was also varied, having the look and feel of an Italian town. The harbour had a man made sea wall to protect it, while it's spacious waterfront had a road along it, filled with restaurants, bars, and many other retail.

The boat turned and backed towards the ferry wharf, and we got the call to depart the boat. As we got in line to leave down the steps, Mark said with stupefying sincerity.

'Thank fuck for that; I couldn't take another ferry journey.'

Roger and I looked in astonishment at each other, not quite sure if we had heard right. Which part of the itinerary had he not been involved in? Which part did he not understand? How many times had he been told?

'But Mark, in two hours time we are catching another ferry to Rhodes.' Said an incredulous Roger.

'We are?'

'Yes, you blithering idiot, a ten hour one.' I emphasized.

'Well nobody told me that.'

'We fucking did, loads of times.'

'Are you sure?'

"YES!" Together.

'Well I don't know if I'm going to be able to do that.'

'Fine, we'll leave you here and pick you up in a few days time, how about that?'

No, he definitely didn't like that idea.

'What's the problem anyway? Are you scared of boats?' Asked Roger.

'No.'

'I bet you are.'

'Bollocks, I was on boats before you were knee high to your Mothers ankle.'

'Were you part of the sailing team at Millfield?'

'As a matter of fact I was.'

'Were you team captain also?'

'No.'

'Admiral then?'

'Very funny Rog'.'

'It won't be a boat like we've just been on you know.' I said.

'It won't?'

'No, it will be more like the boat we took from Athens. It will have stabilizers. You won't feel a thing.'

'Thank fuck for that.'

'So are you gonna' come?'

'Yes, I never said I wasn't.'

'You get it then?'

'What?'

'That we're catching another ferry?'

'Yes; I do now anyway.'

I had to shake my head in bemusement several times, it was another bizarre moment in the world of Mark. Roger couldn't get over it for ages and was a constant source of instant mirth for him.

Hungry, time to kill, we sought out a place to eat and sat down to some good honest food at an outside table, close to the busy waterfront street. Mark decided he wouldn't eat and actually came up with something sensible for a change. He proposed to go find a supermarket and buy some stuff for the trip i.e. beer, snacks, beer, cigarettes, beer and beer; and it was going to be on him. Terrific Roger and I thought, go ahead, but then I got to thinking about his propensity to get lost rather easily and how we had just got into a new place that was built up; and the streets behind the harbour frontage would be confusing to someone not quite concentrating on where they were, in proximity to where they had just come.

'Now you know where we are don't you?'

'Of course, here.'

'So if you happen to get lost you'll be able to find us?'

'Yesss; I'm not that bad.'

'So how come you always get lost then?' Asked Roger spoiling for a fight.

'I don't.'

'You do.'

'When?'

'Ever since you got here.'

'I know where I am.'

'So what's the name of this restaurant?'

'I don't know, but it'll be easy to find.'

'But all these restaurants look the same down here.' I pointed out.

He was getting annoyed, impetuously looking around.

'There.' He indicated. 'You're right by the statue.'

There was a carving in stone of somebody important by the harbour wall, positioned so they were imaginatively looking out to sea. It reminded me for all of a moment of Mark.

'I can bloody well find that can't I?'

At this stage I wasn't overly concerned about him losing his way, as we had at least an hour and a half until the boat sailed and he had a marker to get back to. Roger and I watched him walk away and then turn up a connecting street.

'Think he'll lose himself?' Asked Roger.

'Who cares? I'm still trying to come to terms with the fact that he genuinely didn't know we were catching another ferry to Rhodes tonight.'

'Is it the alcohol?'

'Yes, so let it be a lesson to you. You don't want to end up in a few years time in some strange Greek town unaware of where you're going. Or, even where you've come from, because I'm not sure he knows that either.'

'Nah, won't happen.'

'Could do.'

'I don't drink cider.' We laughed.

'He's fucking nuts at times isn't he?' Said Roger.

'Fucking bananas too.'

Our agreeable food came, with a litre of house white served in the common Greek way, a coloured metal jug; which seemingly always gives the impression of pouring more from it than it actually holds. We ate and drank up our fill, lit a cigarette each and waited for Mark. I checked my watch.

'Forty five minutes.'

'And?'

'He's lost; got to be.'

'Shall we go find him?'

'Piss off, he can find his own way back.'

Another ten minutes elapsed and still no sign of him. Roger went to the toilet and I said to myself under my breath,

'I knew it, I fucking knew it. He's an idiot.'

Roger came back. 'Well what do we do?'

'Wait by the statue I guess.'

So we picked up the bags including Mark's, and just as we were about to leave the restaurant.

'There he is.'

I turned to look where Roger was indicating. Coming along the harbour wall path was Mark, laden with two heavily filled plastic bags and sweating. He didn't look that pleased, and when he got to us erupted.

'You fuckers, I've been waiting for you!'

'Where?'

'Down by the statue! Why did you move?'

'But we haven't moved.'

'You must have done, I've been by the statue.'

'What that statue there you mean?'

I indicated the statue by the wall, the one he had just walked past. Instantly realizing his mistake he held his mouth tight, trying not to laugh or smile.

'Isn't that the statue Rog'? Where he was going to find us at?'

'What the one of the bloke looking out to sea you mean?'

'Is he? I hadn't noticed.'

'You arseholes! Fuck! Why me?'

'So you found a super-market then?'

'Yes!'

'How long ago?'

'Does it matter?'

'Well yes we were worried about you.'

'Oh you were, were you?'

'So there's another statue right?'

'Yes, down there.'

'But we're here.'

'I know that now.'

'But why didn't you know it then?'

'Because, it looked like the statue.'

'Was it looking out to sea?'

'I don't fucking know! Do I?'

'So how far have you walked to get here?'

'Fucking miles!'

'Where's this other statue?'

'That way.'

'How come you ended up all the way way down there?

Where was the supermarket?'

'Somewhere behind here.' Before I could further question him he blurted:

'I caught a taxi.'

'Why?'

'I didn't know how to get back.'

'So you took a taxi and he dropped you at the wrong statue?'

'I got the beers.' He lifted both bags up proudly.

'How much he charge you for the ride?'

'Who?'

'The taxi driver.'

'Can't remember. A couple of euros.' More like ten I thought, knowingly.

Mad Brits and Englishman...

The embarkation area for the impending ferry to Rhodes was getting very busy, so we went and joined the line. There didn't seem to be many tourists like us, it was mostly locals. The boat was making two stops before Rhodes, to the islands of Samos and Kos. So who knew who was going where. We opened up a can of beer each and waited that long, proposed another; when the ferry arrived. Because Ermoupoli faces east and the boat was coming from the south along the coastline, it emerged without warning; a huge platform of electric light, moving at a rate of knots and turning into the harbour entrance as soon as it could. The thing was enormous, much bigger than I'd been expecting.

'Look at the size of that bloody thing.' I said to nobody in particular.

The size of the hulk appeared to fill the harbour, as it slowed and manoeuvred to back up to the wharf. It's majesty and power holding one and all in thrall. Well us anyway, I'm sure the locals saw this thing a hundred thousand times over their lives and thought nothing of it, just another ferry. Actually, when we got our tickets checked and clambered on to the escalators, which ascended at a steep angle for some way, it became clear that maybe people were paying attention to this ferry, as it was obviously brand spanking new, the pride of the Blue Star line. It's name escaped me though.

On reaching the next level, what appeared to be an over dressed waiter directed us to where the main bar area was; sussing correctly that we were economy and unable to afford the luxurious first class areas or the cost of a cabin. In all respects it was a floating five star hotel. The bar lounge was a ballroom in scale. Plush carpet underfoot, soft cushioned chairs and sofas, plasma screen televisions here and there on the walls.

The boat had come from Piraeus and was already filled with people, so we found a small table near the bar and three comfy spare chairs from around, and made camp.

'Boy, this is the life. What a boat.' Said Mark.

'Amazing isn't it?'

'How long we on this for again?'

'Nineteen hours.'

I was now taking to lying with him to see if he noticed.

'That long?' He didn't.

'Are we stopping anywhere?'

'What, us or the boat?'

'Us.'

'Other than Rhodes you mean?'

'Yes.'

My mind boggled.

'Well it does call at Istanbul, so we might get off there and take a look around for a day.'

'Really?'

'Chance we might call in at Beiruit too.'

'Beiruit?'

'Yes.'

'Isn't it dangerous there?'

'What's a bit of danger on a trip like this?'

'McCloskey you're having me on.'

'I am, sorry.'

'So Mark, how many ferries have you been on?' Asked Roger.

'More than you Roger.'

'Have you ever been on a cruise liner?'

'Yes.'

'Where'd you go?'

'Can't remember, I was too young. Disneyworld I think.'

'Disneyworld?'

'Yes; and I was also on the very first hovercraft to France.

Ever been on a hovercraft Rog'?'

'You were on the first passenger hovercraft?' I asked slightly
indredulous.

'Yes.'

'Does this involve your Dad?'

'No, the chairman of the company was a Millfield old boy,

so as house captain I got to go along with a chosen few.'

Not for the first time, Roger and I looked at each other in querulous
mode.

'Were you also on the first space shuttle into space? Asked Roger.

'Now your being silly.' Said Mark.

'Are you sure the head of NASA wasn't at Millfield too?'

'He might have been, they get around you know.'

'Tell you what, I'm going to have a look around myself. See
what they've got.' So I did.

Around the corner from the bar, rows of fixed high backed chairs like an airplane's stood largely empty. Beyond, as I toured the deck, lay games rooms, a shop, internet, DVD rental, cash machines, telephones, restaurants - self-service and silver service - and a fast food outlet. At the back end, plush business and first class lounges dominated. The boat had everything you could wish for while traveling in style, even if you were hauling two bags of cheap beer, an abundance of snacks, and hugging a table in the crowded main bar for the masses. The surrounds alone made you feel a million euros.

Below our deck, lay three decks of cabins in varied grades of comfort, I imagined what the most expensive were like. Ken Adams and his James Bond sets came to mind. The deck below was also the site of the main desk, from there I got some pamphlets on the boat and our journey. Perusing them, I discovered that the toilets also had shower rooms, so as soon as I got back to the boys and gave them my Marco Polo tour account, I grabbed towel and shampoo and went for a well earned wash.

Two hours later, cleaned up and beered up with the time approaching one am, I told the squabbling pair that I was going to find somewhere quieter and join in with what most of the other sensible passengers were doing, catching forty winks. I went around to the airplane seats thinking that the arm rests would lift up and I could stretch out along the row, unfortunately the rests were fixed so I tried falling asleep in the chair itself, but to no avail as I could not find a comfort zone to nod off in. After about forty five minutes of this I simply lay down on the floor along the row of seats I was in. Having no pillow, I lay down on my back and rested my head against the carpet.

One of the notable things about the boat according to the pamphlet, was it had the very latest in stabilizers for coursing through rough sea. Indeed, I was aware that in comparison to the roughish trip from Paros to Syros, this wonderful boat was remarkably stable on the water. Problem was, all that engineered comfort had a downside; that when you put your head to the floor, you could feel and hear this constant steady vibration and rumbling, inscrutably designed to prevent you from sleeping in said position. Did I move? Did I bother to get up? No, I was Paul McCloskey, a man who could sleep anywhere and had proved it time and again; in deck chairs, in bath tubs and on stoney ground. I could sleep through anything and did; loud ear piercing music, gales, explosions; all proved mere bumps in the night. But not this bloody time. The more I tried to relax, the more resonant became the vibration. The more I tried to concentrate on something else, the more aware I became of the noise. I simply couldn't sleep, tired as I felt. Crazily I just lay there for ages, keeping my eyelids closed and running a multitude of things through my mind. Eventually fed up, I decided to take a walk around again.

As I entered into the bar area, I could see the majority of people stretched out on the sofas and chairs wrapped in blankets. I felt for sure the boys were at least resting in their chairs by now, but as I followed around the bar I came upon a picture I shall find hard to forget. Still in situ were Roger and Mark, wide awake, effortlessly chatting. Upon the table were two ashtrays over filled with fag ends and a huge pile of empty tins of beer, with no room left for anything else. All around them, people asleep or trying to sleep above their noise. They were an oasis of Britishness and I just had to laugh at the sight.

'Look it's McCloskey.' Said a merry Mark.

'Where have you been?'

'Around the corner.'

'Did you get anything?'

'What do you mean?'

'Didn't you go to the shop?'

'No.'

'My mistake, as usual.'

'I thought you two would be asleep.'

'No, we had all this beer to drink.'

'I can see. So what have you been talking about all this time?'

'You.'

'Oh really, and?'

'We haven't come to any conclusion...yet. Want a beer?'

'Fuck no.'

'Rog' you ready for another?'

'Absolutely.'

Mark handed him a tin and they opened the pull rings with relish, the release of gas sounding through the lounge.

'I'm going for a walk.' I said, in mock admonishment.

As I wandered around an announcement was made in Greek and then English, the island of Samos neared. I rushed to the open viewing deck on the upper level, discovering quite a number of people there resting on the benches in sleeping bags. So this is where all the mad backpacker tourists ended up I thought.

Vathy, the capitol of Samos, resides on the shores of an open bay with no natural protection from the sea. It looked interesting enough as we closed in, nestled between the mountains and the sea, it's lights shining brightly in the darkness. But being the middle of the night not much stirred, it was like a sneak visit. The boat docked at the jetty and off loaded a surprising amount of people, cars and trucks. Within minutes they had disappeared into Vathy and beyond, and after the disturbing hustle and bustle, the place returned quickly to it's slumber and the boat picked up a few passengers and vehicles, and set off for it's next port of call, Kos. Which according to the Lonely Planet guide, was a lively tourist destination. Just the sought of place for us to hop on the way back. I stayed on the viewing deck watching with fascination the lights of Vathy get smaller and smaller, until with little chance of seeing anymore of the island in the dark I returned to the boys.

A good number of fellow ship mates had left the bar lounge for Samos and that made some sofas available, which we grabbed and layed out on. It was our cue for getting some shut eye finally, much (I well imagine) to the general relief of those in there. The bar staff looked at the departed table and it's debris with unconcealed displeasure. "Bloody English." I could hear them thinking.

About two hours later, I was awoken by the announcement of our arrival at Kos Town. The boys slept on undeterred, but like Pavlov's dog I heeded the call and I made my way to the viewing deck again, avoiding the large number of passengers making for the off ramp. Still being dark the appearance of the town was again measured by it's numerous lights. Hills and mountains were not much in evidence and the town appeared to spread out, from and along a long plain. Close to the landing was an old fortress. Unlike Vathy, the docking area was busy and we took on many more passengers and vehicles, particularly lorries and their varied loads.

I stayed watching our departure beside the island, south, noticing the lit-up towns that dotted along the coast line and wondered what each place might be? A holiday resort or just a normal town? Or a small riviera of hot, fun spots? I liked that idea best and went back to the lounge, with the abiding thought that our next port of call was our getting off point, Rhodes. I checked the guide book again and re-read what it had to say about the place. Rhodes Town was famous for it's old section, the largest inhabited medieval walled town in Europe; largely intact even after many wars and occupiers. Otherwise it was an important governmental and commercial center, steadily sprawling outwards, with recent apartment blocks dominating; it was cosmopolitan, with good beaches and a vibrant night life. The guide listed a few resorts along the favoured south eastern coast line but it failed to highlight a stand-out place, they all sounded much the same, perhaps there wasn't one?

One place listed was Lindos, I'd heard of it but didn't know that much about it, other than a girl I had been intimate with many years past, had once gone there and come back with a fabulous tan and a new boyfriend. It intrigued me, but all the guide seemed to say was that it was a mecca for day trippers from the cruise ships that docked in Rhodes Town, and was mostly a picturesque ancient village with an interesting acropolis and accommodation in short supply. Didn't sound very lively.

So where would we go when we got there? Rhodes Town? Not likely, as Roger had recalled the previous day when reading the guide book, that he and his parents had actually been there some years before and it wasn't all that exciting, though it was worth a visit to the old town. We could very well be turning around in a day or two and heading to Kos in search of excitement, with a great deal of time wasted. I dropped back off to sleep again with no idea as to where I'd be sleeping later that night, although I kept that little nagging concern to myself.

Island of the Sun...

The first thing I noticed upon waking was the sun was up and it was bright out. I went straight to the viewing deck, where the sea air was blustery but warm. All around us were islands in the distance, apart from the one in front which lay about five miles away. Given the time I assumed it was Rhodes. I went back to the bar lounge to tell the boys we were nearing. When I got there, Roger was sitting up coming to grips with the world.

'Almost there.'

'Whaz thu' tyme?'

'Eight o'clock, got about half an hour 'till we dock.'

He shrugged and lay down again. Mark was still passed out, I took a can of beer and opened the pull ring right next to his ear. He screwed up his face and opened his eyes.

'Breakfast is served m'lud.' It didn't humour him.

'Fuucck orrff.'

'We're landing in half an hour.'

'Bollocks.'

Great, we were soon to off load not knowing where to go, and two of us were to all intents and purposes, dead to the world and very likely to stay that way for some time yet. Which meant that I would have to take the lead and carry the load, so to speak. I went back to the viewing deck to watch our approach into Rhodes Town, which lies at the northern tip of the island and was purportedly home to the noted Colossus, one of the ancient seven wonders. The place certainly looked big enough and important; it's extensive deep water port near to the old walled town could contain a number of big vessels, including the massive cruise liners which dwarfed even our impressively sized ship by some height and length, and three of which were, "Lying in state".

Roger appeared, looking worse for wear, come to take in the sight.

'We're here hey?'

'Yes, I see the old part, it looks amazing. There were some beaches further down looked okay. Hotels and stuff.'

'You want to check them out?'

'Maybe. How's Mark?'

'Asleep.'

'Have to keep an eye on him, case he has another turn.'

'Think he will?'

'Fuck knows, but with this traveling to get here and him drinking all night, the chances are good aren't they?'

'Well you can deal with him.'

'Thanks Rog.'

'Pleasure.'

The announcement went off for our impending alighting, so we went to get our bags and Mark; and forgo our sea legs and set foot on dry land once more.

It was the boat's final stop, so all the foot passengers, including the crew it seemed, filed off and walked down the long wide quay towards the town. A long procession of big and small vehicles from the holds of the boat, rode quickly past us, not caring if anyone was foolish enough to be in the way or not. I guess if you had been on the boat from Piraeus for sixteen hours you'd be a bit keen to get away. We walked by one of the cruise liners towering above us, it's outer skin sparklingly white and pockmarked by many rows of chromed portholes. Mark, who had been ominously quiet all this time, stopped to stare at it. Walking on, I turned to look back for him.

'Mark, come on, what are you doing?'

'Look at that fucking thing? It's fucking enormous.'

'Yeah, so?'

For a moment I thought he was having a flashback from the Magic Bus ride.

'How does anything that big, float? How can it?'

I could have gone into the physics of buoyancy and displacement but it was too early in the morning for all that.

'Because it does.'

'Ah! Got y'er.'

We moved on until reaching an information booth, which was basically selling tours to the old walled town and other places of historical interest, like Lindos. We gathered there to discuss our plans. By now, Roger's drawn face had gone from looking like a corpse on a mortuary slab to resembling somebody who looked like him. The powers of recovery never cease to amaze, especially time and again in Roger's case.

'What are we going to do then?'

'Well we could stay here or go somewhere else.' I helpfully suggested.

'I don't think we should stay here first, maybe tomorrow or

the next day, but not tonight.'

'Where are we anyway?' Intruded Mark.

'Rhodes Town, you nonce.'

'I didn't know. Excuse me for asking.'

'Should we ask here?' I asked.

'About what?' Said Roger.

'Where there's a good place to go?'

'What does the book say?'

'Well, there's a number of places we could go to.' I again said
helpfully.

Roger stared blankly at me, taking in the helpful suggestion; then lit a
cigarette, getting some all important nicotine into him. Three or four
drags in, refreshed and prompted, he surveyed the scene.

'Let's ask the taxi drivers where to go, they'll know.'

So we went over to a nearby taxi rank and approached a couple of
savvy drivers.

'Yassas; do you know a good place on Rhodes
where we can go?
Like a busy holiday place?' Asked Roger.

For a pregnant moment there was no response. They clearly were not
used to tourists like us getting off the early morning boat, seeking out wild
party destinations on their island. I thought they were going to tell us to
turn around and head for Kos. Either that or they couldn't get over the
state of Roger's hung over face. I interjected.

'We want a place where they party; girls, beach, clubs.'

They looked at me like they couldn't believe what a man in his late forties was saying. "Come off it mate." I could hear them thinking, "You're way past all that." Actually, they discussed the matter between themselves for a couple of minutes, while we hung on their very answer.

'Falaraki.' One of them answered.

'It's a good place?' Asked Roger.

'The best. Girls, party, very nice beach. I take you there for ten euros.'

It sounded good.

'Well?' Roger asked me.

'Best offer I've had all morning, let's go.'

I turned to Mark who was sitting on the ground aways.

'Mark! Come on we're going.' He rose up and got in the taxi.

'Where's he taking us?' He asked.

'Peru.'

'Peru?'

'Yes.'

'I need to take a piss soon.' He stated blithely.

'You'll have to wait 'till we get there.'

'Get where?'

'Where is it we're going again?' I asked Roger, with a sudden case of the Mark's.

'Falaraki. I've heard of it somewhere. What's it say in the book about it?'

I looked it up but it didn't say much, other than it was a resort with lot's to do.

'Seems to have everything we need. That's all.' I said, not much the wiser.

As we passed by the medieval walls of the old town, I noticed numerous irregular indents in parts of them.

'Is that cannon ball damage?' I inquired historically, pointing. But nobody answered, so I consulted the guide. Indeed, it was the scars of long fought battles that brought about the fall of the Knights of St John. Hence the prevailing disinterest.   We carried on through a more recent vintage of the main town, which wouldn't have been out of place in Athens; concrete to the fore. Quickly leaving it behind, we drove past a long chain of commercial premises dotted either side of the road, including to our surprise, a Lidl's.

'Look a Lidl's' Cried Mark, exalted.

'Do you want to stop and go in? Asked Roger jokingly.

'Can we?' Replied Mark in great expectation.

'Hell no.' I answered firmly, then looked at his disappointed face and softened. 'Later, yeah?'

'Good idea.' He said, seeing the virtue.

'Anyway, might be different than the one at Clapham

Junction." He added. We never did find out.

The taxi came into more open terrain which looked very arid and rocky, with large patches of bare ground baked hard. So far Rhodes reminded me of my teenage days in Bahrain, looking and feeling rather similar, especially the fifties and sixties style buildings.

Ten minutes or so later, the driver took a left turn and drove into an area of private residential buildings and small hotels. At road's end we took a right onto a in-your-face resort road, lined with bars, restaurants, eateries, markets, rental places, nightclubs, exchanges, miniature golf, amusement arcades, big and small hotels, all vying equally for your attention. What in the garish hell was this I wondered? I was beginning to get a sneaky suspicion, especially after I happened to notice some businesses stating their location as Falaraki.

'Is this Falaraki?' I asked the driver.

'Yes, soon.' He replied.

'Sure you want to stay here?' I asked Roger as he surveyed the surrounds.

'Looks like a place to get a shag.' He said, rightly.

'True.'

'You want to go somewhere else?'

'No, let's give it a whirl. You've made me see it in a new light.'

'Mark?'

'What?'

'Never mind.'

Roger asked the Driver if he knew of a reasonable place to stay, the Driver replied that he had an uncle that owned rooms right in the center of things; close to the main beach and he could check with him. Journeyed out, we just wanted somewhere quick so we said fine to that. The Driver took a left and drove down to a small square next to the beach and stopped.

Getting out, the first thing I noticed was a McDonalds on the nearby street corner. All I can say is, it wasn't what I came to Greece for. The Driver went over to a small group of elderly men sitting on a bench in the shade of some trees, and chatted awhile. One of the men nodded, got up and came over to us with the Driver.

'My Uncle is not here, but this is my paternal Godfather.'

No, he didn't say that, but you felt he might of done. He said:

'This man has rooms for you.' We thanked and paid the Driver and he left.

The elderly man was smartly dressed in a short sleeved shirt, grey trousers and braces; a look slightly spoiled by the wearing of flip flops, barefoot. He was portly, grey haired and thinning on top, and he couldn't walk very fast. Roger, went into full Canary Wharf mode, negotiating the business deal. Yes, he had three rooms. Yes, the place was just behind that building to the right, in front of us. Yes, the price would be forty euros a room per night.

'Seems a bit high.' I said.

'Try another place?'

'God no, I'm knackered, anyway it's a good spot.'

'Thirty euro a night?' Roger asked.

'No.' Came the insulted reply.

'I'll share a room with Mark.'

'Sure?'

'Yeah, it'll be fine.'

'What if you pull a bird?'

'He'll have to sleep on the beach.'

'What if he pulls a bird?'

'He'll have to screw on the beach. But come on, he won't pull a bird will he?'

'Two rooms, two nights? They share?'

'Yes; come.'

Two nights? Here? With a McDonalds just a few yards away? What were we doing? I was beginning to think that Benidorm might have been a better destination after all. On the bright side of things, we had a great spot to stay and perhaps Falaraki might just be the best fun on the planet. You don't know until you try it; and you should always try something once, right? Apart from anything that knowingly threatens your existence of course. But what is it about the sound of places? I don't know what Falaraki means in Greek, perhaps sparkling water or glistening sands or summer breeze, but when you say the word it sounds harsh, like uttering a really bad expletive when angry. It just doesn't sound nice and that often, though not always, characterizes a place; that's all I'm saying. In truth, we had found Blackpool in Greece and without turning our refined noses up at it, had instead concluded that such a place offered the best chance of getting our leg over; and we were going to take part as willing contestants.

Firstly though we had to check the place out, get some money and a cup of coffee. We strolled past the McDonalds which was closed.

'Ah no, it's closed.' Exclaimed Mark.

'It's a fucking McDonalds, Mark.' I chided.

'I know, but I really fancied a burger.'

And went up a main thoroughfare filled with bars and, well, bars mostly. They all appeared closed, and there was hardly a soul about as we walked steadily up the middle of the road taking account.

'Quiet, isn't it? Where the hell is everybody?'

'What's the time?'

'Almost ten o'clock'

'There should be more people than this around hey?'

'I reckon everybody is in bed still, sleeping it off. Got to be.'

Not everything was closed, one of the larger bars was cleaning up from the evening's business, readying for the day. The open exterior had a sort of frontier look about it, and a number of wall and ceiling mounted tv's were broadcasting Sky Sports News, loudly. We walked on by like three cowboys just rode into town, looking for amusement or a bank to rob. A tumbleweed came blowing down the street. It didn't, but at that moment it felt like a wild west town and the music from For a Few Dollars More was playing. I kid you not; I half expected the Man With No Name to step out and challenge us to a draw.

Reaching the crossroads things got livelier, with places open and people around. We got some money from the bank and I paid Mark his daily share, and gave Roger money I owed for the room. For some strange reason, we avoided the busier part and went back to the large bar we'd encountered for some breakfast, sitting outside on the deck in the warming sun. A really nice girl from England served us, friendly and very efficient. Somebody you would want to employ if you had a business. We ordered bacon, eggs, toast and coffee three times.

'Could be this place is closing for the season.' I proposed.

'Think we got here too late?' Said Roger.

'The place is dead.'

The girl came back with our coffee.

'Is Falaraki quiet' Roger asked her.

'No it's been busy, why?'

'Nobody around.'

'It's too early, wait 'till later.'

'Especially in the evening I guess?'

'It's not as busy as it was a few weeks ago, but it is end of September now, so you expect it to be a bit quieter.'

She left to attend some more customers.

'Sounds okay then.' Said Roger hopefully.

'Wait and see hey?' Said I guardedly.

'What are we doing today?' Asked Mark.

'Eat, sleep, beach; sleep, eat, drink; shag hopefully, sleep. How's that sound?' I answered.

'And tomorrow?'

'Same thing. Roger, anything to add?'

'No, sounds about right.'

'So we're staying here, not going anywhere else?'

'For two nights yes, after that we don't know yet.'

'Why don't we stay in one place guys, wouldn't it be easier?'

'Because that wasn't the idea of the holiday was it? How many times do we have to tell you that?'

'So two nights here?'

'Yes, and then maybe Kos, then the ferry back to Paros on Saturday night. That okay?'

'I don't care. I'm with you blokes wherever you go.'

'What if we went to Hell?' Said Roger.

'As long as you're going, I'll be there.'

On that cue, Mark and I broke into singing the old Four Tops song, much to Roger's bemusement and whoever else was in the bar. The girl came over with our breakfast, smiling,

'Yer' sound happy to be here.'

'Well we just got in.'

'Who'd yer' fly with?'

'We didn't, we came by boat.'

'Boat? I wondered, because planes don't usually com' in on a Tuesday from the UK.'

'Took a ferry from Paros.'

'Where's that?'

'It's in the Cyclades.'

'Where's that?'

'An island chain near to Athens.'

'How long did it take yer'?'

'About fifteen hours in all, from when we left Paros.'

'That long?'

'We traveled through the night so it wasn't too bad.'

'Did yer' get in at Rhodes Town?'

'Yeah, asked a taxi driver where to go and here we are.'

'Are yer' just travellin' around then?'

'Yeah, island hopping, going where the fancy takes us.'

'How long yer' got?'

'Two weeks, arrived in Athens Saturday morning.'

'Most people who cum' here fly in on a week's package.'

'Where are you from?'

'Yorkshire.'

'Whereabouts?'

'Wakefield.'

'I've been to Wakefield, nice place.' I meant it too, it is.

'How long you been working here?'

'Two years, came 'ere wi' me boyfriend three years ago. Liked it so much I came back to stay.'

'What you live here?'

'Yeah.'

'Good for you.'

'Anyhow's, I'd better get back to work.'

'Sure.' She went and busied herself.

I for one was impressed by her bustle and determination.

'I was in Wakefield doing rep once.' Mark announced.

'What acting?' I asked.

'Yes.'

'What was the play?'

'I think it was The Mousetrap.'

'Agatha Christie? That old pot boiler.'

'Who'd you play?' Asked Roger. 'Colonel Mustard in the Conservatory?'

'That's Cluedo, Roger.'

'Is it? I'm sure you must have played him.'

'I'm not answering if you don't talk sensibly.'

'Alright, which part did you play?'

'I didn't, I was understudying.'

'Yeah, but which part?'

'One of them, can't remember.'

'So you didn't actually take part in the play?'

'No, well yes, I was understudying.'

'And that meant what?'

'It meant I got paid to stay in the pub most of the time.'

'That explains a lot.'

'So if you could have acted in it, which part would you have wanted to play?'

'None, I didn't like any of the actors; they had a different style than me.'

'Style? What's that mean?'

'I couldn't get them to react to me, they were useless. There was nothing there; they couldn't respond You'd need to be trained as an actor to know what I mean.'

'Obviously.'

'You mean a proper actor?'

'YES!'

We were clearly touching a soft nerve with Mark over this, so we dropped the subject and finished breakfast.

A Bit of Bother...

We decided to head to the beach early, so we went back to the accommodation; changed, took what we needed and sauntered over to the sands close by. The beach was long and wide, though it ran mostly northwards from our position and came to a stop just southwards of us. Masses of sun beds filled our area and beyond, perhaps a thousand in all. About a quarter of the beds had already been taken, mostly by married couples with young children, of differing nationalities. We took three beds and settled in. Then I noticed Mark had walked over in his regular shoes.

'Mark, where's your sandals?'

'Sandals?'

'The ones you bought in Paros?'

'Oh, I lost one.'

'You lost one? How?'

'On the boat.'

'For fuck's sake.'

'Think I did, anyway.'

'What's the matter with you?'

'What?'

'How come you keep losing everything?'

'I don't.'

'You could have fooled me.'

'Have you ever lost anything big Mark?' Asked Roger.

'Like what?'

'A house? Your mind? Suitcase of money maybe.'

'An oil tanker?' I added.

'No, I don't lose stuff. You two keep making out I do.'

'I bet you have.'

'Hang on, I did lose a car once. No, I didn't lose it, I just couldn't find it, so I left it.'

'When was this?' Thinking I'd heard most of the good ones.

'Oh, a few years ago. Furie and I went to some rave party in the country.'

'And?'

'We got wasted and couldn't remember where we parked the car amongst all the others. So we thought fuck it, we'll get a ride to the nearest station and come back and get it later.'

'And you didn't?'

'No.'

'You lazy bastards.'

'The car was only worth a hundred. It was about ready to break down anyway.'

'You just left it there?'

'Yes.'

'In some farmer's field?'

'Yes.'

'Degeneracy.'

'No, consumer choice.'

'You going to buy some more sandals then?' Chirped Roger.

'Yes, when I feel like it, Roger.'

'Get some cheap flip-flops mate, that way if you lose them no big deal, you just get another pair.' I sensibly proposed.

'No, I want sandals, good ones.'

'Expensive ones.'

'Yes.'

'Alright, don't say I didn't warn you.'

'Warn me what?'

'Never mind.'

'Maybe you could buy just one sandal.' Said Roger.

'Don't be stupid.' Replied Mark.

'Great idea; mix and match. Can you buy just the one?'

'Fuck off, the both of you.'

Each of us started to read a book but before long I began to feel tired. Mark was already curled up, eyes closed; and Roger didn't look too far either and the three us nodded off. An hour or so later and I wakened, Roger was back reading his book and Mark was nowhere to be seen.

'Where's silly bollocks?'

'Toilet.'

I looked around, the place was much busier and a good sixty five percent of the beds had been taken. Mark appeared with a couple of beers.

'You're up then?'

'Yeah.' He handed one of the beers to Roger.

'Where's mine?'

'You don't drink at lunchtime.'

'True, could have got me a Coke though.'

'You were asleep boyo.'

Mark leaned down next to my ear and whispered excitedly,

'Have you seen all the tits?'

Of course I had, it was one of the things I had taken notice of when I awoke; hard not too really. He was spot on though, there were a lot of bare breasts on display, in that lovely easy European way. There had been a few in Paros but here in Falaraki it was everywhere you looked, including the bed near to me with the young mum. Look, but just don't ogle like a pervert is best. Perhaps we'd come to the right place after all. It certainly perked Mark up anyway.

It was time for a swim I felt, a proper swim, maybe a mile swim. I was in the mood for one and I had my goggles along. The sea looked calm, very few waves. Orange buoys marked the limit of safe public swimming from the beach; they looked to be about two hundred meters out roughly, so five laps there and back and I could call it a mile. I started the swim slowly, building up the rhythm and pace of the stroke and was soon into a familiar groove. I completed four laps and made back for the orange buoys on my last. Reaching them, I paused for a little break and looked around. Just to the right and north of my swimming area, was an expanse of sea given over to jet skis, and the speed boats that operated paragliding, waterskiing, and fun rides like the banana boats and the ringos. They raced back and forth from the beach, to way out beyond the orange buoys and side markers.

Incredibly, for such a busy resort there was no lifeguard system in place. Which was amazing, when you consider all the children present during the summer, and all the hangovers suffered by crazy young adults dead set on trying to destroy themselves. I don't know what the drowning figures are for Falaraki but I'd be astonished if there weren't a couple at least during the summer season.

So there I was contemplating at the buoys, watching a paraglider flying high in the sky thinking that I'd like to try that, when I set off for the last length back to the beach, except this time feeling fit and energized, I tried swimming as far as I could underwater, as fast as my stroke could go. But when I eventually popped my head up out of the water I had a bit of a shock, my direction was completely wayward. Instead of nearing the beach, I had gone off on a tangent and was now in the play area; which felt a bit like trying to cross the road during an F1 race, and, for some strange reason, the speedboats and jet skis were all headed in my direction, seemingly oblivious to my presence. I was in a spot of bother.

So what was my reaction? No, I didn't swim like crazy but my heart rate certainly rose, especially after automatically recalling all those dread stories of swimmers getting killed by oblivious boat propellers, and the present vehicles whipping close by. The worst thing you can do is instantly react, because you'd likely tire very quickly and drown all too sharpish, and the holiday would be ruined. When the area around me looked clear, I decided to swim to the buoys in small stages and check around me each time I stopped. It worked fine and in the process I was never in any danger, but I wouldn't want to try it again in a hurry let me tell you.

I got back to the boys and told them what had happened, they looked about as interested as a commuter on the train to Feltham. I could almost hear them saying, "Silly bugger. What do you expect if you go swimming like that on holiday?". It was a good time to have a beer, and sit and pay some attention to the bare breasts. When that grew stale, I enticed Mark to walk the beach with me. I showed him the spot where I'd had the "bit of bother" and he was suitably impressed. 'That FAR out there? He said, pointing in a completely different direction from where I was trying to indicate. We carried on walking northwards along a never ending sandy beach it seemed, passing massive hotel complexes to our left, until we got to a point where very few people were and we turned around to head back.

'Fuck, I don't remember walking this far.' Said Mark.

'Do you mean to say we've got to walk all that way back?'

'You want me to hail a taxi?'

'Couldn't we get a dune buggy?'

'We're the Monkees now are we?'

'Yea, The Monkees; you're right, it used to start with them in a dune buggy didn't it?'

'One bit of it yeah, I think.'

"Hey hey we're the Monkeees, keep on messin' around now and don't care what people say." Mark sang it at the top of his voice, repeating it. What the hell, nobody was around so I joined along, but I didn't go as far as Mark, who danced and jumped around with the all the freedom of a lunatic.

"Hey hey we're the Monkees..." Good fun, moments worth living for; even if sharing space and time with a forgetful dipsomaniac.

Yabba-dabba-doo...

Long day at the beach finished, we headed back to the rooms and agreed to meet up at the big bar from the morning, at around eight o'clock. I crashed out pretty quickly, while Mark watched TV. I came too an hour and a half later, Mark still watching TV.

'Ah, there you are. Did you know you snore?'

'Yes, often and loudly.'

'I'm going to have to get some earplugs.'

'Cotton wool will work.'

'Have we got any?'

'I don't.'

'I'm glad you've woken up, I need to take a shower.'

'Go on then, leave some hot water for me.'

'Why don't they have a lot?'

'I don't know, hope so.'

He picked up his towel and his soap bag, re-living his boarding school days, and went into the bathroom and closed the door. Before long he'd opened the door and stuck his head out.

'There's no shower curtain.'

'I noticed.'

'Is that normal?'

'There's a drain hole in the floor, so don't worry.'

'Okay.'

He closed the door and ran a shower for the next twenty five minutes. Which in my book is enough water to clean yourself ten times over, with a full mop of hair on your head. Eventually, shit, showered and shaved, he emerged with the towel around his waist.

'Sorry, it's a bit of a mess in there.'

I wasn't sure what he meant by that, so I took a look. The floor was awash in an inch of cold soapy water; problem was, the drain wasn't very efficient.

'Shit, I'll have to wait for that to drain a bit.'

I lay back down on the bed and watched Greek TV, quite how Mark could have watched an hour and a half of it I don't know.

Mark had washed a t-shirt while in the shower, and went out onto the balcony to hang it on the line that hung across the gap. As he did, his towel dropped to the ground leaving him exposed to the elements; and to the eyes of two middle aged women, enjoying an early evening drink on their facing balcony.

'Oh I say, very nice. Any time you like dear.' Said one of them loudly.

Mark scooped up the towel and darted back into the room, closing the curtains, and collapsed on his bed in hysterics. While I just laughed my head off; both of us streaming tears. Ten minutes later I chanced taking a shower, the water still filled the floor so it had to be quick. Mark was dressed and ready to leave.

'I'll see you at the big bar.'

'Jimmy's.'

'Is that what it's called?'

'Yes. Are you going there now?'

'No, thought I'd get something to eat first.'

'Aren't you going to wait for me and Rog'?'

'I'm hungry.'

'Why not eat together?'

'No, I need to eat now.'

'Okay, see you there.'

He left, and I assumed he was not only keen to eat but also to save money for the night ahead; that's why he was opting out of going to a restaurant with Roger and myself. I imagined he'd seek out the numerous Greek gyros shops, and get himself something freshly made and filling for a couple of euros. Course I might have known, the temptation to surrender to the dubious delights of McDonalds overcame him. As I walked past the place to go to Jimmy's, I spotted him in there. All that way to experience Greek culture and he succumbed to a fucking Big Mac.

Roger was sitting at a table on the deck when I got to Jimmy's, tucking into a bottle of Mythos lager. I ordered one too and told him about Mark. The lovely lass from Wakefield came over.

'Evenin', did y'er hav' a good day at the beach?'

'Almost killed myself, apart from that wasn't too bad.

Plenty of people there anyway.'

'There's a few around. Where's your friend?'

'At McDonalds.'

'What's he doin' there? I won't go in, it's rank.'

'Mark likes microwave burgers, so McDonalds is like quality.'

'Where y'er goin' t'er night?'

'Don't know yet, got to eat first. Check some bars out I guess.'

'Know any good places?' Asked Roger.

'Not really, everywhere's much the same t'er me.'

'What's the food like here?'

'It's good. Breakfast was alright wasn't it?' It was.

'You do steak and stuff like that?'

'Yeah, burgers, chops, roasts.'

'Roasts?' I queried.

'Beef, lamb and pork; Yorkshire pudding. Fancy s'um?'

No, but I fancied some of her, she was a delight.

A tall, fit looking, overly tanned bloke in his sixties, wearing a bright patterned Bermuda shirt, interrupted.

'Can y'er go an' check if we've got any Bacardi left over the road luv'.' He said to our lass in a thick Aussie accent.

'Evening lads, Jimmy's the name, welcome to Falaraki.' He held out his hand for us to shake.

'Roger.'

'Paul.'

'Pleasure to meet y'er, been here long?'

'Got here this morning.'

'Well this is my place and across the way.' He proudly stated. We looked over at another large bar, dominated by pool tables and dart boards. I could see our lass in there, grabbing a bottle of Bacardi from the barman.

'Anything you need don't be afraid to ask, Jane'l see y'er right.' He pointed at our Wakefield lass and moved onto other tables, doing the meet and greet or renewing acquaintances. It was old fashioned customer service and he knew how to work it large, in a genuine way. Perhaps that's why he had two big bars, he knew how to cultivate good trade; even if the place we were in, was a cross between an outback bar and a British pub and his other place, the sports hall annex.

Mark showed up and walked right past us looking around. Our lass said something to him and then pointed at us.

'Did you just come in?'

'No, but you did. We watched you walk right past.'

'We were hoping you wouldn't notice us.' Said Roger.

'But then you wouldn't have anybody to take the piss out of.' Retorted Mark.

'Where'd you go to eat?' I asked.

'Up the road.'

'What did you have?'

'Nothing much.'

'Did you have a gyros? Asked Roger.

'What's that?'

'Like a kebab.'

'Yeah, one of those.'

'Are you sure?' I asked.

'Of course I'm sure.'

'Sure it wasn't a Big Mac?'

'No it was a gyp thingy, what Rog' just said.'

'Chicken or pork?' Roger asked.

'Chicken I think.'

'Not a Big Mac with fries?' Said I.

'No.'

'That's funny because I saw you in McDonalds eating one.'

He did what he always did when he got caught out, he chewed his mouth up, trying not to laugh.

'Alright I had a McDonalds. It's not a crime is it?'

'I don't mind if you have one, that's your business; but why have you got to lie about it?' I asked him.

'Because I'd never hear the fucking end of it from you two, would I?.'

'Wanker.' Said Roger.

'Pillock.' Said I.

'Get me a beer.' Said Mark.

I got our Lass's attention. 'Three beers.'

'Mythos?' She queried.

'Mythos.'

Finishing that beer, Roger and I left Mark at the bar and went in search of somewhere to eat. We walked up to the junction. On the right side corner was a large open air display of tall metal gas burners, that rotisseried whole chicken on winding spits, with about thirty on the go.

'That's where Mark should have gone.' Said I.

'Bloody McDonalds for chris'sakes.' And again.

We crossed over to it, admiring the wares and turned the corner to go down the street. The frontage turned from an outside take away into a restaurant, and a large sign on the window read: Mixed Grille, ten euros. Includes: Half-chicken, steak, pork chop, lamb chop, sausage, chips and salad. It was very tempting, I for one was hungry enough to eat a horse.

The place looked busy and there was a smell of freshly grilled meat coming from inside.

'What you think Rog'?

'Let's check the street first, come back if we have to.'

A squat, rotund Greek man, wearing a smart pair of slacks and a very fine red short sleeved shirt, came out the door. He also wore, two thick gold wrist bands, a gold Rolex watch, gold neck chains, and some large gold and silver rings. Other than that he looked inconspicuous.

'You like? You want eat?' He asked as we walked away.

'What's the meat like?' Asked Roger.

'It is the best. In all of Rhodes the best.'

He was a bigger salesman than Jimmy I thought.

'Fresh quality, not frozen. We cook everything here, look.'

He pointed to the open style kitchen inside, with a further bank of gas burners and rotating meats.

'How big is the mixed grille?'

'More than you can eat, I promise. Many people eat here, always come back.'

'You do house wine?'

'Yes of course, in litre, half litre.'

'Let's do it.' I said to Roger.

So the owner took us inside, sat us at a table and took our order of two mixed grilles and a litre of house white. The place had a busy canteen feel about it, but it was obviously well established and popular. About a glass of wine in from the liter jug, the mixed grilles arrived, delivered by our man, the owner. His name is forgotten sadly but he was a great guy.

Larger than life and a pleasure to know; even if he was shamelessly selling himself to another rolex, for the other wrist.

'You do not like, I only charge five euro each.' He joked.

There was no chance of that happening, everything he'd said was true; both of us could not finish our plates of plenty and the meat was great. I shook my head thinking how much Mark must have paid for his McDonalds, and we'd just eaten like kings for not much more. What a berk. Ah well, do not mock the afflicted I told myself, even if you couldn't help it. When we'd paid the bill, the owner came over with three shots of Raki, the not so smooth Greek vodka, and we toasted the occasion and said our yassoos.

Mark was happily ensconced at Jimmy's watching Friends on the overhead TV. I told him he was a fool for missing out on a grand meal but he wasn't bothered in the slightest. If we hadn't suggested moving on to some other bar to get the night rolling, he would have been happy just to stay there like a pig in shit; no cares, no bothers, just one Friends show after another and beer after beer.

The action in the street was so-so, it was livelier than Paros but it wasn't exactly teeming with revelers. The bars we observed looked a quarter full, desperate for custom. Two young male Brits came up to us and pushed cards into our faces.

'Two free shots in Champers, three if you mention my name.'

'Yeah? What's your name?' Asked Roger.

'Chris.'

'Best bar in town.' He said confidently.

'Does it get any women in there?'

'Loads.'

They moved on looking for more candidates to cajole.

I looked at the card, it was a business card for Champers bar and stamped on the back in red ink was "Two free shots".

'What's it mean?' I asked Roger.

'You get two free shots of something they give you.'

'Two free shots? Really?'

'Yes. What's wrong with that?'

'Nothing, I'm just amazed that's all.'

'What, you don't get to choose your own drink? Don't know if I like that.'

Said Mark, looking a gift horse in the mouth and semi refusing a drink of all things. Two other young guys came up, this time they were Australian, they had flyers instead of cards.

'Two free shots guys, y'er can't beat it.'

Well you could, we had the offer of three already. But for doing nothing other than walk a few yards up the street, we had five drinks waiting for us before we'd even bought a drink; how good is that? Alcoholics paradise.

'Who are these blokes anyway?' I asked Roger.

'Door whores.'

'Door whores?'

'Yeah, they work the doors of the bars trying to get people in the place, help tidy up and shit.'

'What they get paid?'

'Yeah, not much but they probably get laid a lot. It's a way of staying for the summer.'

Lucky bastards I thought. What I'd be doing at twenty-one again.
Probably not much more than the only time around. I looked at the card
and the flyer.

'So are we going in any of these?'

'Champers bar is right there.' Said Mark pointing to our left. The
image of a semi-naked girl lounging in a champagne glass against a
silverized background, adorned the space between the entrance level and
the roof.

'Shall we go in?' Asked Roger.

All I could think at that moment was, I don't really like shots and I'd
already had one, with five guaranteed to come. I was a bit chary of so
many shots over a short period, so soon into the night's play. The boys
could more than likely quaff them down in their sleep but I was
contemplating what their likely effect would be on me; that I'd die from
alcoholic poisoning after too many.

'Think it's a good idea?' I said.

'Yeeaahhh; come on let's get pissed tonight! This is what
coming on holiday is all about.'

'You're right.' I replied, half heartedly.

We walked into Champers Bar and were warmly greeted by the four
bar staff there, as if just back from the British Antarctic Expedition of
1905. "You made it, you brave fellows. Welcome home. I bet it was
really cold at times." We sat down at the long elliptical central bar and
ordered three beers, and showed them our certified cards to quick
inebriation.

'Chris said to mention his name for an extra shot.' Said Roger, with the air of a man just back from the 1905 expedition.

'Who's Chris?' Said the bar man earnestly.

'The bloke who gave us the cards.'

'Never heard of him. Chris you say?'

'Yes.'

'What's he look like?'

'About four feet, with a face like a crumpled crisp bag.' I said, smiling broadly.

'Shit! Thought I had you fooled there. Smart arse.'

'I could just tell.'

He brought us our beers and then poured out a pink looking substance from an unmarked plastic bottle, into three smaller than usual shot glasses and gave those to us, pouring one out for himself too.

'YAMAS!' He broadcast around the less than busy bar and out onto the street.

'Yamas.' We replied, downing the shots. Which tasted remarkably of sugar and water. "Well I'm not going to get banjaxed on that." I was relieved to note. "Bring on the other two." Which they did in quick succession and were downed with a collective "Yamas" each time. They may not have been strong but they did have a way of loosening your up-tightedness.

Before long we were all smiles and laughter; joking with the staff and the people in there; hoping to catch the eye of damsels who needed to be in distress. For some reason the bar guys loved us for it and we became the center of attention; helping to draw in more customers it seemed. Such was the happy mood we were creating by our presence, they started to reward us with more shots, but this time proper shots. Out came the dreaded Jagermeister, followed by the black Sambuca.

My inhibitions to shots of alcohol blown away I relaxed beautifully, helped by the fact I wasn't getting instantly inebriated. All that meat inside me was obviously keeping me sober, well, relatively sober that is. The guy Chris showed up.

'So you guys came in?'

The three of us were all over him like a long lost friend, buying him a drink and asking him about how long he'd been working there, and how the season had gone, and did he have much luck with the ladies? Yes, lots of luck, more than he could shake a stick at. Except in his case, being a good looking bastard it wasn't luck, as any plain looking bloke knows. He asked us.

'How long you going to be in Falaraki?'

'Two nights maybe.'

'Two nights? How come?'

We explained our situation and then he said something interesting, which when you looked at us could have been likely.

'Are you guys in the army?'

"No." Said us. "What gave you that idea?"

'Well looking at you, you could be.'

He had a point, all three of us had our hair cropped short and in both myself and Roger's case, we looked tanned and fit in the exercised sense.

'Do you get many military blokes here then?'

'We get a few.'

'Any from Iraq or Afghanistan?' Asked Roger.

'Yeah, some.'

'This is the first sort of place you'd want to be after that shit
isn't it?. I know I would if I was doing that.'

The idea that we could be thought of as military stuck in my mind, I actually felt elevated by the suggestion; stupidly.

Our new mate Chris went back to his duties and we decided to move on to the next place on the free shots list, we said a very warm "Yassoo" and left promising to return, if not that night then the next. God knows what the next bar was called but it had a fake 'Rock' frontage, like something out of the Flintstones. I half expected to bump into Fred, Barney, Wilma and Betty in there, with intermittent cries of "Yabbadabbadoo!" going off. We weren't quite the same focus of attention either, but we did have our two free watered down shots and tried to chat to some pretty females, who were mostly being kind to Mark and I. At one point, pissed enough, the three of us got up to dance. If I don't mind saying, I'm a good dancer, Mark's not bad, but Roger, well, how should I put it? Let's say he dances with spirit and enthusiasm, but resembles one of those tin robots whose arms are half raised at waist level close to the torso, then twist and judder side to side a lot, like a loose bolted down spin dryer. Mark finally had something over Roger that he could tease and mock him about. Did he? No. But like me he laughed heartily at his contortions. It never stopped Roger though, largely because he was usually drunk before he did dance and because it never bothered him; he was far too self-confident to care.

I don't know where the time went, well I do, but you know how sayings are; anyway we were on our fifth or sixth bar, no free shots anymore but enjoying the beer, when somebody handed us another flyer, this time for a nightclub nearby, which offered us the best of this and the best of that, and the most up to date sounds and there was no other place like it on earth or at least on Rhodes. It had promise. It also presumably had lots of women. Women who were merry like us and looking to let themselves go with a kindred spirit, in similar thought and deed.

'Shall we go?' I asked.

Roger raised his arms high and wide and uttered 'PARTY!'. I assumed that was a yes. Mark looked at me blankly.

'Well?' I asked him.

'Think the women will be interested in us?' He asked dourly, dampening the mood.

Hey, we weren't all that bad. I was a little conscious of my age, as I should have been, but Roger always said he couldn't believe I was forty eight, and that as far as he was concerned I was his age almost. At important times like then, I believed it. Roger could attract interest and Mark, well, Mark in fact could be the biggest charmer in the world if he put his mind to it, and if he wasn't so mind bogglingly addled half the time. Forty minutes later, with the bar about to close we decided to go there. There was a little map on the back of the flyer and we tried to follow it, but soon got lost amid the open ground behind the bars.

'Where are we?' Exclaimed Mark.

'Fucking lost.' I replied.

'I'm going home.' He declared.

'Don't be stupid, we're lost now, how the hell are you going to find your way back?' I insisted.

'Easy, follow my nose.'

'If this wasn't an island you'd be half way to China.'

He slumped down on the dirt ground, then some people came by.

'Do you know where this place is?' Roger asked, showing them the flyer.

'Follow us.' They said in a Scandinavian accent.

So we did, and after twenty yards or so they stopped and indicated at a very brightly lit, neon signed building just off the path.

'That's it.'

'Thanks.'

'Bye.'

'Aren't you going in?' I asked with some surprise.

'No we go somewhere first.'

'Enjoy, maybe see you later.'

I'd hung the question out there, to see what the reaction of the rather lovely looking ladies in the group was, there was none and they departed forever. I looked around at our location, the street of bars was just a few feet away. We walked right by the highly illuminated nightclub in the darkness not noticing it, how did we do that I wondered? You couldn't help but notice it.

'Right let's go clubbing then. C'mon Mark.'

'I'm going home, I want to sleep.'

'No you don't.'

'I do.'

'Rog?'

'I'm up for it.'

'What about Mark? How's he going to get back?'

'Just point me in the right direction.'

'Are you sure?'

'Yes.'

So I helped pick him up from the ground and walked him to the street of bars, and faced him in the right direction.

'It's down there mate, remember?'

'I thought it was that way.' He pointed behind us.

'No, it's that way, McDonalds is on the corner.'

'Is it open?'

'Hope not for your sake.'

'Ah, I'll find it.'

'Can you?'

'Think so.'

'Well good luck, see you sometime later today.'

'Night.'

'If you can't find the room just sleep on the beach.'

'Which beach?'

'The one made of sand.'

'Oh, right.'

I went back to Roger and we walked down to the nightclub where the two Doormen and the Manager were vetting entrants. For some reason they looked suspiciously at us, like definite trouble makers, but we allayed their fears by being nice to them. So far, it was just like being back in the UK.

Inside, we grabbed a drink and set up shop at a large central pillar that had a ledge to place drinks on. We chatted and kept our eyes open for lovely women, but the atmosphere in there was not conducive to having a naturally good time and it was only half full. I got another round in and we found two stools to sit on. I was talking to Roger when I noticed he was slumped on the ledge, arms folded, head down. The bugger had fallen asleep. So there was I at three am in a crappy nightclub in Falaraki, at forty eight years of age, effectively on my own. Nursing a rum and coke, wondering how it was that the two alcoholics on this trip, had both flaked out; and me, the concerned one, was still going strong. How the hell did that happen? One thing about Roger though, he could just as easily wake up in a few and suddenly come alive with more fun energy than before; I'd witnessed that miracle a number of times with wonderment. So I let him be and concentrated on watching a very sexy girl dancing up a storm on the dance floor. She was a fantastic mover and dancing to stuff I didn't have a clue about then. I was transfixed and desperately wanted to dance with her but that ol' inhibition held me back, so I just sat there trying to look cool and knowing and desirable. Not thinking for a moment that this is probably why I've led a lonely life; that only works if you are devastatingly attractive.

Taking my eye off the girl for a moment, I noticed that the Doormen and the Manager were doing a sweep of the place. As they neared us, the Manager, who was really a surfer type with long dreadlocks, spotted Roger asleep and said something to me over the loud music. I pointed to my ear to let him know I couldn't hear, so he bent his head to my ear and said matter of factly in a forceful tone.

'He's got to go, no sleeping in the club.'

I didn't answer straight away, I just stared coldly at him and his two standby minions and then I looked at Rog', and then I said for some inexplicable reason.

'Give him a break, we just got in from Iraq and we've had a hell of a bad time.'

The guy stood back in awe almost, like we had just walked out of Andy McNab's Bravo Two Zero. His whole attitude altered.

'Oh, okay, well..' He was also lost for words.

'Don't worry, I'll keep an eye on him.'

He simply nodded and moved on, and I had gained instant respect with a terrible lie, one that I had pulled off with a lot of conviction. My demeanour and my tone had shaken the guy a bit. What Chris had said earlier about thinking we were squaddies, had given me the belief I could pull such a fallacy off. Shit, I was a better actor than Mark. Roger came around about twenty minutes later determined to finish his drink, then by mutual consent we left the less than buzzing club. I nodded to the Manager as we left, walking tall. Outside, was the lovely dancer with a friend of hers, as we went by I told her how great she was; but I had overstepped my mark, and in a German accent she said something very uncomplimentary back and I went from tall to small in one easy sentence.

Little Noisy Bleeders...

The moment I woke up I knew something was wrong. My head was feeling dull and heavy for one thing. My body ached all over and I noticed patches of blood on the pillow. Another thing, my left eye was feeling swollen. I got up to take an overdue piss and stumbled into the bathroom. I looked at my awful face in the mirror, my eye was puffed up and there was a stream of dried blood from my hair, I felt my scalp and discovered a very itchy bump. "What the fuck!" I thought. I tottered back to bed and suddenly felt other parts of my body itching badly, with bumps attached, then I heard the dread sound of a mosquito and realized I had been bit to shit. I threw the sheet right over me to keep the hungry fiend off me. Mark was still sound asleep, he'd woken me a couple of times with slurred shouting and odd noises. God knows, I couldn't figure them out either. I went back to sleep and woke again, hearing Mark come out the bathroom.

'Morning.' I said.

'Morning, what's the time?'

I checked my watch. 'Twelve.'

'Is that all?'

'Did you get bit?'

He looked at me with a what on earth are you talking about? expression.

'Mosquitoes, did you?'

'No.'

'I did. I'm covered in mossie bites, look at my eye.'

'Jeezuz, that looks terrible mate. How did that happen?'

'I don't know, must be an allergic reaction.'

'Maybe you got bit on the eye.'

I didn't think of that, but there was no bump and no itchyness. A Mosquito went by and I followed it's trajectory to over by the bathroom door where it settled close to the ceiling, along with about fifty other mosquitos! It was the horror film that Alfred Hitchcock never made. The word had obviously got around that there was easy pickings to be had in the room, and they had all gathered to come and have a morsel of tasty me. How Mark escaped the gathering is still beyond me, other than adding weight to the theory that he is indeed an alien. It would explain a lot.

Roger knocked on the door to say he was going to the beach and to meet him there if we wanted. Mark declared he was all set to visit Jimmy's and have some breakfast, but could I give him some money, I gave him the remnants in my pockets and he left. I had to do something about the dreadful eye and those damned mosquitoes, it was clearly going to be more of the same tonight if I didn't. I was thinking along the lines of one of those big net screens that hung over the entire bed. The sort you saw in old films, usually set in Africa on safari or the tropics. With a sultry temptress lounging on the bed in longed for abandon and some manly man with shirt sleeves rolled up tight around his biceps; struggling to pierce the net and the girl. Yeah, one of those would work, especially if it came with a sultry temptress.

I went and checked my eye again, it seemed to be getting worse by the minute, the entire left side of my face was puffing up in sympathy. I had a quick shower to hopefully aid my condition and help stimulate my senses and prepare me for once out the door. I took what I needed for the beach; one thing Roger told me on the plane out here, was always take your hangover there, that way you didn't waste your holiday time in a room and it helped you recover quickly. It was sage advice, one I've followed ever since. I left the room and headed for the bank first, after which I searched for a chemist or apothecary in Greece. I found one among the many spend-your-holiday-money-here establishments, and asked for some heavy chemical weapons in the fight against mosquitoes, napalm preferably. As a matter of personal interest I inquired if malaria was a problem in this part of Europe. The answer was "No." on both counts but they did recommend some liquid gunk made by some German company, which you spread all over you like sunscreen and the little blood sucking bastards were in effect put off from making a nourishing meal of you.

'Hmmm, really. How much?' I asked tentatively.

If you've been to Greece and know how much they charge for sunscreen in an Apothecary let's just say this stuff was twice the price at best. Before lashing out a sizable debt on my credit card, I undid one of the tops and smelt the contents, as I did I felt the hairs in my nostrils burn away. I checked out the listed contents on the bottle. Everything that made up the potion was something Zine this and Zine that, it appeared to be all petroleum by product. Carcinogen and Cancer came immediately to mind for some reason, even though it had to be passed safe to use. In my mind, I'd be coating myself with a deadly toxin prone to combustion near a naked flame. And between Roger, Mark and myself, there was always one of those around. Besides what if I pulled and I'd just put this stuff on? I'd smell like the fumes from a leaky petrol tank, nice. Fuck that, where's that net? Is there a camping store nearby?

I was about to leave when I remembered the itchy bites, which were bloody murder and you couldn't help but want to scratch. Do you have anything for those under a bank loan? I asked.

'Mosquito bite?' The very helpful Apothercarist asked.

'Yes. See?' I took off my sunglasses to show her my eye.

She blanched at the sight of me. I thought she was about to run out of the shop screaming, but in fact all she did was rush over to a shelf by the door and produce a small tube of anti-mosquito something or other.

'You need this.' She said authoritatively.

'It's good?' Noticing the price sticker of fifteen euros.

'Yes, very good.'

It didn't look or smell poisonous, so I bought it, not believing for a moment that it would help in any startling way, but it might help relieve the bites and prevent malaria; which for all the Apothecarist's assurance was lurking in Greece, as an article I'd read had mentioned the fact. I walked back down to Jimmy's and joined Mark, whose gaze was barely diverted from the overhead TV screen showing Friends. Though as soon as I flashed his daily sixty euros into space, he gave me his full attention; for all of the two seconds it took to pocket the dosh.

'Got to do something about those bloody mosquitos.' I said.

'Hmm.' Said Mark.

'The supermarkets must sell something.'

'Hmm.'

'Remember the old vapona strips you used to hang up?

'Hmm.'

'Honeycombed packaging. Remember?'

'Hmm.'

'They had a yellow stick inside that stank of paraffin?'

'Hmm.'

'I'm going to the toilet, mind my stuff.'

'Hmm.'

Using the mirror in the toilet, I applied the anti-mossie stuff to the bites on my head, arms, torso, legs and feet; thankfully I'd been wearing elasticated briefs, otherwise... Then I smeared some on my swollen eye lid and managed to get some in my eye. Not only did I have a face disfigurement, I now had irritated eye syndrome, with streams of tear solution running down my face. I was definitely being punished for something I'd done or said. I rejoined Mark who was more expansive now that Friends had finished.

'I know someone who tried eating one.' Mark said.

'Eat what?'

'A Vapona strip.'

'Really? What happened to them?'

'He got really ill.' Now there was a surprise and a half.

'Was he alright?'

'Don't know, never saw him again.'

Our Lass came over.

'Do you want a drink?' She asked me, and before I could reply.

'You should see his eye, it looks awful.' Said Mark.

So having no choice I showed her.

'Aarrgghh, what happened?

'Mosquito.'

'Yeah, there's lots of them here. Sometimes they spray but
not of late.'

That was good to know.

'Got any good ideas to get rid of them?'

'There's these things you plug into the wall, their not bad.

You get them from any supermarket.'

Sounded like a winner to me, easier than hanging a net up if a
temptress wasn't included. I ordered a coffee and when she came back
with it I asked her something that had been on my mind awhile.

'Is Lindos any good?'

'Never been. Hear it's just a place for sightseers. Ask Jimmy,
he'll know.'

'Right, well thanks Jane.'

I drank my coffee and mulled Lindos over. I had expected to hear a
more positive response from her. For some reason Lindos had been
slowly calling to me like a siren since we had arrived. In my mind it had
an air of mystique, like a place waiting to be discovered. Most of all it
didn't sound like a swear word when uttered. We'd have to visit the place
at least, just to satisfy my curiosity.

By the time Mark and I joined Roger at the beach the mossie stuff was
working wonders. The itching had abated and the swelling was reducing
by the wrinkle. I told Roger about the mosquitoes and showed him the
eye, and more importantly asked if he had had a problem with them. He

replied in the negative so it was just me they were after, the little noisy bleeders. It was personal now.

Roger couldn't remember much about going to the nightclub so I told him what happened with the manager, he thought my bullshit funny but added it was disrespectful to real servicemen. Which he was right about and made me feel stupid saying what I did. At least I now knew the reason for being punished.

Mark was slapping on factor one thousand sun screen again, which was probably why after four good days in the sun he still looked white as a hotel towel; aside from his lower arms, neck, head and feet (yes feet, toes included.) which had all turned conker brown. Many would describe much of that particular affliction as a "Farmer's tan." but Mark didn't look remotely like the outdoors type. We started to chide him for overdoing the protection.

'Get some bloody sun on you for Chris'sake!'

'No, I'm happy as I am thank you.'

'But if you used a lesser factor and stayed in the sun you'd get a great tan matey. Check your feet out if you don't believe me.'

'I need it. I don't want to get burnt.'

There was no chance of that happening that day, not with the sun fast disappearing under a swathe of grey cloud and the wind picking up. Within an hour it was turning a darker shade of pale. The beach, which hadn't been particularly busy to begin with, began to resemble the last of the few with perhaps under a hundred persons around. It was still warm though and for the brave souls who toughed it out it had it's own rewards.

One of which was the swelling sea and the breaking waves that accompanied it, creating perfect body surfing conditions. Commenting thus, Roger goaded us to challenge ourselves; to be men, to face up to the elements. So for some crazy impetus of a reason, we charged in to the sea and ducked, dived, surfed, tumbled and flipped with the rolling waves. It was cheaper than the Water Park in Falaraki and probably as much fun.

Unexercised, Mark didn't last as long as us in the pounding and went off in search of refreshment. Besides, he'd drawn blood on his leg when tossed and turned and hurled onto the pitiless hard beach by a relentless wave. Not really, but it sounded good; still, he retired like a wounded hero. As time went on it was getting like that though, the waves were getting increasingly powerful and trying to surf a wave got more difficult, Roger and I got battered about as we strove to defy the sea's strength.

Fairly exhausted, all funned out, we retired for the luxury of the sun beds, a good book and a cold beer. First though, I stood at the tide's edge and took in the fermenting weather, manifested in the turbulent sky and sea. There are times when you feel so extraordinarily alive because all your senses are hyper responding to the stimuli of the world around you. An hour previous I'd been nursing a disconnecting hangover but with a charged atmosphere and an invigorating splash about, I was now at top dead center. As far as I could tell looking along the beach, we had been the only ones in the water enjoying ourselves. Sometimes the most fun to be had is when things are quiet and conditions look bad, like that day in Falaraki, or "Falafuckingraki" as we started calling it.

The idea of lasting the day out on the beach and expecting the weather to clear, ended when it began to rain around three pm. We decided to go to Jimmy's and watch the rain pour down from there and discuss our belated plans for the next day. Well that's what Roger and I did at least, Mark sat and watched Friends of course. Without fail, our cheery hard working Wakefield Lass attended to our needs. We told her the fun of the night before and of the afternoon's escapades on the beach. She liked us; indeed I got the feeling most people did on this trip. When up and running, without the breakdowns, our little trio had a friendly fun seeking aura and it rubbed off on like minded souls.

'First time it's rained in ages. March maybe.' She said.

'How come it's so quiet everywhere?' I asked.

'It's turn-around day.' She replied.

What in the hell was turn around day? I sat thinking. Roger could see my difficulty in comprehending her answer.

'It's the day that one group of package holiday makers go
home and another come in.'

'So where are the new ones?'

'Oh, they won't c'um in 'till late ter'night or early morning.'

I sort of got it but I didn't, in time hence I would.

'So what's y'er plans? Hav' y'er decided?'

'Not yet, thought we'd have a chat now.'

'I'll leave y'er to it then.'

As promised she did, which was a shame as it was nice to have her around.

'So any ideas?' Roger asked me.

'I'd like to go check out Lindos. I've got an urge to go there.'

'An urge hey?'

'Yes, fancy it?'

'Sure, and after?'

'Kos for two to three nights.'

'Yourself?'

'I'll be up for Kos. Need to check for ferries. We should make time to see the old town of Rhodes too.'

'Hopefully we'll get it all in.'

'Are we going to spend a night in Lindos?'

'See when we get there I think. If it's no good we'll come back here or go to Rhodes Town hey?'

'Hello boys how's it going?' It was Jimmy flashing that stupendous tan again and a warmer than warm handshake.

'Jimmy?'

'Yes mate.'

'What's Lindos like?'

'Lindos? Day trippers place mate. Only want to spend a few hours there. It's got nothing going for it. Not like here.'

Really? I couldn't believe it, but Jimmy's view of the place was quite adamant. The image I'd been building up had taken a severe knock. So far nobody had anything positive to say about it, even the taxi driver on the trip from Rhodes Town had dismissed my inquiry. The last comment by Jimmy gave me a small ounce of hope though, we definitely didn't want anywhere to be "Like here." after tonight. We'd still go check it out and satisfy my curiosity.

Mark was still eyeball deep in Friends.

'Mark. Mark. MARK!.'

'Yes?'

'We've made a decision about tomorrow.'

'Yes.'

'Thought you might want to know.'

'Yes.'

'We're going to fly to Cairo and go see the pyramids at Giza.
Is that okay?'

'Yes, whatever you guys decide. I told you.'

'Right.' I turned to Roger and quietly spoke.

'Let's leave him here hey? He's got the perfect set-up. He
wouldn't miss us. We could go to Lindos on our own.'

'Cairo? Did you say Cairo?'

'No, what are you talking about?'

'You just said.'

'Said what?'

'About go-'

'Going to Lindos, then Kos.'

'What flying?'

'No, a ferry to Kos.'

'I swear you mentioned about going to Cairo.'

'You're getting worse, that brain of yours is fucked.
Stop drinking bloody cider.'

I turned to Roger,

'Lindos then.'

'Lindos.'

With the rain not letting up and not much to do, we plumbed for eating an early meal at Jimmy's. That done it was back to the rooms for a couple before we started the night off again. First though I located a supermarket and stocked up on mosquito killing gear.

Mark had to spend self imposed time on the balcony as I sprayed the room head to foot in some nasty stuff. Wiping out multitudes of expectant mosquitos, who had congregated on news of a big feast to be had. Mark was not pleased by my actions, convinced we'd die from some terrible reaction to the spray can's contents, or at the very least break out in reactive sores, rashes and suppurating boils. Tough, it was them or me; apocalypse now.

I plugged in the electrical device for keeping any late arriving mossies at bay, it basically heated a small replaceable pad, releasing an odour that acted as a benign repellant. Mark wasn't happy about that either, convinced it would set off some long dormant asthma problem. I didn't get it, all these sudden health concerns from a man who was destroying his liver with alcohol, his lungs with nicotine and his nutrition with microwave burgers. I ask you, what is a friend supposed to do? Easy, ignore him, ignore the chemicals and read a book instead. Which I did for the next thirty minutes, while silly bollocks constantly shuffled about on the balcony, huffing and puffing; placing his hand over his mouth any time he came into the room to do or get something quickly, and generally making a meal of it; while I constantly reminded him to keep the door shut.

Meanwhile, I was perfectly happy lying on the bed reading a very fascinating modern plot about a man who was unlike any other, who outwitted and outfought superior forces lined against him in the most improbable ways and means imaginable. Shakespeare it wasn't, but according to the high praise on the jacket, from noted critics such as Brad Strump of the Patio Subscribers Weekly it ran rings around such a trashy writer. "The greatest writer in the history of writing!" High praise indeed. The bullshit get's better with age.

I heard a loud slap, as if Mark had just hit the palm of his hand on the top of his exposed thigh, with all the force his skinny arm could muster. He had.

'OWWWW!'

'What's the matter?' I shouted.

He came into the room painfully clutching his thigh, forgetting to cover his mouth.

'Look!'

'What is it?'

'I got bit! See?'

He held out his hand to reveal a pulped mosquito.

'That's your fault McCloskey.'

'My fault? How can it be my fault?'

'You forced the fuckers outside.'

I couldn't fault him on his twisted logic, but I could fault him in his misguided confidence that he was immune to bites.

'See? They like you after all.'

'Have you got any spray left?'

'A little bit.'

I pointed the can out and he grabbed it and went out on the balcony, spraying like mad at everything and anything.

'Fat lot of good that's going to do out there.' I shouted.

'It's the same as doing it inside.' He insisted.

'Whatever.'

'SHIT!'

'What now?'

'I've been bitten again. Right!'

He stood in the doorway, and after all his bleatings about the dangers posed by the tin's contents, began to spray the stuff on him; including under his arm pits and around his crotch, like he was going out for the night..

'There, they won't go near me now!' He said resoundingly.

We all met again at Jimmy's at nine o'clock. Mark had gone on a mystery walk half an hour before. I'd warned him not to stray too far, otherwise there was the constant danger of him getting lost, of course I knew he was going to pay McDonalds another visit, although he thought I had no inkling of his intentions and dark desires.

'How were the fries?' I asked him.

'What fries?'

'McDonalds.'

'I didn't go there.' He insisted.

'You did, Roger saw you in there this time.'

He hadn't, I just made it up to draw the sordid truth out.

'That's right.' Said Roger.

'Fuck! I feel like the..what was that TV series about the bloke in the village?'

'The Prisoner.'

'Him.'

'So what did you have this time number six?'

'Not much. Fries and one of those apple thingies.'

'Disgusting.'

'I luv' 'em. Anyway you went there today.'

This was true, feeling a tad parlous from the excessive night's drinking I had sought to obtain a chocolate milkshake, in the belief it would assist my recovery.

'I went to get the only thing worth getting from there.'

'And what was that?' Asked a rather dubious Roger.

'A chocolate milkshake. And guess what?'

'What?'

'I couldn't get one.'

'Why not?'

'The bloody machine was broken down. Anyway what are we going to do tonight? The place looks dead.'

Turn around day also meant nobody around day. It wasn't looking very promising for the evening. Even our lovely lass was working the other bar tonight. Roger came up with a temporary plan.

'Let's go across the road and play pool, and whatever else they got going.'

So we picked up our drinks and walked over, much to the delight of our Lass.

'Glad y'er came over, it's been really quiet.'

Yeah, the place definitely needed our help, with no more than five people present. The incredible thing about Mark is that for all his ills, there are times when he surprises you with his energy and independence. I suppose having gone five days without cider for breakfast, was helping to restore his forthrightness. Eyeing up the situation he proposed that we participate in a pentathlon of pub games. It would include, pool, darts, pinball, fussball and some skittle type game that was there. I dropped out due to unfeigned disinterest after the first three competitions, preferring to chat to our Lass at the bar. Roger and Mark meanwhile went at it hammer and tong, driven by a fierce rivalry and will to win.

Unfortunately for Mark, Roger won the contrived tournament, confirming his smug arrogance and an innate ability to drive Mark to untold heights of inner rage. After months of having the piss taken out of him by Roger (in a playful way I add.) the last thing he wanted to do, was lose to him in an arena he felt he was in with a good chance of winning. It was funny yet sad at the same time.

There was Roger smiling, declaring himself "King of the Pub." While Mark had to sit there taking not only that gem but all the rest of the jibes.

'I told you I was better than you.'

'You're not.'

'Fancy another game of fussball?'

'No.'

'Go on, I'll give you a three goal lead this time.'

'Piss off.'

'Thought you said you were good at darts?'

'I am.'

'Well we won't play double to start next time.'

'Anymore?'

'When you play pool does your hand always shake like that?
Or is that what happens when you drink too much cider?'

The simple answer to that was yes, years of it. Not to be outdone,
Mark came back with a slagging of his own.

'Tell you something you're not good at, Roger.'

'I'm all ears.'

'Acting.'

'Acting?'

'Yes. You couldn't do what I do.'

'You mean turn into an unemployed alcoholic wreck?'

'Yes; I mean no! Oh fuck it, why have you always got an
answer to what I say?'

'Not difficult Mark, you keep setting yourself up.' I entered.

'Who asked you?'

'Me.'

'One more game. Let's play one more game.'

'No.'

'Why not?'

'I've already won.'

'Come on Rog' one more.'

'Okay, but when you lose you have to print loser on your
forehead and wear it all night.'

'How can I do that?'

'Have you got any lipstick on you Jane?'

'Yes.'

'Well?'

'Fine, because I'm not going to lose.'

'You will.'

'No I won't.'

'You've lost so far.'

'I won the skittles.'

'Still lost overall.'

'My luck could change.'

'It's not luck.'

'What is it then?'

'You just can't beat me.'

'I fucking can.'

'You blokes are funny; you always like this?' Asked our Lass of me.

'Periodically.'

'Yer' should be on stage or sum'thin'.'

'Oh Christ don't say that or Mark will start going on about treading the boards.' I said.

She looked at me with a what-did-I-say look to which I replied, 'Technically he's an actor.'

'That's what he claims anyway.' Said Roger.

'You two are...' Uttered Mark, suddenly lost for a word.

'What?'

'Bastards.'

'Ah, but good bastards.'

'Maybe.'

'Are you really an actor?' She asked.

'Not anymore.' Said Mark.

'Pool or darts?' Asked Roger.

'Neither, I'm not playing now.'

Two beers later we decided to head for the dizzy climes of Champers Bar again. Our Lass looked disappointed.

'Com' back if your bored, keep me company.'

'Where's your boyfriend?'

'He's workin'. He might cum' out later but I doubt it.'

'We still haven't met him.'

'I know; he does exist I can assure yer'.'

'We'll say good night then.'

'Are y'er definitely leavin' tomorrow?'

'Fraid so. Going to Lindos. Kos day after that we think.'

'Make sure yer' com' ter' Jimmy's an' say gud'bye.'

'We will.'

So Roger, the inaugural "King of the Pub", led the way to Champers where we were greeted with great fanfare and doused with free shots. We chatted to three splendidly buxom Welsh girls who were game for a laugh but just when we thought we were in, their unmentioned boyfriends showed up. Wouldn't you know it? We then chatted to the owner or manager of the bar, he liked our entertainment value. We tried to buy him a shot but he wouldn't have it.

'It's the end of the season, enjoy. I give you shots because
I like you. It is my pleasure.'

It's enough to understand the part of the world he was coming from and to appreciate his hospitality. We left Champers and went to one other bar, where Mark got involved with some crazy German tourists in their sixties who insisted on us singing Beatles songs with them, presumably because they thought we'd know the words, so did we, but we couldn't remember hardly any. For Englishmen who grew up with them it was shameful, talk about your mind going blank. Thankfully we didn't mention the war like Basil, or nineteen sixty six; and ended up having a good drunken laugh with them, particularly Mark who for all his faults can certainly entertain a crowd at times. He was definitely better at it than Roger and I.

Being a quiet night out, and knowing we were leaving in the morning we shuffled off home early, grabbing a gyros on the way. It was the first time I'd had one and it was delicious. Chicken, sauce and salad, open wrapped in a toasted pitta and all for two euros, bloody marvelous. If you were doing Greece on the cheap, one of these a day and you were set.

My night time's sleep was interrupted by Mark, with bursts of loud jiberish, odd sounds, and the shouting out of some indecipherable words. I tried spraying him with the mosquito spray but it did little good, he was in some deep type of coma. Not only that, I had been bitten again and I could hear the mini tormentor buzzing around my ears. In the end I slept under the sheet one ear pressed to the pillow and the other pushed uncomfortably against my arm. How I slept at all is a mystery.

Smack Between the Eyes...

I was dreaming that I lay in a small apartment infested with mosquitoes and a strange man in the next bed was moaning loudly, as if in tormented pain or deep sexual pleasure. Long drawn out moans, that ended with piercing shouts of indeterminate meaning. As I awoke to the pronounced audible nature of the vision, I found that the moans were continuing and further more, they were coming from the strange man in the next bed.

'Mark'

'WWWWWAAAAAARRRRRGGGGHHHH!'

'MarK.'

'NNNNNOOOOOOOOYYYYYYUUUUUUCCCCCCAAAAAA!'

'MaRK!'

'EEEEEZZZZZZMMMM!'

'OI MARK! WAKE UP!'

'WHAT?' He answered without opening his eyes.

'You're making weird noises, shut the fuck up!'

'Okay.' And he promptly fell asleep again.

Not me, I was annoyingly wide awake. The watch read eight am, three hours until our planned departure time; what the hell was I going to do? I thought about going for a walk but I'd seen all I'd wanted to see of Falafuckingraki. What I really wanted to do was go to Lindos there and then, perhaps check it out before the boys were alive to the world and report back, but that wasn't very feasible. No, I'd have to wait it out for two hours then rouse the dynamic duo into action or rather into renewed alcohol and nicotine.

Killing time is the least fun one can have on their own, but knowing the fact didn't prevent me from trying it out that morning on the balcony. I imagined, sitting in the sun reading a book would be a nice relaxing thing to do, a sensible and rewarding use of the time. What a mistake; the book read terribly, the watch was in slow motion and I couldn't relax. The thought of moving on was too much. At least Mark had stopped his utterances during this time. Indeed he was sleeping like a new born baby, so it was with some small measure of guilt that I awoke him at nine thirty; thirty minutes earlier than planned.

'Waaaaaassssuuupp?' He slurred.

'It's ten thirty mate, time to get up.' I lied for good purpose.

'Whyyy sooo earlyyy?'

'We're leaving this morning remember?'

'Uuuhhh, do we have too?'

'Do you want a cup of coffee? I'm going to get one.'

'Nuuhhh.'

'Don't go back to sleep now. Remember,

eleven o'clock is checking out time.'

'Fuuccchhh.'

I went for a coffee, and returning knocked on Roger's door.

'Yes?'

'You up mate?'

He came and opened the door, a half read book in hand. He stared at my inviting coffee.

'Where's mine?'

'Back at the shop. Left it there, sorry. Been up long?'

'About two hours.'

'Don't tell me you've been reading a book all this time?'

'Why?'

'So have I, we could have been gone by now.'

'Mark up?'

'He soon will be.'

'Meet you at Jimmy's in half an hour.'

'Right.'

Affirmative action, you can't beat it.

True to form Mark had gone back to sleep. If I'd set the room on fire before I'd left, he'd have returned to the land of nod no problem.

"Paul, what are you doing?"

"Nothing much mate, just setting the room ablaze.

You just doze off now."

"Thanks, I will."

But perhaps I needed to try a more conventional route in waking him, otherwise I'd have a lot of explaining to do and it would take awhile longer to get to Lindos. Hence.

'Mark?'

'Yeeaahh?'

'Roger and I are going now. We'll be back in a few hours,

meet you at Jimmy's later hey?'

He bolted upright, alarmed that he'd be left alone.

'Hold on I'm coming with you.'

'Well you'd better be quick, taxi's waiting outside.'

'Fuck why didn't you wake me?'

'I did.'

'When?'

'Ages ago.'

He rushed into the bathroom and locked the door.

'How long you going to be?' I asked, hesitating to learn what he was about to do in there.

'Don't leave without me!'

'Oh Mark.'

'Yes?'

'I lied a little.'

'About what?'

'Leaving right this moment.'

'When are we leaving then?'

'Within the next hour.'

'You're a cunt.'

'I know. Meet us at Jimmy's when you're ready.'

'I might go back to bed.'

'We have to vacate the room by eleven.'

'What's the time now?'

'For real?'

'Yes.'

'Ten thirty.' Wriggle your way out of that I thought.

Roger and I went up to Jimmy's and waited on Mark. Our lass wasn't there but Jimmy was, he welcomed us with all the gentle force of a hurricane. He noticed our bags.

'Are yer' leavin'?'

'Yes Jimmy, going to Lindos.' I said.

'Lindos? Yer' won't like Lindos mate. Nothin' there.'

Nah, won't like it, tellin' yer'.'

'That bad hey?' Said Roger.

'Terrible mate, it's like goin' to church. Nah, Lindos,

don't want to stay there. One night maybe, that's it.

Anyway what can I get yer'? Drinks on me.'

We could hardly refuse so we ordered three beers. Mark timed his appearance perfectly, just as Jimmy came back with the order. He'd included a beer for himself.

'Boys, it's a bit early for me. I don't normally do this but

here's a toast, glad ter' meet yer'. All the best for the

rest of yer' trip.'

We raised our glasses, thanked him for his great hospitality and sipped. He knocked his beer straight back and left us to it.

'So Mark do you know where we're going?' Asked Roger.

'Yes.'

'You're sure?'

'Positive.'

'Where then?'

'Lindos.'

For once he was on the ball. Roger and I had nothing but sudden respect for his awareness. All of a minute that was.

'What time is the ferry?' He asked.

'The ferry?'

'To Lindos.'

'We're not going by ferry.'

'I thought we were?'

'No.'

'How we getting there then?

'By bus or taxi.'

'How can we do that?'

'Lindos is on Rhodes it's just a few miles up the road.'

'Aren't we going to another island?'

'Tomorrow maybe.'

'Wish you lot would make your mind up.'

Roger and I gave him five out of ten for effort. He was trying to get to grips with the itinerary at least.

Our delightful Lass turned up especially to say goodbye even though it was her day off. She also brought along her elusive boyfriend and a puppy dog they had acquired. The "Fell'er" seemed a nice bloke, I was pleased for her and I hope they live happily ever after. It's as much as she deserved. Soon, the time came to leave, we gave our Lass a hug, a kiss on the cheek and wished her all the best. Shook Jimmy's big hand and waved back at their smiling faces as we walked up the road to the bus stop, Jimmy convinced we'd be back by sunset.

'See ye'r around six, fellers.'

Falaraki may have been Blackpool abroad, it may have been garish, ever so shallow and over the top. But it did have a good beach and some great people who welcomed us with a friendly open nature. even though they mostly wanted our money. We'd miss them but not Falaraki. Hell, for all it's lurid atmosphere we didn't even come close to getting laid there. As Mark said poignantly.

'If I'd fallen into a sea of nipples, I'd have come out
sucking my thumb.'

We walked up to the main road from Rhodes Town to Lindos. The grey clouds and rain of yesterday had been replaced by a shade seeking hot sun. Locating a bus stop we checked out the timetable; their wasn't one. I suggested we wait but Roger sensibly flagged down a passing taxi and negotiated an all inclusive fare to Lindos, while Mark and I watched from the shaded shelter of the bus stop.

'Twenty euros.' Roger shouted at us.

'How far is it?' I shouted back.

'Thirty minutes.'

'Fair enough.'

So we dove in, Roger in the front and Mark and I in the back. Mark started to laugh.

'What?' I asked.

'You just said something funny, witty even.'

'I did?'

'Taxi; fair enough. Get it?'

'Yeah, well, I'm clever that way.' Sometimes I make a very good liar.

'Balls, you didn't have a clue you'd said it, did you?' But not this time.

'Not really, but it comes automatically to me. I can't help it.'

'What? Being full of shit?'

'Occasionally; if I need to be.'

The Driver was a woman who came across as sixty but could have been forty. She'd had a hard life from the look of things and even though it was hot she was wearing a heavy leather jacket over a t-shirt. Her English wasn't great either which came as a bit of a surprise, as almost every local encountered on this journey spoke it well. Maybe she was Albanian? I was told many of them worked and lived in Greece as cheap labour. What I did surmise correctly was that she was superstitiously religious, in a big way. Plastered all over the dash was iconography, statuettes, crosses and prayer beads. She kept one well worn loop of beads on her thigh and at regular intervals would fiddle with them. She also had a rather unnerving habit of crossing herself and saying a holy vow under her breath every time we passed a church or monastery, or any number of intimately known roadside shrines that appeared the length and line of the road to Lindos. New shrines, marked by fresh flowers indicating some recent roadside tragedy, got extra treatment with several crossings and repeated oaths.

How worried could you be? I wasn't expecting anything to happen but who knew? From the amount of shrines, the odds on meeting with a bad crash on Rhodes were pretty good, just ask Robert Plant. Least ways she seemed convinced that without constant devotion to God while driving, a fatal car crash would be forthcoming. She didn't drive fast enough to warrant a crash though. In fact she drove at a very steady ideal pace, allowing ample time to view the rocky arid landscape with some attention.

For the first few miles we passed by other towns and villages a distance from the road, they were older looking settlements unlike the crass modern nature of Falaraki. The only road side attractions were a Golf course, some pottery workshops, plenty of abandoned building projects and an odd assortment of holiday studios, retail businesses and residences.

In due course, the road inclined and we drove up towards a tight U bend that marked the location of a monastery of some standing. Our credulous driver was in a near frenzy of religious fervour, and I was sure Roger would need to take hold of the wheel, to help negotiate the turn as our Driver's hands shot up towards heaven. Fortunately, she didn't have enough faith in divine intervention and she held on.

Past the brow of the rise we drove along the outskirts of Arhangelos, Rhodes second biggest settlement,; before another steep rise brought us to a grandstand view of the approaching land for miles ahead. Below us lay a wide plain with dry river beds, to our left the sea and the curving coastline. Far out in front, the next great incline in the land. Through it all you could follow the wavy line of the road, shining in the sun. As we descended the driver pointed ahead.

'Lindos.'

I gazed hard to see where she meant. Along the coast at the far end of the plain, lay the built up outlines of a resort but I knew from the guide book that Lindos had an Acropolis and bays so that couldn't be right. Roger came to the rescue.

'There, see it?'

'No.'

'To the very left of the far end hill.'

I narrowed in on what looked like small dollops of soft icing upon a separated promontory. In the heat haze I could just make out an Acropolis and some buildings.

'I see it.' I said in a perky tone, being rather taken by this first distant encounter; followed by a strong instinctive sense of where we were headed and what we needed to do.

'We've got to stay the night.'

'Want to?' Asked Roger.

'Without a doubt. That beats Falafuckingraki any day.'

'I can't see it.' Said Mark leaning forward.

'Follow the coastline to the end then look to the left.'

'Where?'

'The far left.'

'Got it.'

'Nice huh?'

'The hotels look big.' He said and sat back, perplexing Roger and I again.

By the time we had descended to the plain, the idyll had gone from view and ten minutes later we were coming to the end of the coastal plain and driving through the resort area and town of Kalathos.

'There's your hotels.' I said to Mark.

'Right.' He said glancing out the window.

'Which one are we going to stay in?'

'We booked the penthouse apartment in this little
five star number.'

'You didn't? Really?'

'End of season internet bargain.'

'Brilliant. Can we afford it?'

'Yeah, Roger got a deal on it.'

'Fantastic; well done Rog'. Your useful for some things
at least.'

'Like to do my best Mark.'

'We're only bloody joking.'

'Ah, that's not fair. You bastards had me going there.'

Excitingly, we were closing in on our destination. As the road curved upwards we began to spot caves in the bare rock to our right.

'Hey, I could come here and live. One of those would do me.'

Said Mark half jokingly, perhaps aware that in time to come the bailiffs would finally come knocking.

As we rode the rough rocky rise we could look down upon the massive shore line hotels, the long stretching beach, the numerous umbrellas and beds that catered for the guests and the wide expanse of wonderously blue sea. It was quite a sight, especially as you could also see the sun bright coastline for many kilometers back and the mountainous terrain that followed.

The road began to level out and soon we encountered a lone building minus a roof; a pleasure garden nightclub called Amphitheatre. Curiously the Taxi Driver hadn't crossed herself in awhile and there was no appearance of our destination, yet it had to be hereabouts; but then suddenly she absolved herself, the road dropped and there ahead and below us in startling immediacy, stood a walled acropolis atop a singular vertical mass of rock. Presiding high over winding clusters of white sugar cube buildings, that pervaded the landward base and crept around towards the larger of two bays. Lindos; it struck me like a fabulous pearl in it's open shell.

'Wow.' I said.

'That's it then?' Said Mark.

'Yes.' I replied a shade or three dazed.

'Nice.'

'Interesting.' Said Roger.

It surpassed my perception that's for sure.

With the road levelling out again we lost sight of most of it; ahead left sides, lay a parking area filled with big coaches and people being marshaled by tour guides. The taxi Driver told us the obvious,

'Lindos! Busy, busy.'

She made a left turn onto a road that led to the village. A chain of people were walking the right side of it coming and going. We motored slowly down it while local taxis whizzed up in the other direction. Coming around a bend we rode the last few yards into an engaging square which was no bigger than half a football pitch and had a tree in it's center, the trunk painted white. A busy Policeman kept the traffic in order as groups of people milled around. We pulled over and as Roger paid our grateful Driver, I extracted dreamlike from the car and took in the special feel of the surroundings. Towering above was the Acropolis and to the open side of the square, a sweeping view of the near enclosed main bay, with it's two beaches; it's small wooden jetty moored by tour boats and an assortment of private boats anchored about. Without any doubt we had come to the right place, this was what I had come on holiday for. I thought of what Jimmy had said and knew he was wrong. I was going to stay and not just for one night either, I was already seduced by Lindos's specialness.

The three of us stood there taking it in, aware of our next move but unsure how to go about it. There appeared to be no fishermen around so the best thing was to ask a local taxi driver, which Roger did and he took us to a bench where some old ladies sat in state. In bouts of English and Greek they determined we wanted three single rooms for at least one night possibly two. They wanted forty a night so we asked for two rooms instead, as I didn't mind sharing with Mark again to help ease his budget. We waited for some guy to come and show us the rooms, and while we did we sat in a restaurant lining the square and had a beer. The guy showed up quicker than we thought so we told Mark to stay there and mind the bags, the beer and the bill; which worryingly for him he couldn't pay.

'You're coming back aren't you?'

'No, we thought we'd leave you here.'

'But I've got your bags.'

'You can have them.'

'What?'

'Their yours.'

'I don't want them.'

The guy led us from the square through the winding, irregular stoned paths of the village very much in the style of Parakia's old town but somehow different in character. After taking us this way and that, we came to an entranceway of a small courtyard which led to a large room with four beds in it and not much natural light. Something had got lost in the translation. I'd have been quite happy to stay there but Roger wanted his own room so we re-explained our requirements.

The guy got on his mobile and talked to someone in an apparent volatile fashion and when finished, calmly explained.

'I have just talked to my sister, she has some very nice rooms near the beach.'

'Two rooms?'

'Yes, she has.'

'How much?'

'Fifty but the place is very nice. Good location.

In high season she ask eighty euros.'

'What you think?' I asked Roger.

'If it's nice I'll take it.'

'Okay, can we go see?'

'Yes of course.'

So he called the sister again, explained in the same tone and manner as before and finished.

'Come, she will meet us in the square.'

So we walked back to the square realizing that the passage looked wholly different from before; this was more of a maze than we'd thought especially on first encounter.

'Good job we didn't get that place.' I said to Roger.

'Why?'

'Can you imagine Mark trying to find it in broad
daylight sober? Let alone drunk or in the dark?
Hell, I'd have a job finding it.' I laughed.

'We should get a St Bernard for him.'

'Now there's a thought.'

Getting back to the square the Guy's sister was there waiting, she was a small tough middle aged lady with a smattering of workable English. We grabbed Mark, our bags, and paid the outstanding bill and followed her direction. We had to pass by the crammed donkey station, virtually the first thing you encounter when entering the village from the square. During the day it did a roaring trade carrying tourists up and down to the Acropolis. Delighted customers could also purchase an unasked for photo of themselves upon the poor ass as a holiday memento. Talk about a license to print money.

The direction we took happened to coincide with the donkeys route and we had to avoid their passing back and forth along the way, and their natural bodily evacuations upon the ground. Of more concern though was keeping up with our guide, who use to such things ploughed on and we had to keep chasing after her. Thankfully at around one hundred meters the majority of beasts, tenders and riders ascended some steep steps to the Acropolis. How the donkeys managed to bear the burden of overly large persons on hot days at steep angles, gave cause for concern.

At least this route was easy to follow and remember. Mark should be alright on his own I thought. A few meters further and a small rotund

Greek church with an extended triangular yard, marked the last buildings to our left, and the downward path edged the sloped rock mass that formed the southern side of the bay. From hereon we could witness a panorama of bay, main beach and the ridge road we came in on. Just ahead the path forked and we took the rising track to our right, which passed by some properties fronted by high walls. Not far along we stopped next to one such abode, it had new wooden front doors and two windows either side, above head height.

The Landlady opened the left door and invited us in.

'Please.'

We encountered a small sunken patio, done in the Lindian custom of using black and white stone pebbles to create a ground picture with patterned borders, resembling a mat or rug. The black stones typically defining the pattern and the image. Studio rooms to our left and right, were in the process of being cleaned, we waited while the Landlady talked to the cleaners about something she wasn't happy about.

'Come.'

She led us up the set of white painted steps immediately in front to the main terrace level of the property. There facing the bay was a staple shaped porched building, embodying six studios designed to accommodate the likes of us. She showed Roger his room first on the left sided end, then took Mark and I to see our assignment on the right of the porched area. We walked in to a lovely big room with three beds, kitchenette, bathroom, TV, fridge, A/C, and keenly noted by me, a bug zapper above the entrance. She drew back the curtains and opened the big windows to fill the space with warm sunlight.

Outside under the porch was a big table, with a cushioned bench and some chairs all resting on a large pebble picture floor. Either side of the entrance way steps, were two taller levels forming small terraces. In reality the roofs of the studios on entering, they were fenced by waist high white pillared walls.

Aside from the cleaners we looked to be the only ones there. Was it possible? Did we have the whole place to ourselves? Sadly not, the Landlady explained that two couples were also staying in the studios on the right sided end.

'You like?' She asked, getting down to business.

I looked at Roger who shook his head in the affirmative, I gave the Landlady a big smile and said,

'Yes, we like.'

'Tonight only?'

'Yes and tomorrow maybe.'

Her face looked pleased by my answer. She wanted her one hundred euros up front so I explained we'd need to go to the bank and get it. She tried to convey in her best limited English where I could find her but due to a complete failure to communicate, she beckoned me to follow her out of the building to her place of residence, which was along the near side alley and at the back of the property.

I came back and found Roger on one of the small terraces surveying the all round view and joined him.

'Some place hey?' I said.

'Certainly is, struck gold here.'

'What were we doing in Falaraki? Look at this.'

'Where did Jimmy get that, "Nah, nuthin' there mate." from?'

'Never coming here probably, or maybe because he's a

top businessman.'

'You think?'

'Got to be. How can you not like this? It's bloody beautiful.

Look at that bay. And look at that incredible thing.'

I pointed back to the Acropolis above us.

Roger nodded.

'Impressive.'

'Where's Mark?' I asked.

I found Mark lying on the bed, television on, curtains drawn over the

opened windows.

'What are you doing?'

'What's it look like?'

'Have you seen what's out there?'

'I'll see it later.'

'Friends isn't on is it?'

'No.'

'Thank fuck for that, otherwise it might get in the way

of the special moments in a holiday.'

'Ah it's not that bad. I like it.' I wanted to hit him.

'Rog' and I are going to take a look around, you coming?'

'Yes, why not. '

'Good.' Realizing it was only because Friends wasn't on.

Our first priority was a cash machine, with the amount of people around I was worried they could run out of daily cash all too quickly. We found one near the donkey station and thankfully got our money without a hitch. I gave Mark his eagerly awaited daily ration and we headed into the unknown village eyes open.

Initially, the main thoroughfare was shaded by a canopy and lined with shop after shop, selling everything the average tourist felt a need to buy. Whether it be a fresh orange juice, a gyros, a t-shirt or a tacky souvenir, something along the lines of a cuddly toy donkey say. Needless to say we weren't about to let the side down. Mark purchased a Gyros and T-shirt, I got a juice and Roger got a toy donkey. No, not really; he got a flash lighter with a laser light built in.

Around the corner lay the main Greek orthodox church, small in scale but large in proportion and decoratively bewitching inside. It's customs and traditions more closely tied to the true eastern origins of the Christian faith. Hardly more so than in Lindos, as it is where my namesake Paul the Apostle landed two millennia ago, to bring Christianity to western Europe. How's that for a close link? Talking of which, facing the church was a travel bureau and another cash machine. We popped in to get ferry times for Kos but were told we would have to go to Rhodes Town for assistance or use the internet. It didn't matter for the moment, I was fairly confident we'd all want to stay here longer anyway.

Taking a right onto the main spine through the village, we began to encounter restaurants, our first bars, more quick food outlets and small grocery markets. It was all so absorbing I didn't feel bored for a moment. We came to a spot that could be loosely described as a small square, five paths wheeled from it and it's focus was a tree encircled by a low white painted wall. As in the main square the trunk was also painted white; presumably to stop branches developing lower than head height? Filled with leaves, it's branches began high up on the thick trunk and splayed far and wide to the surrounding buildings, to create a natural cool cover.

It stood in front of a bar called the 404 and between the tree and the entrance were two small tables, chairs, and stone benches that formed part of the singular building.

Again the sirens were calling and it seemed the most natural thing in the world to visit the bar and sit at a table by the tree, and watch the neighbourhood go by. Entering, we walked in to a space that was mostly floor, six stools and a bar. Another entrance door faced the right side of the building and a spiral staircase in the right hand corner nearest us, led to toilets and a store room below. A very nice blonde haired English girl called Zoe served us, we were the only customers.

'Where hav' yer' all come from?' She asked.

'Falaraki.' I answered.

'Falaraki? What were yer' doin' there?'

'We've been asking ourselves the same bloody question.'

'Are yer' stayin' long?'

'Don't know yet, see how it goes.'

'What are yer' just travellin' around like?'

'Yes.'

'Mark you can explain this time.' I said.

'Explain? Me?' He looked worried by the suggestion.

'Where we came from.'

'From London.'

'No, how we got here to Rhodes, where we've been.'

'All I know is we caught a plane and some ferries;

but I couldn't tell you the names of places.'

So not for the first or last time I explained (hereafter known as the "explanation" to save overly repeated description.) our journey, at the end of which Zoe asked.

'When do yer' go back to the UK?'

'Not for another ten days yet.'

'Have you been to Kos?' Asked Roger.

'No, I've only ever been here.'

'We're thinking of going there after this.'

'I don't know what it's like, I couldn't tell yer'.

Taking our beers outside we sat and people watched, just taking in the calm relaxing air. Finishing the round we thanked Zoe and headed back to the studio determined to make the beach, plus I had to gratify the Landlady, if you see what I mean.

In the event, the three of us took a diverted stroll down to the main beach to check it out instead; and out of nowhere thick cloud came rolling in and thunder erupted. After admiring what it had to offer, we negotiated the slope of the rocky base up to the donkey path and onwards to our studio. I went to the Landlady's place, knocked on the door she had shown me and waited until she opened the door to a kitchen essentially, but serving as a living area too. A Man was there, her husband I assumed, I don't know for we never met. He was permanently settled in a comfy chair whenever I saw him.

'Everything good?' She asked, vaguely concerned.

'Very good. I have the money.'

I handed her the lolly and her face lit up like a firework display.

'Tomorrow?' She inquired.

'Yes, I'm sure.' I confidently said without consulting the others.

'Good, good.' Stated like she only understood the yes part. She ushered me out the door as if glad she'd been right about us and we waved goodbye. As I walked down the alley to the studio a few spots of rain fell and I suddenly felt the urge to walk back down the slope and go for a swim. So I did, leaving the two reluctants to either sleep, watch TV or read.

By the time I'd swam half a mile, climbed the base wall and run up the path; as if like the famous ad to secretly deliver the box of Milk Tray chocolates. The steadying rain turned into an instant heavy downpour and I sprinted for the shelter of the studio. Absurdly, I had just voluntarily got soaking wet and here I was avoiding getting wet. To my great surprise the boys were sitting at the table under the porch (not a proper porch more a overhang of the building above; also containing studios on another terraced level of this surprisingly big complex which our Landlady either owned or ran for somebody.) chatting, smoking and drinking a cuppa' of all things.

'Want a tea?' Asked Mark.

'Yeah.' I replied, looking inquisitive.

'I found some PG tips in the cupboard.'

'That was handy.'

'Yes, this place gets better and better.'

'Don't it just, can't beat a cup of char.'

I changed, hung up my cosie and towel and joined the wise mens club. We watched the rain lash down then ease off.

'I think we should stay another night at least;

what say you both?' I asked.

'I just want to stay in one place anyway.' Said Mark

'Yeah I'll go with that.' Said a lulled Roger.

At that, the entrance door opened and two couples entered; back from the deserting beach by the soaked look of things. We introduced ourselves. They were very pleasant, German and Hungarian respectively and in their sixties. They didn't stay for tea and retired to their rooms. The rain was at an end by now and the cloud covering was brightening.

'What shall we do?' I asked.

'What's the time?'

'Four.'

'Got any good suggestions?'

One of the things I had developed a great liking for on this trip was Greek salad. Just on it's own it could make for a nice healthy filling meal especially with bread. Considering we had fully equipped kitchenettes I made an offer they couldn't refuse.

'Fancy a big Greek salad with fresh bread If I make it? I proffered.

"Yeahh." They spoke as one in a famished tone.

'What just salad?' Asked Mark.

'Don't worry, it will be filling enough.'

'Salad?'

'Where you going to get the ingredients?' Asked Roger thoughtfully.

'I thought I'd get them at one of those markets by the bar
we were at. What was it called?'

'The 404.'

'I need detergent also, to wash me smalls. How about you?'

We'd now been on holiday for six days and our one week anniversary
was looming. I'd been washing my underwear while taking a shower and
hanging them out to dry in the sun, easy going really. My worn T-shirts
needed a soak wash though. As noted, Roger wasn't particularly fussy
regarding such matters. His two polo shirts were seeing him through.
Though he had broken his own rules and splashed out on another designer
shirt at Heathrow, but had yet to wear it. Weirdly enough, his belief about
only needing two tops while on the move was bearing true. The only
people who would notice a lack of sartorial selection was Mark and I.
Mind you the dark blue horizontal number was getting overly familiar.

'You doing some washing then?'

'Yeah my own.'

'Thought you were offering.'

'Won't take you long to do two shirts now will it?'

'Three.' He reminded me.

'And when are we to witness the new number?'

'Tonight if you're lucky.'

'I don't believe it, you'll be wearing that I guarantee
you. You love it too much.'

'I love it!.' He laughed, knowing I could be right.

'Are we doing anything now?' Asked Mark.

'Yes, I'm going to the market to get some stuff.'

'Are you going to get some beers?'

'Beers? I could. What sort?'

'Any.'

'Okay.'

'And some cigarettes. And chocolate. Err, and milk.'

'Milk?'

'For the tea.'

'Seriously?'

'Of course; I like tea, don't you?'

'Fuck it you might as well come with me.'

'Let's all go.' Said Roger. So we did.

There were two markets side by side, I chose the one on the right and we piddled about in there until we had filled about four bags full of stuff other than what we had gone down for. Unconciously we were settling in for a stay. We paid the nice lady owner and decided that as we were here now we may as well go for another drink at the 404, besides because of the rain there were more people milling around, especially some fine looking girls back early from the spoiled beach. The bar was way busier this time, though we still managed to grab a wet table outside. Zoe was there but busy serving, spotting me she asked if I wanted three beers, I said yes, and she said she'd bring them out to us when she got a chance. As I sat back down, a tall heavy set guy in his thirties with shoulder length straight blonde hair, T-shirt and jeans, came striding purposely towards the bar carrying a foam container of food. Minutes later he came out with our beers and placed them on the table.

'Three beers gentlemen.'

'Oh thanks.' I said, not sure who he was.

A few minutes passed and a woman in her thirties with two energetic young girls came to the bar and took the remaining table, other side of the door. Our deliverer of the beers came out with some drinks and sat down with them. Unrestricted, the playing girls took a shine to Mark, who feigned engaging interest in their toys they had with them. Showing them to him, he began to pretend that he didn't understand how they worked or what they did, just like a clown. It got them laughing and excited.

'Girls, leave the poor man alone. Sorry.' Said the Mum.

'Oh no it's fine I'm used to this, my sister's got three girls.' Said Mark.

'Yeah don't worry we don't mind.' I added.

So the girls, looking for diversion and fun decided we would be it. They grew more bold and began to involve Roger and I into their little world, as Mark continued to make them laugh and shriek with his antics, drawing out all his thespian talents as a kids entertainer. Meanwhile the Mother continually apologized to us and the man kept a careful eye on things.

'Come on girls let's go and get a toy.' Said the man.

With that they dashed away from us shouting,

'Yes please Uncle Rob, yes please!'

'I'm so sorry, their not normally like this.

Their bored I'm afraid, they've been in the house all day.'

'Well we're enjoying their company.' I assured.

'I hope so, because I know they can be a pain.'

'No, it's fine, believe me.' I said honestly.

Fact was we were enjoying the attentive girls' energy and innocence. In a way they were bringing out our fatherly instincts. Mark in particular was reveling being an entertainer; the girls were bringing the best out in him and it made you realize what a great dad he could be, minus the drink problem.

'How old are they?' Asked Roger.

'Jane's seven and Claire's five. They can be a real handful. Especially as their Dad's not here.'

'Where's he?'

'Australia; we live there, emigrated six years ago.'

'Whereabouts?'

'Near Brisbane.'

'Like it?'

'Love it. We've got a Honda dealership. It's hard work but we wouldn't go back to England now.'

'So you're here on holiday?' I asked.

'Yeah, we went to the UK first to see family and we've been here a week to see Rob. Back to the UK tomorrow and then Brisbane on Sunday.'

'Just you and the two girls?' Cried Mark.

'Yeah, but they've been great up 'till today.'

'So how come you're husband didn't come?' I pried.

'Couldn't leave the dealership, we've only had it two years and it's just us running it.'

'Well good luck.'

'Thanks. How long have you been here?'

It was Roger's turn to give the "Explanation" so he did.

'So you've never been to Lindos before?'

'No, we didn't know much about it. It's a complete surprise,
had no idea it was like this.'

'Do you know Rob?' She asked.

"No." We said collectively.

'Who is he?' I asked.

'Rob's my brother, this is his bar.'

'I wondered.'

'You should tell him what that bloke said about Lindos,
he'll like that.'

The two girls suddenly came running back excitedly shouting.

'Mummy, mummy, look what we got!'

Rob followed behind them smiling at their joy. They both had water
bubble kits. Rob prepped one of them for the elder girl, while Mark
offered to do the same for the younger.

'Rob, they've just come from Falaraki, you should hear
what somebody said about Lindos there.'

'Oh yeah? What they say?'

So I told him what Jimmy had said.

'Coming from a shit hole it's a bit hard to believe.

Tell you what, they must be hurting down there
if their saying that.'

'I think they are, it was dead last night.'

'Falaraki, fuck. Anybody wanting to go there are wankers.

Just don't come here I say.'

We nodded agreement, knowing by default we were technically in the "Wanker" category. Zoe came out.

'Rob I've got to go.'

'Yeah, alright Zoe.' Said Rob.

'I've got to work the bar. Do you lads want another round?'

'Yes.'

'Right.'

We stayed for two more beers, as the girls and us had fun blowing bubbles. Mark blowing the biggest of the lot, often to the utmost breaking point, causing untold merriment for the girls, us, and onlookers from Yanni's, the bar next door. And as young persons do after too much fun, the girls got tired and irritable, and became physical and obstructive. Mind you I could say the same thing about adults.

Before they got in any more trouble with a sorely tested mum trying to maintain authority, we said our farewells and went back to the studio where I slaved over a cold counter and put together a decent Greek salad for us to eat; and in striving for authenticity, wine served in a coloured metal jug. We dined up on the right side terrace using the plastic chairs and table provided for our comfort, and gazed at the prospect around us with it's saturated hues and tones created by the setting sun. It was another of those perfect moments, when there is no hurry, no concerns, just a simple contentment with where you are and what you're doing.

'I'm glad we went to Falaraki.' I said. 'If only just to compare and also to say you had.'

Roger and Mark each gave a nod of agreement.

'We did have some fun.'

'I'm so glad we came here though.'

'Yeah, much better.'

'Another thing.'

'What?'

'I haven't encountered one mosquito yet.'

Done, we cleared our grubbings and resolved to siesta before the night to come. We'd savoured the welcoming delights of Lindos by day, now we had to uncover what went on at night. One thing was for sure, this was no day trippers place only, given the bars we had seen. But what would come out of the woodwork?

Lindos by First Night...

About nine thirty we left the studio to head into town. The three of us had scrubbed up and by the strong smell of things, had shaved as well. Roger was wearing his new shirt for goodness sake. Inadvertently we did a bit of exploring, diverting to our left to see where a side route took us. It led us to a continuation of the bazaar which wound this way and that. Shop after shop offering, among many things, hand stitched Greek linen, jewelry, fine pottery, ornaments and the inevitable trinkets. One shop caught our attention, it sold small models of ecstatic faced pigs copulating in various positions and scenarios. It was the funniest thing and I wanted to buy one, but when I saw the price I stopped laughing and we moved on.

Soon our curiosity found us wandering back paths devoid of commercial hubbub, taking in the architecture, particularly of the lovely "Captains Houses." Which are famous in this part of the world and date back to the sixteenth century. Their notable feature is a blocked upper level room that allowed for, according to the story, the reconnaissance of the sea or harbour by the salty occupant. Some we encountered, sat partly upon a tall arch which spanned the path.

Unsurprisingly, they are highly sought after and not cheap to buy, even in bad condition. We rambled on with only a vague idea of our position, much to Mark's growing consternation.

'Do you two know where you're going?'

'No, of course not.' I answered.

'Well how are we going to find a bar?'

'Easy, just wind our way along 'till we come out somewhere.'

'How are we going to do that?'

'Follow me.' I said with utmost confidence.

Sure enough, we made a right here, a left there, another left, followed by a right and there we were, down a blind alley.

'Fuck McCloskey you've got us lost!' Said Mark.

'You can't get lost in a place like this, it's too small

for God's sake. Side tracked yes, but never lost.

Eventually you'll find where you need to be.'

'Oh yeah?' Said Mark in annoyance.

'I think we need to go back that direction.' Said Roger helpfully.

'I agree.'

We back tracked and took a right instead of a left and there it was, up ahead the main street busy with people.

'Thank fuck.' Said Mark.

'See I told you. Piece of piss really.'

'We should have stuck to the route we knew.'

'What's the point of that?'

'So we know were to go.'

'But now we know another way, don't you see?'

Mark was singularly unconvinced as we reached the street and took our bearings.

The people walking along were not the donkey riding tourists of earlier in the day. Most appeared tanned and dressed up for the evening. Generally, men in short sleeve shirts, women in sleeveless dresses. A large smattering British to boot. There was no sense of hurry, everybody was ambling along, as restaurant and bar touts tried to entice people inside; the "Door whores" as Roger had so eloquently put it. Electric light from the businesses bathed the narrow street in brightness and a healthy glow radiated from people and things.

We called in the first two bars we encountered and had a beer. What looked like groups of single women were present, there was nothing special about the bars though, other than they played loud dance music and we quickly moved to the 404 which was busy outside and in. It too was playing loud music, mostly Brit rock from the nineties and current alternative. It was difficult to hear yourself speak let alone listen. I waited at the bar until Rob spotted me.

'Mythos? Three?' He shouted.

'Yes. Busy now hey?'

'What?'

'I said it's busy.'

'Usually is.' He replied, a tad indignant.

I looked around noticing that the crowd was a broad range of ages. I got the beers and the three of us sat out on the wall surrounding the tree. It didn't take long for lot's of eye candy to be walking by, as a steady stream of folk strolled by in either direction.

'Check this out.' One of us would say.

'Cor she's lovely.' One or both of us would reply.

God knows what they thought of us. Lechers probably. I was hoping we looked handsome, suave and desirable. Who was I kidding? I'd learnt enough in life to know that I was no matinee idol to the opposite sex, physically I took myself to be plain looking, brutish even. But there was no doubt when hopelessly confident with myself, I could be attractive to women. Being on this trip, being in Lindos, we did feel pretty good about ourselves, though Roger had the best chance I always felt.

Beer finished, we followed the stream and ended up in Socrates bar, Lindian House and Sixties bar. Having a beer in each, generally not getting into much conversation with anyone. Finally we walked into the last bar on the street, Luna bar it was called. An ante-room led into a large open air courtyard with a staircase up to a patio. In front, through two open arches lay a long u shaped bar, a dance floor and a DJ booth from which a Guns n Roses song was playing, barely anybody was in the place.

'What yer' think?' Asked Roger dubiously.

'Fuck it let's stay and have a quick beer.' I said, as it was my type of music.

We approached the bar and the bartender, a very muscular bald headed Greek guy.

'I haven't seen you before.' He said.

'No, we just got here today.'

'First time Lindos?'

'Yes.'

'What you think?'

'It's amazing.'

He smiled and set out five shot glasses on the bar in front of us. "Five? The guy can't count." I thought. He looked over at the DJ booth where a very attractive girl was talking to the DJ, and gave a piercing whistle. She turned around smiling and came over and into the bar serving area, as the barman poured some evil black looking substance into the glasses. She bounced up to the counter and smiling, said,

'Hi, I'm Ulla.'

Whether it was her lovely face, her perfect blonde hair, or her well tanned not-an-ounce-of-fat body showcased in a tight white vest, or her low slung shorts over lovely legs and a bum to match I couldn't tell you, all I know was the three of us were immediately smitten. We shook hands with her, introducing ourselves. The bartender spread the shots out and picked his up.

'Together now.'

Not wishing to upset him we quickly picked up our shots.

'Yamas!' He shouted.

'Yamas!' We shouted back.

And we promptly knocked the shots back, apart from Mark who managed to send some of his down the wrong way and suffered the consequences. Hacking and coughing, spluttering and choking; it sounded exactly like it did every morning when he was first up and about, except this time the alcohol was having an adverse effect.

'Don't worry, he does this all the time.' I said to the captivating Ulla.

'He does? Why?' She asked innocently.

'Because he wants attention.'

'Really?'

'No, I'm kidding.'

'Perhaps he is in trouble?'

She may have had a point, clearly he wasn't getting air very well, choking quite badly.

'Mark, you okay?'

He hacked and hacked; bending over double, patting his chest hard before putting his hand up to sort of indicate he was okay.

'Where's the toilet?' He asked in an unusual voice, his glasses misted up and tears streaming down his face.

'Where you come in, to the left.'

'Don't be long, it's your round soon.' Said Roger.

'Leave the money here just in case .' I added.

I think Ulla was beginning to understand our humour.

'Are you always like this to him?'

'No, only when he deserves it.'

'And he always deserves it.' Ended Roger.

'Where are you from?'

'From London, how about you?'

'From Germany, from Frankfurt.'

'Do you work here?' I asked.

'Yes.'

'And is this your boyfriend? I asked pointing to our barman.

'No, that is Perri. My boyfriend is there.'

She pointed to the DJ who waved back, destroying two hearts in the process.

'You arrived today?'

'Yes from Falaraki.' Said Roger.

'From Falaraki?' She said shocked.

It was time for the "Explanation" once again, so even though it was my turn to deliver it, Roger and I shared the tale, enraptured by this beautiful girl. So wrapped up by the telling were we, we failed to notice that Mark had not returned.

'Where is your friend?' Ulla asked suddenly.

Yeah, where was he? I rushed to the toilet expecting a prone, blue faced, leg twitching, oxygenless former alcoholic. The last thing I reckoned on was that nobody would be there. He had disappeared. I went back to the bar.

'Well?' Asked Roger.

'He's not there. Don't know where he is.'

'Are you sure?' Asked Ulla with concern.

'Yes, he's gone.'

'Did you check the women?'

'No, but I'd like to.' I joked. 'Yes, I did.'

'Perhaps he went outside.'

'He'll be back wherever he is.'

Sure enough, two minutes later Mark walked back in brandishing a packet of cigarettes.

'Are you okay?' Asked Ulla.

'Fine, why?' Acting as if the choking episode had never happened.

'There was slight concern you might have
asphyxiated in the toilet.'

'Oh that. No.'

'So where'd you go?'

'Had to buy some cigarettes.'

'I thought you got a whole carton at the market today?'

'I did.'

'What and you forgot to bring some out tonight?'

'Sort of.'

'Sort of?'

'Well, yes.'

'Plonker.'

At that moment, a group of five noisy English women in their late thirties walked in. They clearly knew Perri and the DJ well as they hugged and kissed them. Meanwhile Mark could not get the wrapping off the soft pack of cigarettes he'd bought.

'For Chris'sake give them here.'

My teenage years came rolling back as I expertly removed the top wrap, carefully tore and peeled the foil back, and tapped the pack to give a staggered formation of easy to take fags.

'How'd you do that?'

'An errant youth matey.'

He took a fag, and patted himself down in search of an elusive lighter. So far the lost lighter count on this trip was: Me, nought. Roger, nought. Mark, one hundred and twenty four (counting the one just lost). I embellish, but you get the idea.

'Anybody got a lighter?'

'Yes.' Said Roger.

'Can I borrow it?'

'No.'

'What do you mean no?'

'Get a deposit off him first.' I added.

'A what?' Laughed Mark.

'Please Roger lend me your lighter, I need a smoke.'

'I have a lighter, here.' Said Ulla to the rescue.

'Thank you Ulla.'

'Make sure you get it back, he has a habit of pocketing

other people's lighters.'

'Shut up McCloskey.'

He took the lighter but the lighter would not work, even after ten
attempts.

'It is strange, it has worked every time before now.'

Remarked a quizzical Ulla.

'Here, try mine.' Said Roger relenting.

Mark took the lighter and pushed the button on the side, a thin bright
blue line of light shone. Mark put his cigarette to it in an effort to fire up.
Not being a flame, he had a little difficulty.

'Why won't it light?' He said.

The three of us saw the problem immediately and started laughing.

'Because you've got the wrong end you nut.' I said in fits.

'What do you mean?' He couldn't understand.

'Try the other end.' Said Roger.

'The other end?' Said Mark.

He looked at the other end, noticing the flipping wheel for the flint
and the release valve and jet.

'Hey?'

He checked out what he had been trying before.

'So what's this?'

'It's like a laser light. It's just for fun.'

'What and I've been trying to use it to light my Cigarette?'

'Yes, you fucking idiot.' I said splitting my sides.

He bent forward and beat his hands down on the bar top in hysterics.

'You guys are crazy.' Said Ulla.

Unabashed, Mark eventually lit the fag and then like a child couldn't get enough of checking out the blue light. Shining it on his clothes, up his nose, along his arms, all over the ceiling, the far wall, and cheekily on the back of Perri's head.

'Hey you'll use it up, get your own.' Said Roger grabbing it back.

'I will, where'd you get it from? I want one.'

'From the shop.'

'What and you didn't tell me?'

Our attention was diverted by the sound of a large crashing sound. Above the center of the bar was a loose hanging brass plate, Perri had given it a good whack with a soft ended drumstick. It was shaking and swinging back and forth.

'What was that?' I asked Ulla.

'When we feel like it, we hit that. But if you buy shots
you may also.'

The three of us looked at it like why would you do that? But then one of the women was allowed behind the bar and she had a go, her eye catching stance shouting sex appeal. Hitting the thing first time, her delighted friends went wild and the boys were struck themselves.

'We should go talk to them. You game?' Said Roger.

'Nah, I'm happy here.'

I was, a very beautiful woman was right in front of me and I was on speaking terms.

'They look alright.'

'You wont get anywhere.' I proposed.

'How do you know that?'

'I can tell.'

I didn't really, although all my instincts told me they were prick teasers or at the least hard work. Whatever, I didn't like them for some reason; they reminded me of bad nights in English nightclubs when younger.

'C'mon Mark let's talk to them.'

So Roger and Mark went to chat them up, hoping to get somewhere without being made to feel like they were wallies.

'You are not going with them?' Asked Ulla, surprised.

'No, I don't like girls like that.'

'Why?'

'They strike me as being not very nice.'

'I think you could be right. I have met them before.'

Mark and Roger were chatting up a storm however and Mark waved for me to come over and join them. I ignored him until one of the women actually came to me and said.

'Why don't you come over?'

'I'm quite happy here.'

She grabbed my arm and pulled on it.

'Come on, we won't bite.' I begged to differ.

So I reluctantly joined the party, though the boys could sense my discomfort as I tried to muster the required enthusiasm and failed to do so.

'C'mon mate, we can have some fun here.'

Said Mark of all people, worried that I might let the side down and hence his and Roger's chances of pulling. Not that I could see any sign of that happening for all of Mark's optimism. Mind you I've got too agree, I wasn't helping the cause much and I should have been. Getting moody at a moment like this was against the esprit de corps of the trip, at least it wasn't on a par with Mark's first night shenanigans. I tried to get into the spirit of things, but something about this group of women just rubbed me the wrong way and meeting them didn't change that sense. Talk about being seventeen again.

So I made a show of it in the hope that the boys would succeed and I could go back to talking to Ulla. The compromise was fleeting anyhow, done with their visit they upped and left leaving us with a "hope to see yer' later" routine that left the boys a bit bemused.

'I thought I was doing alright there.' Said Mark. And truth be told he was, sounding and acting like his old gregarious self after years of having gone missing. Roger meanwhile took it all in his stride. "More fish in the sea." was his attitude. In fact chatting to the women had got his juices going and he ordered a round of shots including one for the DJ Nikos.

Meanwhile the group of women whom I didn't like were likely walking away cackling.

"Useless weren't they? Especially that miserable bastard
who didn't want to know us."

"One of 'em was alright."

"Which one?"

"The rich one."

"A bit cocky mind."

"I wouldn't have touched the other two with a barge pole."

"The tall, baldy one he was funny."

"Would you have though?"

"Only if I was pissed out of me head."

"He was a plonker though."

"Which one?"

"Old misery guts."

"Definite plonker." And they all chortled.

The six of us gathered around the bar and took our shot glasses, shouted "Yamas!" and knocked back the elixir. I felt a sudden retch but managed to hold off being sick, just. Perri smacked the gong again and handed the drumstick to Roger.

'Come on, you must try.'

Roger relished the chance and like an excited audience member chosen to come on stage, clambered over the bar and tried his luck. It looked easier than it was. With his first effort he missed wildly causing untold merriment, especially with Mark and I. But his second effort caught it smack in the middle and he raised his arms in triumph, his face a broad smile. We all applauded, adding more weight to Roger's burgeoning ego. Mark desperately wanted a go but the rule was you had to buy a round of shots, which by now he couldn't afford to do. Having almost thrown up I wasn't about to offer one anytime soon.

'Where are you going from here?' Asked the delightful Ulla.

'Why, do you want to come with us?' I asked.

'No, I am too tired. I must go home.' Shame.

'Where's a good place to go?' Asked Roger.

'You can go to Arches or Qupi's.'

'Are they bars?'

'No, they are clubs.'

'Fancy that?' Roger asked Mark and I.

'Absolutely.' I answered.

We had another beer, by which time my watch was reading close to two am. It was time to move. We said goodbye to Perri with firm handshakes, waved to Nikos the DJ with a crumpled hand, and caught Ulla in the courtyard returning from the toilet.

'You are leaving?'

'Yes, to the clubs.'

'Does that balcony go anywhere?' Asked Mark.

'No, there are some chairs and tables only. Why?'

'Just wondered.'

'Come, I will show you something.'

She led us to the staircase and took away the chain that blocked passage and we followed her up to the balcony level.

'In my opinion it has the best view of the Acropolis.'

She wasn't kidding, I don't know how, but in our evening's walkabout we had managed to miss the fact that the too-big-to-ignore Acropolis was fantastically lit up at night to create a stirring spectacle. Well we couldn't miss it now, there in front of us above the sprawled rooftops was an incredible sight of nature and Man's efforts to crown it.

'Beautiful yes?'

"Awesome." We said opened mouthed. Not in some vacuous American surfer speak way but in the true sense of the meaning. It was a hell of day for revelations.

Following the directions given us by Ulla we managed to find Arches nightclub, but if it hadn't have been for a trail of people headed in that direction we could have easily walked by it, as there was no discernible sound indicating it's whereabouts. The residents of Lindos mandate that noise levels are kept to a minimum after midnight; which for bars means lowering the music and closing all doors and windows. But for night clubs they are required to be sound proofed and vacuum entranced. By that I mean they operate a sealed two door system for letting clubbers in and out. Entering a sound proofed ante-chamber one door stays open and one door stays closed; that way the residents of Lindos get a good night's sleep or try too at least, because they can still suffer the comings and goings of drunken happy souls wandering the village in loud revelry virtually all night long or should that be morning?

As with the night club in Falaraki there was no entrance charge and Arches was impressive and popular. The reason for it's name was obvious as soon as you entered. From the center of the floor space, a large arch rose up to bolster the walls and high ceiling of the structure. Along with the grey stone walls, there was an old cathedral look about the place but the mood was modern, slick and cool; helped by a sophisticated lighting system that traced, spiraled, and spattered patterns of bright coloured light in near constant motion around the place. It acted in unison with a contemporary dance sound that was way over my head but excited the large crowd present and throbbed your insides. It had one large bar against the far wall and a DJ booth centered at the far end. In many ways it was like the first day at a new school and you weren't sure what it was all about, yet it was familiar.

The crowd was half Greek with the other half mostly British but with a smattering of other nationals like Italian, Swedish, and Dutch. Everybody looked noticeably happy and there were lots of eye catching women about. It was difficult to converse because of the continuous high volume music and like so many clubs on first encounter, it's design merely served to dislocate you from it's trappings; even though it appeared to be doing the opposite. It lacked a warmth, a spontaneity. Maybe I was just to old for the place but I didn't think so. We had one beer and left, using sign language to convey meaning and intent.

I don't know quite how we managed it, but when we stepped out of the entrance chamber we bumped into the group of women I didn't particularly like, and were persuaded all too easily to go with them up to Qupi's, the other nightclub Ulla had mentioned. Being more inebriated than I was earlier, they didn't appear quite so charmless as before. We made a left out of Arches courtyard taking the path upwards, climbing some steps which left Mark looking like he couldn't quite make Everest this time around. Roger and I grabbed an arm each and helped carry him up the last obstacle and onto the path that ran to Qupi's.

Not far along, we turned into a doorway and climbed more steps finding ourselves on an open air courtyard with a full face on view of the majestic Acropolis again. There was an area to our right with a stone bench running around it complete with coloured cushions, it was a spot to chill out on. The place had an older dreamy acid house feel about it.

   We entered via the sound proof doors into a small homely bar area, with a cute little thing working the bar, she gave us a melt-your-heart smile. Around the corner in a basic L shaped pattern, a long room served as dance floor and main bar. It wasn't as busy as Arches and it lacked the expensive light system of it's sophisticated competitor, but it did have a more inviting feel with it's candles, patterned lanterns and warm colours. Within the small entrance bar area at least you could talk in comfort, plus the courtyard was a hell of a place to sit outside and whisper sweet nothings into a girl's ear or take time out. Not that there was much of that going on. So we hung with the women awhile, drank rapidly and danced on the main bar with them; and took shots of red vodka poured from the bottle by some mad American guy called Tommi, who was jumping around like an electrocuted chimp. As expected the (still) unflattering women left us high and dry again and sometime around four thirty am, spent, we left. Mark had left at around three am, but after wandering around lost returned uttering, 'How do I get back?'.

   We called in at the twenty four hour gyros shop on the corner near to the donkey station and loaded up on protein and fat. It was late September and the early morning temperature was a wonderful seventy degrees fahrenheit. Inside the gyros shop with all the burning heat, it was about a thousand degrees, if you worked in there all summer stepping outside into seventy probably felt like winter time. We ate and meandered the route home with Mark having to stop and rest every few feet.

'I couldn't take one more step.'

'Come on we're almost there.'

'You guys go on I'm staying here. Are you sure we're going
the right way? I don't remember any of this.'

'I know what you need.' Said Roger.

'Oh and what's that Roger?'

'You need a donkey to get home.'

Mark laughed like mad at the concept, picturing himself hanging on to the donkey's neck as it made it's way to the studio, coming to a halt outside the entrance and him sliding off onto the ground. Well, that's what I was picturing but no doubt Mark was too. The laughter revived Mark and we all made it safely back to our beds, our lovely welcoming beds and the sleep that entailed. What a memorable day it had been.

Fearless and Fright...

The cleaner tried to wake us at ten and got short thrift in the nicest possible way. If Mark had been making weird noises in his sleep I wouldn't have known, soon as I'd hit the pillow it had sent me to temporary oblivion. Around eleven thirty am I desperately needed to piss, my bladder had been informing me of the fact since the cleaner called. The non-existent phone rang.

"Hello?"

"This is your bladder calling. You are to proceed to the nearest evacuation area and excrete the beyond the limit contents as soon as possible, otherwise I shall not be responsible for the consequences. Understood?"

"Yes, I'll do it in half an hour."

"Remember what I said."

The bladder must have called five times. Eventually I heeded it's advice and blearily stumbled to the bathroom to alleviate the pressure of over imbibed, well filtered alcohol; and to look into the mirror with one eye and wonder why my face sagged. With great satisfaction I relieved myself, I don't know what the alternative Guinness Book of World Records would state as the longest sustained urination, but I must have come close to setting a new world time that morning.

Splashing some water onto my face I was a new man, it was an old trick handed down through the ages from father to son. Sure I was worse for wear and tear, my mouth felt as dry as a rusted exhaust pipe, my head was fixed in a pool of wobbly jelly, and my eyes were weighed down with lead weights off a long case clock. Other than that, I felt perfectly chipper. Surprising what a bit of cold water can do to revive your being.

I determined to go to the cash machine, get myself some blessed ultra-reviving coffee and pay the landlady for the day. I didn't bother with a shirt, I just slipped on some shorts and flip flops, put on the obligatory sun glasses and set off; I must have looked a right bloody sight but I didn't give a damn. As I made my merry way in the gorgeous warmth of the sun, I discovered the answer to a question I had been considering since witnessing the toilet habits of the donkeys that worked the tourist trade. How was it the path to the square was not knee deep in droppings and running with fluid? Answer: they have a little man that cleans up after them with a bucket, spade and broom. And it is said he is well paid for it too. Problem solved my blissful morning was only disrupted by the hordes of day trippers filling the main streets. I had to navigate through a thick slow moving stream of headless souls with one thing in common, stopping me from getting where I wanted to be at my normal pace. Fortunately in my state I was too laid back to care. At snail's pace I eased through the bazaar collecting my money, gathering my fresh coffee and orange juice, and sat by the tree in the main square and watched the hustle and bustle from my care free vantage point.

Mouth less dry, head less wobbly, eyes less weighed down, I sauntered back to the studio and caught Roger leaning over the terrace looking out,

'Morning squire. How's the head?' I asked.

'Really good.'

'I'm surprised.'

'Where have you been?'

'Bank; it's busy in town.'

'Beach looks busy too.'

'Ready to go down?'

'In about half an hour.'

'Any sign of his lordship?'

'Not yet.'

Mark was still sound asleep when I entered the room, and out of the goodness of my heart I made him a cup of tea to wake him up with. I tapped the mug with a teaspoon next to his ear.

'Wake up. Oh, Mark, rise and shine. Time for the beachy weechy.'

He opened one eye slowly, chewed his mouth around and scratched himself. Darwin was right.

'God, you fucking snore.' He said coming to his senses.

'Do I? I wouldn't know.'

'Is that for me?'

'Yes.'

'Two sugars?'

'Yes, and fresh milk squeezed from a goat.'

'Goat's milk?'

'Yeah, the landlady keeps one out the back there.'

'Cobblers.'

'I'm not joking, I just went to pay her the rent and she gave me the milk from her goat.'

'I'm not drinking tea with goat's milk in it.'

'Why not?'

'It's not fucking right.'

'Of course it is, we're in Greece ain't we?'

'So?'

'Most of the milk comes from goats.'

'You're full of shit McCloskey.'

'Just checking that you're awake. Enjoy your tea, we're going

to the beach in twenty five minutes.'

'The beach!'

'Yeah.'

'Do we have too?'

'Not if you don't want too.'

'Good.'

'But look at it out there, it's splendid.'

I flung back the curtains and threw open the windows.

'See?'

Mark looked up putting his hand across his face to shield the shining

light, like a caught out vampire.

'Oh God.' He moaned, as his body started to smoke.

I went and paid the Landlady and she gratefully received the money as
before. I told her there was a good chance we would stay yet another
night and she was happy with that. I'd let her know in the morning I said.
Roger was ready to go beaching when I got back but Mark was less
encouraged.

'I can't go to the beach.' He said.

He was dressed for it, sporting his snazzy black football shorts and his new tourist t-shirt: white with a picture of a donkey on it and the words Lindos taxi. He was holding a beach towel.

'Why?'

'Because I don't have any sandals.'

This was true, since the ferry he had largely been wearing jeans and his brown dress shoes, and unlike Falaraki where we were on level ground and he could just about go barefoot to the nearby beach, here he had to navigate the rough slope down from the studio.

'Well wear your shoes.'

'I'm not doing that! I need to buy some new ones.'

Agreed, but if he didn't come with us now to sort out a location on the busy beach he'd have difficulty in finding us; no, he wouldn't find us and he'd likely get all bent out of shape again.

'Okay this is what we shall do, I'll lend you my flip flops to get to the beach and you can buy a pair down there.'

He thought about it as if there was a catch to the suggestion.

'How are you going to get to the beach then?'

'In my bare feet.'

'You can't do that.'

'Why can't I?'

'Don't know.'

'I've been walking around a lot in bare feet in case you hadn't noticed, so it's no big deal.'

'Are you sure?'

'Yes, I'm sure.'

'Ah no, that won't work.'

'What now?'

'They'll be too small for me.'

'No they won't, I take a size eleven remember?'

'Fuck you've got big feet.'

'Almost as big as yours.'

'Have you two women finished? Can we go to the beach?' Said Roger.

'When I've finished doing my hair.' Mark said in a theatrically camp voice.

'What hair?' Roger replied.

'Oh you're so butch.' Mark camped.

'Sometimes I worry about you.'

'What do you mean sometimes?' Said I.

Getting down the slope was an episode in itself, Mark should have gone bare feet. He looked precarious navigating the narrow coarse trail down and he kept losing a flip flop. "I'm not doing this again." he kept saying and, "Isn't there an easier way down?". Yes there was, but it meant going the long way round. He managed to stub his big toe, which only served to exacerbate his bad mood. "FUCK!" He shouted to everybody in listening distance, families mostly; while balancing himself on one leg, nursing or making a big show of his right digit.

'This is fucking hopeless! I can't do it!'

If he had stayed any longer on one leg I swear he would have toppled off. Fortunately with my goading, he regained his composure and carried on. Meanwhile, an interested crowd below watched with fascination for his next unsteady move. In the end I had to help nurse him down the last part while Roger moved on bored by it all.

'I'm not wearing shitting flip flops again, there useless.

Here, have them back!' He exclaimed, his feet resting on blessed sand.

So I took them back. We must have gone about twenty yards along a sandy path when Mark hopped about.

'Shit! Shit! Ow!'

'What the hell's the matter now?' I asked as Roger disappeared up ahead.

'I got stung for fuck's sake!"

'Stung?'

'Yes!'

'What by?'

'Something on the ground!'

He sat down and nursed his foot. I took a look, he hadn't been stung.

'It's a splinter. You've got a splinter.'

'Where?' He demanded.

So I showed him and he pulled it out as if drawing a knife from his back, and I half expected him to say "Et tu Brute?". I felt the ground, it was full of bits and pieces ready to stick in your feet, wood, glass, metal, you name it.

'Give me those flip flops back.' He commanded.

'I can't possibly walk on this.'

Yards ahead a latticed wood boardwalk began, providing relative ease for walking across the sand. Roger stood waiting for us on it, at the middle point of the beach.

'How about here?' He asked me.

One side of the boardwalk were two restaurants and a shop; the other, sun beds, umbrellas, sand, sea and a bevy of beauties getting scantily browner by the second.

'How about the quieter end of the beach? Away from all this.' Said I.

'Up to you, I'm staying here.' Said Roger unamused.

We secured three sun beds as close as we dared to a group of appealing women, pretending not to be interested in them. Actually Mark wasn't, he simply wanted his daily ration.

'What if I give you fifteen?'

'No I want it all.'

'Why?'

'I've got to buy some shoes!'

'I know that but if I keep hold of most of it then
you've got money for tonight.'

'But I'm not going to spend it all now am I? I'll just go
to the shop that's all.'

So I deferred to him, as he was an adult, and of course by shop I thought he meant the one close by. Roger greased up with protection and started a new book. I had to go for a quick swim, the wobbly jelly feel was very wobbly. Feeling only slightly better after the immersion I lay down on the bed and closed my eyes to the marvelous calming sounds of the beach. About an hour later I woke up to find myself alone no sign of Roger or Mark. I took to reading my own book, flipping between pages, observing the lovely women and the scenery in general. Forty odd minutes later Roger returned.

'Alright, where have you been?'

'The restaurant down there.'

'What you have?'

'Steak.'

'Any good?'

'Really good.'

'Seen Mark?'

'No.'

'Where the hell's he got to?'

The answer to that came some time later, when he turned up eating a gyros, with another wrapped in paper.

'Well?' I asked.

'What?'

'Did you get some flip flops?'

'No I got sandals, I can't wear flip flops like you do.'

I looked down at a pair of designer label sandals.

'How much?'

'How much what?'

'The sandals.'

'Not much.'

'So they were a lot.'

'No!'

'Roger, how much do you reckon Mark paid for his new sandals?'

'I'd say about fifteen euros.'

'Wrong.' Said Mark.

'Twenty euros then.' I said.

'You're both wrong, they cost thirty euros.'

'Are you fucking mad?' I blurted.

'Yes, I am. I bought a spare gyros, do you want it?'

'No.'

'Roger?'

'No.'

'I'll eat it then.'

Roger and I went back to reading our books and cooking in the sun. Mark ate his spare gyros in the shade.

'Guess what I found?' Mark blurted.

'Some expensive sandals.' Answered Roger.

'Not funny.'

'What?' Said I.

'An English pub, near the Gyros shop.'

'Oh great.'

'Guess what it's called?'

'The Kings Head?'

'No, The Sunburnt Arms. Do you get it?'

'Yeah, not bad.'

'Not bad? It's brilliant.'

'You went in?'

'Just to check it out.'

'And?'

'It's good. We should go there.'

'I didn't come to a place like this to go to an English pub, sorry mate.'

'Are you staying here long?'

'Five probably.'

'I might go back there, they said they'd buy me a drink if I did.'

'What are you going to do tonight?' I asked.

'What d'yer mean?'

'Well you spent thirty euros on sandals.'

'Who said I did?'

'You did, just now.'

'That doesn't mean I did does it?'

'Whatever; that would leave you with twenty five euros.'

'Thirty.'

'But you just bought two gyros, so that's four euros.'

'So what? It's my money isn't it?'

'Did you have a drink in the pub?'

He briefly thought about it.

'No.' He replied unconvincingly.

'Point I'm making Mark is if you go to the pub now you won't have any money for this evening. And Roger and I are not going to be subbing you all night, get it?'

'Got it. Understood; over and out.'

'So why don't you just stay here save your money and come
out tonight?'

'Their expecting me back, I'm not going to stay am I?'

'Alright mate, it's up to you. I'm not your keeper.'

So he finished up his spare gyros and took off with declaratory
pledges of returning soon, which he had no intention of keeping.

'Think he'll be back?' Asked Roger.

'Like fuck will he. No, looks like you and me tonight matey.'

'That's not such a bad thing.'

'You're right.'

'Let's meet some women.'

'Agreed, but not like that bunch last night hey?'

For some crazy reason I decided to do a big swim even though I was
still more than a little fuzzy. Using a leg float for ease, I swam way out to
the orange markers about a half a mile from the beach. Getting there
wasn't a problem but when I turned to come back the beach looked an
awful long way and I wasn't in the best shape. About thirty yards in I hit a
problem. I was swimming but not making any headway, the odd currents
there were proving too strong, holding me. My alarmed reaction was to
try power my way through but all that did was leave me exhausted and
close to panic. The adrenaline was pumping fast trying to rush me in to a
bad decision. I quickly rationalized that I couldn't drown because I had
the leg float to keep me afloat and as long as I stayed clear headed I'd be
fine. In a pool you don't think about drowning but in the sea it's a different
matter; you're on your own and the surrounds can appear overwhelming,

ready to engulf you; as I had just discovered for the second time on this trip. I recalled an incident years ago in France when a trio of us had got caught in a riptide close to the beach and it felt like we were being dragged under. Fortunately one of our party had some experience and he shouted at us to relax and float our way through it, which we did and were helped to safety by a couple of lifeguards. Remembering that, I floated on my back to get my eye off the distance to the beach, and to calm myself down and relax as much as possible. I told myself there was no hurry, that swimming with a hangover wasn't the greatest idea in the world; that I wasn't in a battle with the current. Nice and easy I mantraed, nice and bloody easy.

The currents soon subsided and I got back by counting slow regular strokes. Making the shore every inch of me began to shake as if freezing cold. I also felt like a bloody fool; ashamed. No wonder, I'd undergone a sudden jolt of fear and the thing about fear is you immediately assume the worst scenario and believe it absolutely. But if you want a quick remedy for a hangover or a general malaise, try scaring the b'jeezuz out of yourself. That'll make you feel right on the ball, with every nerve end jangling, ready for anything.

Roger could sense something had happened.

'You alright?'

'Not really; fuck. Tried to drown myself.'

'What happened?'

'I got caught in a weird current and panicked. Fuck, man that was scary, I'm not doing that again in a hurry. Thank Christ I had the leg float.'

'Want a drink?'

'Too right I do.'

'Beer, or stronger?'

'A bottle of Tequila would be great mate.'

Charms of Ulla...

We left the beach around five thirty and strolled back up the slope to the studio. When we got there Mark was nowhere to be found, not that we were bothered or surprised, we just didn't want him to screw up the night. Roger was going to crash and we decided to start the evening sortie at nine. I was hungry so I went and grabbed a gyros, when I got back Mark was in the room drunk as a skunk.

'Yousegoingoutlater?'

'Yes, at nine.'

'Wakemewillyou? Iwannacometoo.'

'Yeah sure.'

'Dontforgetwillyou?'

'Of course not.' I lied. No way was he coming with us.

I knocked on Roger's door at nine, having managed to take a shower and get ready to leave without waking droopy drawers, passed out atop of his bed.

'Yeah?'

'Ready?'

Roger opened the door and looked beyond me.

'Mark not coming?'

'In his dreams.'

'Let's go get lucky then.'

So we strolled into the village, slowly working the bars along the main drag looking to chat to available ladies and puffing out our display of peacock feathers for them to see. In Roger's case his favourite dark blue striped polo shirt, in mine a white shirt of all things. Why of all things? Because I never wear a shirt, yet I'd put it in the bag so I was going to wear it once to justify it's inclusion. One good thing, it bought out my so called tan.

The fourth bar we went into Roger got talking immediately to some fine looking girl, while I got the beers. She was from Birmingham and had a wicked sense of humour; she also had one of the best bodies on earth. I thought Roger was in until her boyfriend came back from the toilet to ruin everything. He wasn't put out in the slightest and we ended up chatting up a storm with them for about half an hour, having great fun. Gin was her name and she asked me what I was hoping to do that night, I told her as honestly as I could. 'Meet some lovely lady and have sex together Gin.' And in that great brummie accent of hers she replied. 'Paul, you are a minx. Best of blu'ddy British mate.' I got a kick out of that and it made me think that I'd never met a brummie I didn't like. Even when they are miserable they sound humorous.

Fun over, we moved on to a bar called Antika which was like a display case for the beautiful people but it didn't stop us from trying to fit in. A number of pretty Greek and Italian women were present and I decided to give Roger's "Distance" theory a test by trying to smile and small chat to them. I was met by a wall of indifference; theory proved. Next, we stopped in at Yanni's close to the 404 and sat on the large outside patio, people watching. Four very attractive girls came and sat at the table next to us. One of them, a raven haired, bronzed goddess asked me for a light, which I gave her and we got talking.

'Where are you from?' She asked in a northern accent.

'From London.' I answered; not sure of the reply, because northerners can be a bit strange about London and southerners in general. I've met northern English in the middle of nowhere in a far away country, and the first thing the men will generally say to you when they discover you are from "Down south." is, "The beer's crap down there. Don't know how yer' drink it." Quite where that comes from is beyond me; a good pint of English bitter is good wherever you get it, there's no demarcation line distinguishing where it starts or stops being good. Refreshingly she simply followed on.

'What d'yer do?'

'I'm a builder.'

'Oh, you don't look like a builder.' She said with a note of genuine surprise.

'What do I look like then?'

'Something more important.' She replied without putting me down.

'Well I did try to be a film director at one time,

but it didn't work out.'

This was true, though it went down like a lead balloon.

'And what do you do?'

'I'm a hairdresser.'

'Hard work hairdressing, how's your legs?'

'Not too bad 'cause I own me own shop.'

'You do? Whereabouts?'

'In Sheffield.'

'I know Sheffield, great place. I lived outside of it for awhile a few years ago.'

'Where?'

'Clifton, near Maltby.'

'Yeah, I know it.'

The other raven haired bronzed goddess looked to Roger.

'What d'yer do?'

'I'm an investment banker.'

That sounded so much better than builder let me tell you and it did impress.

'In London?'

'Canary Wharf, heard of it?'

I thought Roger was trying to take the piss when he said that but they registered no response, perhaps they didn't know of it. Beauty and brains don't always go together. I got the impression that they thought initially we might be a couple of wealthy playboys with the money and personality to match, but now they were taking us for a couple of southern wide boys and the bullshit detectors were out. A strange mixture of interest and disinterest had evolved, a bit guarded if you please. As we strained further it was made clear they all had boyfriends, all of whom had been left behind while they came away on holiday for a girls week out.

It ended up with me engaging the two ravens while Roger took on the other two, who were brunette or blonde. The chatter was never comfortable even though I for one made an effort to be easy going. It was at times like these that you needed to be an Onassis and invite them onto your luxury yacht parked in the harbour. Some may call that shallow but I say very attractive women need to be impressed to break the ice. Not being able to do that, they soon lost interest in us and said goodbye and left. It was a strange interlude.

'Well?' I asked Roger.

'Waste of time.'

'What is it about English girls?'

'What do you mean?'

'Why can't they be nice and natural and confident? I mean we just met four lovely looking ladies, two of whom were stunning and throughout it all I felt like I was trying to break down the walls of Jericho.'

'You either get on well with them or you don't.'

'But we're not exactly boring are we?'

'They had boyfriends.'

'So? That shouldn't stop you from being yourself. Take Ulla, she's got a boyfriend, she's highly attractive and yet she's natural; she engages, why can't those women be like that?'

'Because that's the way it is.'

I couldn't question his logic, it made perfect sense.

We took a few steps over to the 404 and settled in there for two beers and got chatting to a group of Scottish women outside; who were in town for a wedding on sunday, their men out on the stag somewhere. They were a good antidote, cheerful, friendly and funny. Roger and I couldn't be faulted for making an effort with the opposite sex but it would have been nice to meet some who were like us, single and on the make; it would have made things a lot easier. I wasn't complaining though, in fact I was having a great time generally.

Around midnight we went up to Luna bar, the place was busier than the previous night. A hen party was there, fifteen quite large women dressed as vikings, and we sat the far side of the bar attempting to steer clear of it all. A smiling Ulla served us.

'Hi, where have you been so far?'

So we reported the evenings events, in between Perri came and shook our hands and told Ulla to issue us a shot on the house. Ulla had one herself after which she looked at the empty glass and stated.

'I needed that.'

I could sense something wasn't quite right with her.

'Why what's the matter?'

'I don't know if I should say this.'

'You don't have to tell me anything if you don't want.'

'Okay, last night I see Nikos kissing one of those women you did not like.'

'When?'

'At Qupi's. I saw them outside.'

'Are you sure they were kissing?'

'Yes, he was kissing her!'

Sorry Ulla I thought, I only meant to say that I couldn't believe your fool boyfriend preferred one of those girls over you. What an idiot. What a young horny male bastard.

'Are you talking?'

'Yes, he says he loves me.'

'What do you say?'

'I am not sure.'

'This other girl, was it the blonde one?'

'Yes.'

'Thought so.'

'He says she means nothing to him.'

He would say that; if he could have got away with it he would have done. At his age I would have done the same damn thing.

'Did he say why he was kissing her?'

'Because he was drunk.'

'Really? And you believe that?'

'No I do not.'

'I wouldn't either.'

'What must I do?'

'You must do what is best for you.'

'I do not know. I am confused.'

Now it's at times like this in the romances that the caring, listening hero takes the distressed damsel in his loving arms and comforts and ensures her that the future is safe with him, and that he will rescue her from the evil clutches of her misguided love and live happily ever after; right? In reality of course it's a golden chance to seduce the poor upset girl, savour her physical delights and see how you feel afterwards before you go making any silly promises. Except there was one thing holding me back from being so cynical, apart from not wanting to be cynical of course. I was twenty eight years older than her, which more than likely was her father's age. In the short time I had met Ulla, it was clear that we got on well for whatever reason, but then again she was intelligent and beautiful and I was neither so why wouldn't we? I would have had no qualms sleeping with her of course.

I'm not that prudish and I was single, and seemingly attractive to younger women, but having burnt my fingers in the past I err on the side of caution. I decided her cry of help was to someone she felt she could trust not to someone she fancied. I also knew that in situations like these you often got played as the sap for bringing the two disjointed parties back together again. So softly-softly was the approach, just in case I was a fool either way. If things came about how I wished they would then great, and if they didn't? Then fine, it was a pleasure to know her and be in her company.

'Where are you going later?' Ulla asked.

'The clubs probably.'

'Qupi's?'

'Yes.'

'Then I will come with you.'

Wow, maybe things were about to happen beyond my wildest dreams I thought. But no, part of her reasoning was clearly to avoid confrontation with Nikos when they finished work, he was after all working the DJ spot in the bar while we talked, and he was watching her hawk eyed.

In between talking to Ulla while she worked, Roger and I had got friendly with a group of Scottish people who had come in; three young couples out for a week and were on their last night determined to enjoy themselves, so we wanted to enjoy it with them. We had a few drinks, banged the gong a few times, laughed a hell of a lot and danced on the bar. At one point joined by the mad American, Tommi, who dashed in for five minutes and like a barefoot tourist on a red hot beach, jumped and bounded around on everything two feet off the floor and did his party trick with the red vodka and left. The whole thing was slightly surreal but a lot of fun.

'Who is that guy?' I asked Roger

'Must be the owner.'

'Think so?'

'Greek-American I bet; comes here for the summer.'

'You're right, he looks rich.'

Energized, bar closing, we all set off for Qupi's. The couples and Roger went ahead, as Ulla and I followed behind them chatting, keeping the conversation away from her love ills.

'Have you worked here long?'

'Three years now.'

'How did you know about Lindos?'

'I come here with my family when I was young.'

'Oh, so you know it well?'

'How do you like Lindos?'

'I like it very much.'

'Me too.'

'Do you work in Germany?'

'No, I go to university. I have two years left.'

'Will you stay in Germany when you have finished?'

'Most likely but I like it here also.'

'You like London?'

'Yes, I do. I've only been there a few months.'

'Where are you before?'

'California for fifteen years.'

'Really?'

'Yes.'

'Oh, I always want to go there.'

'You would fit in very well there Ulla.'

'Why did you leave?'

'Because I prefer this.'

'It's better?'

'Yes, it's better.'

We got into Qupi's which was busy, and Roger went mad and ordered some cocktails. Ulla knew quite a lot of people there and she went off to do some socializing. I noticed Nikos turn up and saluted to him, and he saluted back smiling. A few minutes later I saw him and Ulla go outside to the courtyard for a long chat. Whereupon, to add flavour to the situation, the group of women from the previous evening turned up, offending blonde included. As things were working themselves out, us party goers were having a right good time. More cocktails, a round of shots, some dancing, engaging with the other like-souls there. The kind of classic fun night that people familiar with Lindos have known over the years. I assumed Ulla and Nikos had worked out their differences and gone home but when I went outside to use the toilet, I saw Ulla sitting on the bench on her own. I went up to her.

'Hey, things okay?'

'I think so.'

'Where's Nikos?'

'He is at Arches, he must work there tonight.'

'Are you coming inside?'

'Yes, soon.'

Ten minutes later she came inside and she joined in the fun for awhile but then confessed to me that she had agreed to meet Nikos at Arches. Amazingly she invited me to go with her, but I didn't fancy the idea so we said good night.

An hour later smashed, it was time for me to go home. Roger was picking up on some girl at the main bar and looked like he was on his way to becoming more than friends. I caught his attention and indicated I was leaving, he gave me the thumbs up and I left. I made my way to the gyros shop. Being close to four am the streets were largely deserted and the shops boarded up with wood shutters, a lovely calm atmosphere pervaded. I walked slowly back to the studio eating my gyros contemplating lovely Ulla, the night, Lindos. It was Saturday and we'd been in Greece a week, what's more I was having the time of my life.

Garda-Da-Vida...

Ulla was in the bed. Her warm soft naked body pressed to mine, her skin smelling of fragrant soap and sweat. I went to kiss her forehead but I was distracted by the sound of a boiling kettle whistle. Followed by the sound of somebody running in to the room and removing the offending noise. Followed five minutes later by the sound of a spoon against china.

'Tea mate. Lovely day out there.'

Tea? Lovely day? Ulla? Merely a dream, bugger. I opened my eyes to see a mug of tea on the bedside table and a long thin white body with strange brown markings, wearing black shorts, moving away to the door.

'What's the time?' I uttered.

'Eleven.'

'Eleven?'

'What time are you going to the beach?'

'What?'

'The beach, what time?'

'Oh, two hours yet.'

'Two hours?'

'I need more sleep.'

I could see where this was leading so I sat up half eyed, sipped my brew.

'Got any money?'

'Don't know; maybe not.' A worried frown came over his face.

'Hand me my jeans.'

He did so, and I rummaged my pockets for spare cash then checked my wallet. Incredibly, I had twenty euros left.

'Here.'

He took it gratefully.

'You missed a good night.'

'Did I?'

'What did you do?'

'Slept mostly.'

'Good for you.'

'I did try come and find you.'

'You did? What time was that?'

'About one o'clock.'

'We were in Luna bar.'

'I thought so.'

'And you didn't find us?'

'I couldn't find it.'

'How could you not find it?'

'I don't know, I got lost.'

'It's the last bar on the main street, just past Sixties.'

'I don't think I went that far.' Clearly not, I thought.

'How about 404? Did you go there?'

'Where?'

'404, where we sat out day before with the young girls, remember?'

'No?'

'Yes you do, where the tree is outside.'

'Oh the tree; no, didn't go there.'

'Bet you found the gyros shop though.'

'Found that, but I didn't have any money did I?'

'So you came back here?'

'No, I had a drink in the Sunburnt Arms.'

'Thought you didn't have any money?'

'I didn't, I've got to go back and pay for it now.'

Oh shit, I thought, now their giving him on-the-slate drinks. What bloody maniac does that to an alcoholic? But something else rang true in my head, Mark's accounting of his predicament to his new found hosts.

"So they won't give you any money?" Said mein host to Mark.

"Only every now and again."

"It's a disgrace is what it is. You poor man, you just wait 'till I meet these so called friends. I'll have it out with them by Christ." Said mein host's wife.

"How come they've got control of your money?" Said mein host.

"They took it from me."

"They TOOK it from you!?" Mein host and wife and others at the bar said together.

"Yes, in a manner of speaking."

"This isn't right. I'm going to the police and have them kicked off the island!" Said the wife.

"Oh no don't do that, it will make things worse. They've got my passport too."

'That's terrible, you poor man.'

"Have you even eaten lately?" Asked mein host.

"Not really, a day ago I had a gyros."

"I've never heard anything so awful before in all my time in Lindos." Said wife.

"Where are they now?"

"In town somewhere."

"Spending your money I bet."

"More than likely."

"Well you just sit there, I'm going to buy you another drink."

"Oh, you don't have to."

"I insist."

"If you insist, fine."

Was I far wrong in my imaginings? Did I exaggerate my unfounded suspicions? Yes; but I'm sure there was a large grain of truth in it.

So I grabbed my two hours extra of sleep, even though it was disrupted by the cleaner coming in to do her job. Clearly unhappy at my dissolute presence and talking to herself about me throughout. The late nights, attempted drownings and the copius intake of alcohol was beginning to have an effect upon me. I was even thinking maybe I should ease off in case I had a heart attack. Eventually I got up, put my shorts on and sat outside at the porch table, supping on a big bottle of water and tried reading my book. Twenty minutes in and Roger's door opened; incredibly some girl did not come out, scampering away, not wishing to be discovered for her supposed indiscretion. No, it was just a pasty faced Roger squinting in the bright light.

'What's the time?'

'About one.'

'Been up long?'

'Thirty minutes.'

'Mark?'

'At the pub.'

'Already?'

'Thought you'd pulled.'

'I did.'

'What happened?'

'Don't know. Woke up in some doorway.'

'So you got hammered, passed out some point along the way
and she left you asleep in the street, is that it?'

'Something like that.'

'Well done. Getting as bad as Mark.'

'What are you up to?'

'Beach; remember the rule.'

'What rule?'

'Hangovers on the beach not in the room.'

'Don't have to live by it do you?'

'You disappoint me.'

And so Roger and I went to the beach to work off our hang overs, but
not before we topped up with cash from the ATM and walked by the
Sunburnt Arms, not daring to go in. One thing Roger said though stuck
with me.

'At least he's in the right spot.'

'For what?'

'For catching a donkey home.'

Just at that moment some donkeys came clomping towards us on their way back to the station.

'He must have called for one.' Quipped Roger.

I half-expected Mark to come out arm raised, shouting.

"That's for me."

I didn't do much on the beach except close my eyes. Roger went and had another big meal but I felt too rough for anything other than just laying there. A day of atonement.

Getting back to the studio Mark was face down on his bed, TV on, blaring really loudly; thankfully the other tenants were absent. I had to ask Roger a question so knocked on his door.

'Hey, are we staying tomorrow night?'

'What and go to Kos Monday?'

'Yeah, if we feel like it.'

'Okay, let's do that.'

So I trundled around to the Landlady's residence and paid her cash for two nights. She couldn't have been more delighted. One night had turned into four nights already, we were proving to be a late season windfall, with the promise of more to come at this rate.

The evening rolled around, even after a day of basically doing nothing essentially resting and sleeping I still felt dulled by too much partying. As we wandered into town for the night I felt like the odd man out, the dead weight; the other two lively and well. Lindos was packed; everybody bar the household pets were out and about. Mark and I needed food, so we left Roger outside the 404 and went and had a reasonably priced meal in

Mikki's - Pork chop, chips, salad and wine for seven euros each. A price you couldn't refuse.

After eating, the three of us went into Antika and chatted to these two lovely Welsh girls. One of whom lived near us in London, Clapham in fact. We were getting on really well when the bombshell hit.

'How long are you here for?' Asked Roger.

'Oh this is it. We're going home tonight.'

'Tonight?'

'Yes, it's turn around night.'

'Saturday is turn around as well?'

'That's why it's so busy, everybody is waiting to go home.'

'What time do you leave then?'

'In about an hour.'

They then dropped another timely bombshell, delivered from a great height.

'It's a shame really.'

'What is?'

'Well, we've been here a week and had a great time, but haven't met anyone we liked talking to until now, shame we didn't meet earlier really.

When did you say you arrived in Lindos?'

As we stood there daggers protruding from our hearts; absorbing the bad and good in their comments. Understanding their drift; pondering the unfairness of chance meeting and brief encounter. Wondering how the hell we hadn't met until then; I almost felt impelled to say.

"Stay! Don't leave! If you do, we'll all have the best few days of our lives. What more do you want? Life is short, take advantage when it pokes you in the eye."

But hang on, how was three going to go into two? Well, let's be fair Mark had already fallen in love. Miss Sunburnt Arms gave him everything he needed for the rest of the stay. Needless to say I never gave a plea to the heart, I merely said what every civilized creature says.

'It's been a real delight to meet you both, it's such a pity you are leaving.'

The interpretation of which was: "It's a fucking crying shame you're damn well leaving us, I could cry."

'Ah, you are so lovely, honestly you are. Come back next year, same time; we'll be here. We've got to go, see you, bye.'

We hugged, kissed and waved them goodbye forever.

'Fuck.' Said Roger.

'Fuck.' Said I.

They were right about everybody leaving; come midnight the bars and paths were dead. An odd feeling for a Saturday night, especially one that had been so lively. We went to Luna bar to see Ulla, things were patched between her and Nikos, although you could tell she'd been hurt and confused by the experience. We didn't stay that long and much to her disappointment went to Arche's and Qupi's early. I ran into the girls from Sheffield again but made a bit of a tit of myself, which left me not in the best of spirits, I decided to go home early; Roger and Mark joined me. Apart from the Welsh girls it was a night to forget, I for one should have had an early night to recharge my batteries. Little did I realize that by Lindos standards I was having an early one, I was in bed by two am.

The Man from Del Montetravolta...

The next day I was woken by church bells ringing. I soon surmised they were coming from the main church and that they signaled it being a Sunday. In a weeks time we'd be leaving Greece, Thursday come what may, we had to catch the ferry back to Syros and on to Paros. Question was should we to go to Kos on Monday and spend three nights there? I was loving Lindos, Roger and Mark too, but not to the same extent. I had a genuine affinity for the place, but our whole idea had been to keep moving on, yet here we were settling in, lulled by Lindos's embrace.

Sunday was a repeat of Saturday. I still felt like shit. Roger and I went to the beach; he went to the restaurant for a meal, and Mark went to the pub after I had given him his daily budget. The only real difference was Mark, by nine pm he still hadn't shown. Just over a week in Greece and he was emulating his back home ways. As ever, Roger and I discussed him as we made our way into the heart of the village for the evening.

'Think Mark is okay?' Asked Roger.

'Oh, he'll be holding court in the Sunburnt Arms guaranteed.'

Roger needed to use the ATM in the square so we happened to go by the said establishment, who should come out as we neared it but Mark. Pissed as a fart, talking to himself; cigarette in mouth and patting his body down for a lighter, unaware of our approach.

'Mark, what are you doing?' I asked.

'Ah there you are, have you got a light? I seem to have lost my lighter. Again!' He started to crack up laughing.

'Here.' As I gave him a light.

'Where are you two going?' He asked.

'We're out for the night.' I replied.

'Can I come?'

'Aren't you drunk enough already?'

'Yes, decidedly.'

'You should probably go home then mate.'

'No, I'm coming with you.'

'That's not a good idea.'

'Are you saying I can't?'

'No, just saying home's a better idea, that's all.'

'I've been home and you weren't there.'

'When was that?'

'This afternoon.'

'We were at the beach.'

'I know you were.'

'How long you been out?'

'Oh a few beers.'

'I think you should call it a night.' Said Roger.

'Should I?'

'Yes.'

'What am I calling night?'

'What?'

'You said, call IT a night. What am I calling night?'

'Piss off Mark, go home.' I said.

'I need a gyros.'

'Then go get one.'

'Am I allowed?'

'Only if you are a very good boy.' I said deflating his accusation. He cracked up again.

'That's good, I like that.'

Roger and I didn't want to seem mean, but when Mark was in this state it generally spelt bad news. A couple more and he could be a major pain in the arse, like the first night.

'Well? Roger asked me.

'He should go back.'

'You sort it out, I'm going to the cash machine.'

Roger left me with the man from Del Monte, whose cigarette had gone out by the simple expedient of him knocking the lit end off, by accidentally sliding his fingers along the length, when attempting to take it out of his mouth.

'Got a light? Didn't I just ask you that?'

'Yes.'

'Thought so.'

'Mark, I'm going. I'll see you later okay?'

'Okay; Roger and out; or rather Roger and Paul.'

I left him standing there laughing at his own joke and went to join Roger. There was a cafe open on the corner that faced the donkey station and across from the gyros shop. I ordered an espresso and sat at the outside table, while Roger got his cash and joined me.

'They do beers here?' He asked.

'In the fridge I think.'

Sure enough he got a Mythos and sat down with me. The village was quiet by the square, only a couple of people around.

'Where is he?'

'Left him there.'

'What's happened to him?'

'Unfortunately he found a pub he likes. Worse thing possible.'

'Think he's got any money?'

'Has he fuck. As it is we've been subbing him last few nights anyway. I'm not too bothered if we're all having fun, but when he's like that, shit.'

'So if he did come with us, we'd be buying him drinks all night?'

'Pretty much.'

'I don't understand how he keeps getting lost.'

'No, nor do I. It's just at night. Day time he's fine. He claims all the buildings and streets look the same.'

'What he needs is a taxi.'

'No cars allowed in the village is there?'

'I know, how about the donkey idea? We could order him one from midnight onwards.'

'Yes, a donkey would be great, that'd get him home or the Acropolis at least.'

'A donkey taxi service.'

'We could call it the Midnight Donkey.'

'Yeah, that's a great name for it. Can you imagine?.'

'Mark's here.'

'Where?'

'In the gyros shop.'

'Fuck.'

Two minutes later he came strolling over, and sat down eating and spilling his gyros in equal measure.

'Have you tried one of these?' He asked in all seriousness.

'No, what are they like?' I answered in all seriousness.

'Brilliant. You should try one.'

'Maybe one of these days I will.'

'I'm sure you've had one, haven't you?'

'Paul and I have thought of a way of you getting home at night, without getting lost.'

'What's that?'

'We're going to arrange a midnight donkey.'

'A what?'

'You know, a donkey. We'll get it sorted so it's available from midnight. It'll come and get you when your ready to go home. What you think?'

'Absolutely marvelous, how much will it cost?'

'Couple of euros I'd have thought.'

'Great. Who's the driver?'

'You are.'

'Me? I can't drive a donkey.'

'Don't worry, it only knows one route, the one down

to our studio. You just hang on. Well?'

He finished slobbering his gyros and burped long and loud.

'Right, where are we going then?'

We headed straight for the 404 and had a beer, then we wandered up to Luna bar, but neither Perri or Ulla were working so we stayed for one drink only and moved back down the empty road. We passed the Sixties bar and for the hell of it decided to call in, as nothing was going on and it looked like a quiet one was on the cards. We were greeted warmly by the two fine looking hostesses and sat at the bar with not too much to say to each other. In the large inner courtyard, a big group of people of a wide age range, sat around the central space that acted like a dance floor. Music from the fifties, sixties and early seventies was played loudly to no effect. They all looked like they were paying the dentist a visit. Then the resident DJ put on Stayin' Alive by the Bee Gees and Mark became energized. Roger and I watched in bemusement as he shot off his stool, went in to the courtyard, and started to dance in a world of his own. John Travolta would have had a hard time keeping pace with all the moves, it was hilarious. The hostesses, the bar staff, the DJ, and the large group, watched transfixed; laughing at the inspired performance. The whole mood of the place had quickly changed.

'Your friend, he dances good no?' Said the barman.

I was too busy laughing to answer but I nodded affirmatively. The DJ wasn't stupid, he kept the disco theme going, keeping Mark as the center of attention. Soon enough, all the delighted women in the courtyard we're up dancing with him, while the men just smiled and laughed, their night made good by a crazy man.

'How does he do it?' I asked Roger.

'Do what?'

'Go from drunken idiot to dancing hero in less than three minutes. Look at him, he's a fucking star out there.'

After five scintillating dances, Mark's smoking habit caught up with him and he had to retire. Much to the disappointment of the courtyard crowd and the bar, for Mark's display had tripled the drink orders. In appreciation of his efforts, we got a free shot of Raki, which tastes as bad as it sounds. To this day I think Sixties bar were missing a trick, they could have offered Mark accommodation, all the beer he could drink, a couple of gyros's a day and in return all he had to do was dance like that every night. He'd have packed the place all summer long with his antics. Meantime things were worse for Mark than I thought,

'I've got to go home.' He said.

'Want us to call the Midnight Donkey?' Said Roger.

'Yes, now, I'm fucked. How long will it take?'

'Can you make it back?' I asked.

'No, can't somebody come with me?'

Shame it didn't really exist I thought, it would solve a lot of problems regarding Mark's nocturnal deliverance.

We went to the 404 and pointed Mark in the right direction.

'Straight ahead mate, remember? 'Til you get to the main church, yeah?'

'Church?'

'You know the one with the bells?'

'The bells. The bells, Esmerelda.' He said in a fair imitation of Quasimodo's voice and offending lump.

'Take the passage by the side and you meet the donkey trail, remember? And it's a right from there.'

'Is it?'

'Yes, it takes you all the way to the small beach.'

'Why do I want to go to the small beach?'

'Because it's on the same route as the studio.'

'Ah yes.'

We watched him toddle off in the general direction, doing a late flourish of dancing to Stayin' Alive; in a very camp manner it has to be said.

'Do you think Mark's gay?' Asked Roger.

'Possibly, he is an actor after all.'

'Does that mean all actors are gay then?'

'No, but it runs in the family.'

'So he is?'

'No I don't think so, he acts like it at times; like now when he's rat arsed and he wants people to believe it. Twenty years ago when I first met him, he could easily charm the knickers off a girl just by being funny. Believe me, I saw him do it plenty of times.'

'So what happened then?'

'If we knew that we could get him sorted out.'

'Don't think this trip will do it then?'

'What do you think?'

'I was thinking 'till today that he was doing good actually.'

'Yeah then he got pissed all day long and it's back to square one.'

'We got to get him laid.'

'I know. How?'

'Try him with a donkey, he won't know the difference at four in the morning.' We laughed at the suggestion.

'Quiet isn't it? Think I might have an early one.' I said with half a bottle of beer left and no inclination for another.

'Don't fancy the nightclubs?'

'Nah, to be honest I'm feeling a bit rough. I can't get messed up and recover as easily as you two can.'

'What about Kos?'

'We don't even know if there's a ferry tomorrow do we?'

'No, but we could spend the night in Rhodes Town, bound to be a ferry Tuesday.'

'We could, we could also stay here.'

'Want to?'

'Wouldn't mind. I'll leave the decision with you mate.'

'Oh thanks.'

'Nah, I wanted to come here so next decision is yours. I'm happy either way.'

He never got to give his reply, as Ulla came walking by at that moment and stopped to chat.

'Hello, are you going to Luna bar?'

'No, we've already been. It's very quiet.'

'And you're not working there tonight.' Said Roger smoothly.

'I must go meet Nikos there. Where is the funny tall one?' She inquired.

'He just left, on his way home.' I said.

'Oh no he's not. He's right there.' Said Roger.

I turned to see Mark standing at the path by the grocery store, oblivious to where he was. We waved, but he didn't notice a thing and walked on straight ahead as if going to Arches. We shouted to catch his attention and he waddled over, at that point, Ulla said goodbye and left.

'What are you doing?' I asked him.

'Trying to get home. Where am I?'

'Outside the 404, by the tree.'

'Fuck, how'd I get here?'

Roger took out his mobile phone and pretended to call.

'Hello?. Is that the donkey station? Yeah, I need the Midnight Donkey. 404. Five minutes? Yasass.'

Roger put the phone away and said very deadpan.

'Be here in five.'

Mark fell to the ground laughing his head off, concerning those watching.

Rob came out.

'Is he alright?'

'He will be in five minutes.' Said Roger.

'Well, he's got to get up off the ground.'

Roger and I decided it was best if we had an early night and escort the man from Del Monte home, otherwise there was a chance some poor unfortunate Lindosian was going to wake in the morning, to the sound of snoring outside their front door.

Ears of the Ass...

For the first time in days I rose early and well. Late nights and copious amounts of alcohol a distant memory seemingly. It was one of those it's-great-to-be-alive mornings; the rising sun was bathing the landscape in a warm golden light, while the sky had not a cloud to spoil it. I stood on the top left terrace and could see the big tour buses winding their way down the ridge road to the village stop. The main beach was getting sun worshipers already and a few people were in the water splashing about. Compact four wheeled vehicles rode by, carrying supplies to the businesses on the small beach. Some early birds walked by caught in the moment like me, stunned by the simple beauty of it all.

I strolled into town avoiding the congregation of day-trippers. Again I just wore shorts and flip flops but if I could have gone naked I would have done, because I felt so free and relaxed. I got some coffee first then went to the store and purchased eggs, bread, butter, marmalade and a container of celebrated fruit juice. Celebrated? Because it claimed to do everything to your system that medicine couldn't, so I thought I'd give it a whirl.

When I got back to the studio I laid my groceries on the porch table, as I did I heard a sound much like a donkey makes, emanate from the room through the curtained open windows. I went into the room half expecting to find a lost donkey in there but it was just Mark making strange noises in his sleep. Every three or four minutes, he'd punctuate the air with this new odd sounding resonance. Amid this, I made myself scrambled eggs on toast and along with the carton of fruit juice, went up to the table on the top right terrace and sat down for a nutritious breakfast, mit lovely view. The noises appeared to have stopped by this time.

Finishing, I lit a fag and pondered it's health benefits against the goodness of fruit juice. As I did, the German couple came out of their studio, all prepared for another long day at the beach. Unaware I was there, I shouted "Yasoo" to them, they stared up and gave me a strange look, replying "Yasoo" and left. As I took the debris back to the room, I ran into the Hungarian couple coming out of their room and they just gave me these big silly smiles and left. I cleaned up and knocked on Roger's door.

'Uh?'

'Rog' it's me; hey, are we staying or what? I got to let the Landlady know.'

'Stay.'

'Are you sure?'

'Yeah, may as well.'

'So no Kos?'

'No.'

'Okay.'

Delighted, I went to see the Landlady. When I told her we wanted to be accommodated 'till Thursday, her face came over all worried, like I'd said something bad.

'It's no good?' I asked with concern.

But then after thinking for a moment, it was all wine and roses. She clamped her hands together and announced,

'Is okay. Thursday good.'

'Sure?'

'Absolute.'

My reading of the situation was she had some people coming to stay for a night and wanted to use our rooms, but simple arithmetic had carried the vote. I arranged to pay her every day, and as I waved to her man in the comfy chair and went to step back outside, she indicated for me to wait and got something to give me; it was a little jar of olives. I've got to say I was quite touched and accepted it gratefully, even though I'm the last person on earth who likes the fruit of the olive tree.

'Lindos, nice?'

'Very nice, special.' I answered.

'Yes, special.'

Without word to the others I went to the beach. I deliberately did not leave Mark any money in an effort to force him to come down. Roger could find me no problem. I had a swim, not taking any chances this time by swimming back and forth the length of the beach. I did a good mile and got back onto the sun bed feeling bloody marvelous. Roger found me and went for a meal first thing. When he got back I asked him.

'Did you hear Mark this morning?'

'No, why what was he doing?'

'Making these really unpleasant noises.'

'Like before?'

'Sort of, but more donkey like, hey? Whatever it is you call what they do.'

'Eyore.'

'Yes, eyore. No, that's a Winnie the Pooh character surely?'

'Yes, but it's named after the noise a donkey makes.'

'Possibly; anyway, if you'd heard it you'd thought a donkey was in the room.'

'Did he?'

'Did he what?'

'Did he have one in there with him?'

'No, course not.'

'How do you know?'

'Sharing the room I think I would have noticed it somehow.'

'Think he'll go to the Sunburnt Arms today?'

'If he does, he'll have to find us first. I didn't leave him any dosh.'

'Why not?'

'Teach him a lesson. Hopefully keep him from drinking all day.'

'He was taking a shower when I left.'

'So?'

'He'll be here soon.'

'If he finds us.'

'Shall we move?' Asked Roger.

'What and confuse him further?'

'Yes.'

'Grand idea.'

So we upped beds and moved further along the beach, greatly amused by our schoolboy antics. Amazingly Mark found us, though he was looking a bit perplexed and sweaty from walking up and down the beach.

'Have you two been swimming?'

'No.'

"Cause I've been looking for ages. This isn't where you always come is it?'

'Since we got here, yeah.'

'I could have sworn it was further down.'

'You're thinking of Falafuckingraki.'

'Got any money?' He jumped in.

'Problem there mate, the machine was out of cash. I've only got ten euros for now. Do you want it?'

'Is that all?'

Which interpreted as, "Too right I want it, you lying bastard."

'Sorry mate but we're all in the same boat. Have to wait for the machines to stock up again.'

He took the money.

'You going to the pub?'

'No, I'll get a gyros and come back here.'

'Okay, we'll see you soon then.'

'What's the water like?' He asked.

'Lovely, good day for a swim.'

'Maybe I'll have a dip.'

'Absolutely, you should.'

'See you in a bit.'

We watched his thin white legs head up the boardwalk.

'A swim hey?' Said Roger.

'Nah, that ten euros is burning a hole in his pocket right now.
Walking by the Sunburnt Arms will be far too tempting.'

'Are the machines out of cash?'

'Not yet.'

'You should let him do what he wants with his money really.
Don't you think?'

'No, I want him out with us at night having fun, not boozing
his holiday away in the day. No point in him
coming otherwise.'

Three and a half hours later we left the beach for the comforts of the studio, wondering if Mark had taken his swim and whether the earth was round or flat. Entering the room I found my answer, Mark was fast asleep in his bed. About an hour later I took a nap myself, not before opening the windows to let the coolish air in, curtains drawn. An hour or so into my nap and I was woken by Mark, making the same moaning and shouting sounds I had grown accustomed to in Falaraki. Quite frankly they were getting a bit annoying.

'Mark shut up!' I repeated four or five times.

He said something in his somnolent state and mercifully stopped the sounds. I then looked over at him and saw a dreadful sight, his naked hairy buttocks were staring at me from under his pulled up blanket.

'Oh God.' I said.

The wind had got up and was blowing the curtains around. I could hear the neighbours movements outside and worried a bare arse could occasionally be pointing their way, so I shouted.

'Mark, cover yourself up.' But to no avail.

I got up and closed the windows instead, and stepped outside to have a smoke in my shorts. The German couple came out from their room and acted strangely towards me again, we said good evening and all that, and they left.

Then it hit me, I realized what the strange looks were all about. They were clearly under the assumption that Mark and I were gay lovers and that the noises they must have heard, were the sounds of sexual pleasure between two men. The Hungarians must have bought into it as well but they were clearly more up on the preference. Besides, there was a fair chance that Mark's nakedness had shown itself through the blowing curtains. I had a really good chuckle just thinking about the whole episode and it's suggestive tendencies.

One Girl Leads to Another...

Later that evening, after a reasonably good meal at a reasonably good restaurant on the main drag, the three of us walked up to the 404 to get the night's drinking events underway. A group of four girls and two blokes were sat outside. Utilizing two spare stools and the low tree wall, we managed to squeeze ourselves a space between them and a couple using the other table.

'Do you mind if I sit here?' I asked the dark haired girl, nearest the spot I had selected for my stool.

'No, help yourself.' She said in a Lancashire accent.

'Sounds like your from Manchester.' I said.

'No Oldham, just outside.' She answered with a big broad smile and a full set of white, white teeth, American style.

'How long you been in Lindos?'

'Me? Oh I've been comin' for years but arrived yesterday.'

'What, all of you?'

'Just the girls. Com' every year. Y'erself?'

'This is our first time.'

'Enjoyin' it?'

'Loving it.'

'When did y'er get here?'

'Got to Rhodes last Tuesday.'

'Tuesday? Did you come by Easy Jet then?'

'No, ferry.'

"Ferry?" All the girls appeared to coo together.

It was time for the "Explanation" again which must have made us rather exotic, because the girls peppered us with questions about how and why, and where and when. Which did nothing to please the two blokes who had been sitting with them. The one with outward signs of displeasure, who was from Manchester and proud of it, was unimpressed by me in particular. I guess I was too southern, too healthy and too happy, I was also probably moving in on the bird he fancied. He was near my age but showing it, his mate was younger and friendlier. We hadn't meant to spoil the party, but we had no idea they were not attached to the girls when we sat down. Hey ho.

'What's your name?' I asked the girl next to me.

'Janet, and yours?'

'Paul.' I said, introducing the others as well.

'What do you do?' She asked.

'I'm a general builder for want of a better explanation. How about you?'

'Nurse.'

'You enjoy it?'

'Use too, hate it now.'

I checked her out more closely; her fringed dark hair came to her jaw line and her skin had that dusky, light brown olive look. Her nose was slightly hooked but attractively so. Her hazel eyes were most appealing. She had a keen intelligence which was obvious from the start.

'How long you here for?' I asked.

'Two weeks.'

'Staying in the village.'

'Apartments up near the Acropolis. Yourselves?'

'Got a place where the road divides, along from there.'

'Where's that?'

'You know, the main path to the beach, the small beach.'

'Pallas beach.'

'What is it called?'

'Pallas, that's the name of the small beach.'

'Didn't know it had a name.'

The other girls stood up to leave, waiting on Janet to finish chatting with me.

'Now you know, that's where we go in the day.'

'We've been going to the main beach. Maybe I'll swim over to you tomorrow, pay a visit.'

'Do, we'll be there, by Scala restaurant.'

'So you won't mind if I do?'

'No, not at all.'

'Right, expect me tomorrow.'

"See you later." They all said and wondered off. The two blokes went inside to the 404 a little peeved.

'You were getting on well there McCloskey.' Said Mark.

'She was nice wasn't she?'

'Why did you let her go?'

'What was I supposed to do? Handcuff her to the stool?.'

'Yes.'

'Well I'm going to see her tomorrow for your information.'

'Oh yeah? When?'

'When I feel like having a swim.'

We went up to Luna bar and chatted to the lovely Ulla, who looked very pleased to see us. She was like that to everybody of course, just that we were besotted with her so thought otherwise; we were somehow special and different in our imaginings. I related the story of Mark's earlier sleeping sounds to her, Ulla was intrigued.

'How does he make these noises?' She asked.

'Like the donkey. You know, eyaah,eyaah,eyaah.'

'Oh yes. And this was coming from where you say?'

'It sounded like he had a donkey in the room.'

'He had one in the room?'

'That's what we thought.'

'What was he doing with it in the room?'

I don't know what it was about that question, but it tickled my funny bone and I reacted loudly with:

'Eeyaah, eeyaaah, eeeyaaahhh!' Heavily suggesting some depraved form of beastiality. The four of us burst into uncontrolled laughter. I further added,

'In fact when I walked in (laughing) the poor animal was in

bed (laughing) smoking (laughing)

a (laughing)... cigarette.'

Tears were streaming down my face I was laughing so hard. So were the others. Mark was exclaiming,

'It's not true, it's not true.'

I then related to Ulla the story of Mark's bare arse sticking out the bed and how the neighbours had reacted to the noises and drawn their own conclusions, and we had a good laugh about that too. The "eeyaaah" became our in-joke that night, with Ulla taking particular delight in using it for some reason. About one am we left to go to Arches and Qupi's, as we passed the Sixties bar the staff in there saw us and shouted and waved for us to come in; but we just waved back pointing forwards.

'What was that all about?' Asked Mark.

'Because of last night of course.'

'Why, what happened last night?'

'We were in there and you brought the house down with your performance.'

'What performance?'

'The John Travolta routine, on the dance floor.'

'Who me?'

'Yes, you!'

'I don't remember that. Did I piss everybody off?'

'No, you had everybody in stitches. You livened the place up when it was dead on it's knees.'

'Me?'

'Even Roger was impressed, hey Rog'?'

'I was.'

'Really? Was I that good?'

'Fanbloodytastic.'

'Maybe we should go back in there for a drink?'

'Later, when they've had sufficient time to recover.'

'Alright, wish I could remember it though.'

'Mind you, I don't know what that crowd from Germany is
going to do without you tonight.'

'There was a crowd from Germany?'

'Yeah, they'll be in there now sitting quiet as a mouse waiting
for your appearance, ready for you to spark them into
dancing again.'

'Well let's go back there.'

The idea of an expectant audience was almost too much for the actor
in Mark to quell, I had to adjust what I'd said to deflate his call to duty.

'They won't be there.'

'I thought you just said-'

'That was their last night. They were leaving on a
jet plane today.'

Mark and I spontaneously broke out into singing "Leavin' on a Jet
Plane". Roger instinctively breaking away from us, to appear separate to
those watching.

Arches was busy as usual, I spotted Janet and her friends but they
were busy being chatted up by some blokes. A small stag party walked in
sporting party wigs of long black, colour braided dreadlocks, a la Winnie
Mandela, they were good fun and we got talking to them. Somehow they
had become separated from a larger group between Lindian House and
Sixties Bar, which is a bit like getting lost from your Mum in the corner
shop. Not only that, but the entire group had also managed to lose the
bridegroom during the course of the drunken trail. Last anyone could

drunkenly recall seeing him was in a nameless bar, in the clutches of three decidedly naughty looking women. In fact the group had been searching for him when they themselves became divided. It was clearly a night of untold merriment for I couldn't stop laughing; and my jaw was hurting as a result. Bedsides, the wigs were funny objects in themselves, appearing to have a life of their own in the way they shimmered and moved. One look at Mark and you could tell he was desperate to own one. He even offered to replace the missing bridegroom in fair exchange; now there was an offer.

Our allocated time up in Arches, we wished our new found friends the best of luck and said our good byes. Stepping out of the two door chamber, we bumped in to Ulla waiting to come in.

'Where are you going?'

'Qupi's.'

'How is it here?'

'Very busy.'

'What will you say if I come with you?'

Roger suddenly did the donkey noises and we all laughed once more at poor Mark's expense, but then again he had bought it on himself. In fact the donkey jokes just kept coming.

'You did get rid of the donkey didn't you?' I asked him.

'Yes, I put her in Roger's room, after he said for the price we should hold on to it for another night.'

'Sensible, especially if we don't pull tonight.'

Changing the subject completely, while Roger and Mark traded donkey insults at each other, I pried into Ulla's emotions,

'You and Nikos okay?'

'Yes, he is very sorry and I accept for now.'

'Be careful.'

'I have not slept with him last two nights, so I will see.'

She wasn't stupid Ulla and she certainly trusted me with confidences, but whether there was any more to it I didn't push to find out.

Coming down the path towards us, zigzagging from one wall to the next, was a very drunk attractive girl in her early twenties. Her ample breasts almost spilling out over her tight low cut dress.

'I know this girl.' Said Ulla quite concerned.

The girl missed a step and fell to the ground with a horrible smack sound. We all rushed to her aid.

'Dee, it's Ulla, are you okay?'

'I'm going home, I'm mashed.'

'Let's get you up first.' I said.

'I am fucking, fucking pissed out of my head.' She said stuffing her breasts back in place after we lifted her up.

'You know her?' I asked Ulla.

'Yes, she works here, she lives not far.'

'She's going to need help getting home.'

'No, I can make it on my own.'

'You can't, you're that pissed you'll fall again.'

'He is right Dee, we must help you home.'

Step forward Mark, the knight in shining armour now appearing as Lancelot in Lindos; "Fear not fair maiden for I Mark of Londinium, shall escort you back to your castle and lay your wearied soul to rest, and close the drawbridge behind me when I leave." Or words to that effect. And her reply to such fair and honest samaritan work?

'Fuck off, I'm not shagging. I've had enough of shagging.'

'He's not going to shag you, he's just going to walk you home.

Trust me he's a good man he means what he says.'

'I'm not trusting anybody. Fucking toe rags. Fucking liars.

I've fuckin' had it with them, they can all piss off.'

'Mark, just take her home, go on mate. She needs help.'

Why I was prompting Mark to escort her I have no idea, what with his talent for not knowing where he was, it would be the blind leading the blind. It's possible she could lead the way but after that, Mark would have no idea how to get back.

'Come on love I'll walk you home.'

'No, shitting hell leave me alone, I'm not getting fucked.'

'I don't want to fuck you.' Said Mark gallantly.

She leaned against the wall and lifted up each leg to take her shoes off, then barged her way through us, to carry on weaving down the path.

"Be careful, take care!" We all shouted; and she lifted her shoes up in the air, as she made for the next wall and bounced off it. As she passed a group of Greek guys by Arches, something must have been said and she threw her shoes at them.

'FUCK OFF!' She screamed.

'Well we tried.' I said.

'She is very drunk, more so than before. I hope she is okay.' Said Ulla.

We carried on to Qupi's, whereupon we walked straight into the missing stag group and explained ourselves and where their allies were. The bridegroom was still missing, presumed in trouble somewhere, but none of them were unduly worried. I spotted Nikos behind the DJ booth.

'Nikos is working here tonight?' I said to Ulla.

'Monday and Tuesday yes.'

That's a shame I thought; I hope he doesn't think I'm giving you far too much attention and he get's all Greek and macho, and decides to attack me with a knife to protect his long founded honour. Was she worth fighting such an action? Well naturally, she was an angel after all. One thing with Nikos being the DJ though, was we knew him, so we could request music he would play. Instead of the usual dance stuff we got a rock vibe going. And soon enough, we were up dancing the night away; ribbing Roger about his dance moves; letting it all hang out and acting the goat; pure unadulterated fun. I went to the small bar to get another round of drinks, the stag group had left. As I waited, the door opened and in walked three dangerous women with a very drunk bridegroom, wig still in place. Interestingly he was wearing a white vest and aside from his head it appeared that his entire torso, arms, and neck were saturated in tattoos. "Wonder what the missus looks like?" I thought. From what I could tell, he hadn't a clue where he was and who he was with. Given the look and intentions of the women, chances were he was in trouble. The kind of trouble most males fantasize about. Poor bugger, I hope the wedding went off okay, otherwise it would have been an expensive night for not knowing anything.

Twenty minutes later I was back out on the dance floor, when Mark appeared wearing a prized rasta wig.

'Where the hell did you get that.' I shouted.

'Some bloke gave it to me outside.'

I looked in to the small bar, the groom and women had gone. I turned back to see Mark or rasta Mark as he now called himself, talking like Lenny Henry doing a rasta. Women were all around him; God he looked funny. The wig ended up being passed around at stages, so various people got to wear it including Roger, Ulla, Nikos and myself. Fun, I guess, is all about making a fool of yourself.

A Safe Occupation...

I awoke the next morning to the sound of cleaners outside, our German and Hungarian friends had departed and the hard working ladies were busy turning out the rooms ready for the next intake. Roger and I made the beach around one pm, after some hearty breakfast at the Bluebird cafe with it's great vantage of the main beach.

'Well we didn't have to call the Midnight Donkey last night.'

'How did he get home?' Asked Roger.

'Came back with us didn't he?'

'Don't remember that bit.'

'Remember the rasta bloke with the jet black dreadlocks.'

'Hmmm.'

'Him.'

'Thought his legs looked a bit white for a Jamaican.'

'Wonder if the stag party hooked up with the groom?'

'Oh yeah, forgot about that. Doubt it.'

'No, I saw the bloke with the women in Qupi's. That's where Mark got the wig from.'

'I know I was there. I doubt it, because when we went and got a gyros-'

'We got a gyros after the club?'

'Yes.'

'I don't remember that.'

'You were busy talking to Ulla.'

'I remember that.'

'And?'

'I told her she should stop messing about with Nikos and have me instead, while there was still time.'

'Did you really?'

'Did I fuck. I think I offered to walk her home but she said no, so there, tell's you everything.'

'She likes you though.'

'I like her but nothing's going to happen.'

'Why not?'

'Just isn't is it?   Anyway, what about the Groom?'

'He and the women walked by the gyros shop.'

'Really?'

'And it didn't sound like they were taking him to his place.'

'So what you think happened?'

'I bet he's waking up about now, wondering why his hands and feet are handcuffed to the bed.'

'And why three naked women wearing long pvc gloves are lying next to him.'

'Yes and why it is his knob is painted red and it's really sore.'

'They were a bit dominatrix looking weren't they?'

'Looked like strippers to me.'

'High end ones. Here, you don't think they were hired by his mates do y'er? That it was all a set up?'

'If so, I wish I had mates like that.'

'Me too.'

Roger and I must have been on the beach for a couple of hours, when I decided to make good on my promise of swimming over to Janet and the girls on Pallas beach. Which I did, catching them by surprise and feeling a bit like an interloper; a dripping wet one. I stayed briefly having a quick drink with them.

'Did you go to the clubs last night?' Janet asked.

'Went to Arches.'

'We were in there.'

'I saw you but you looked busy.'

'Oh aye, we were. We're all feeling a bit delicate today.'

'Did you go anywhere else?' Asked the one called Claire.

'Went to Qupi's.'

'Was it busy?'

'Not like Arches but we had a blast up there; great fun.'

'Paying for it today hey?'

'A little, we've been here a few days now, so I'm slowly adjusting to the alcohol intake.'

'I wish we were.'

'Out tonight?'

'Oh yeah.'

'Hopefully see you then.'

I left them to sleep it off and got back in the water, taking a longer route back to get some exercise in, building up my strength in case anything happened that evening; I just had that feeling.

Mysteriously, Mark never came to the beach to get his money; nor paid the Sunburnt Arms a visit; nor the gyros shop a trip; nor, though we were convinced of it, even came to search high and low for us. He had in fact slept until four pm and spent the interim time lounging under the porch; incredibly, reading a book and smoking a packet of cigarettes in the absence of drink.

'You thin lazy bastard. Four o'clock?' I told him.

'What time did the donkey leave?' Asked Roger helpfully.

'Fuck off.' Answered Mark trying not to laugh.

'So with the others leaving, we've got the whole place to ourselves hey?'

'I think there's some people above us.'

'I mean down here.'

'It's just us, yeah.'

'Let's have a party then. We'll get a barbeque set up and roast a pig. Drinks bar over there, disco on the top right terrace.'

I was getting carried away with myself but it was entirely feasible, something I would have done when I was twenty.

'Got any money? I need a drink.' Said Mark shaking quite badly, clearly enthused by my proposal.

'I've got a better idea, I'll get some beers from the market now and then we can all go out together tonight and start off with a meal somewhere, hey?'

He mulled the proposal around in his tin can, until the ball bearing had stopped moving around.

'See if they've got any cider will you?' Oh, Oh.

'Yes m'lud, anything else m'lud.'

'I need a lighter; for some reason I've lost mine. Get me the one with the blue light yeah?'

'Blue light?'

'You know.'

'No.'

'Yes you do.'

'I don't.'

'You fucking do.'

'Alright I do, two of those?'

'No one.'

'But you'll lose one by the end of the night.'

'No I won't.'

'I bet you a shot of Jagermeister you do.'

'You're on.'

'By the way the loser gets to drink the shot.'

'Hey?' Said Roger.

'There's nothing worse than Jagermeister.'

'Oh I see.'

'Apart from raki.'

'Hurry back with the beers.' Said Mark.

'Thought you wanted cider?'

'Cider then.'

They did sell cider at the market but I ignored it's presence and told Mark they had none, for all our sakes. The early part of the evening was spent hanging outside, lounging around drinking slowly and snacking. We crapped on about this and that, with Roger and I reminding Mark of his humorous indiscretions so far on the trip.

'When?' He answered indignantly each time.

Indulged ourselves in a couple of Roger's scenario games i.e. 'If you were to chose the time you would be born in, which would it be?'. I plumbed for 1947 so that I could have enjoyed the sixties and seventies more fully. Followed by 'During the second world war what service would you have chosen to fight in?'. Mark immediately answering, 'Easy, the air raid service.'

'You mean an air raid warden?'

'Yes.'

'You bloody coward.' I said provocatively.

'They had bombs dropping on them didn't they?'

'Wasn't quite the same as active service was it?'

"Course it was active, they had to go house to house while the bombs were dropping. I know, my uncle was one.'

'Was he?' Asked a disbelieving Roger.

'Yes he was.'

'Where?'

'Ware.'

'Where?'

'Ware; I told you.'

'Where's where?'

'It's in Hertfordshire.' I said.

'It's a place is it?'

'Haven't you ever heard of Ware?' Teased Mark.

'Not lately no.'

'Shakespeare mentions it.'

'Who?'

'Piss off.'

'I bet you decided on air raid warden because of Dad's Army.'

'No, I wanted to be one because you could go around telling people that you didn't like, Roger, what to do and they'd have to do it.'

'Yeah I can see that, give you a black uniform and tin hat and you'd turn into a right little Hitler. Anyway, air raid service doesn't count.'

'Doesn't count?'

'I said which service would you fight in remember?'

'What does that mean?'

'The verb to fight, protect your country and all that.'

'I know what it means Roger, do you?'

I had to change the subject, things were getting heated.

'What's happening about leaving on thursday?' Do we know what time the ferry leaves?'

'Four o'clock.' Roger answered.

'In the morning!?' Exclaimed a worried man.

'No, afternoon.'

'Can't wait.'

'Thought you couldn't take another ferry journey?' I asked.

'I never said that.' Roger and I chuckled at his gall.

'It's ten hours long again.'

'Ten hours?'

'Same as before.'

'Is it? Don't we go to Syria first?'

'Syros.'

'Syros then.'

'No.'

'So that's why it's ten hours?'

'Tell me Mark, when they beamed you down from the
spaceship did they give you the full package or did
they skimp on the download?
The 1.0version or lower?'

'Didn't count on the cider fucking the software up did they?' Said
Roger.

'That's it, that's what happened, they didn't account for the
corrosive effect.'

'What are you two on about?'

'Don't be coy, we know the truth now. We won't let anybody
know; come on what's your real alien name?

'Piss off!'

'So it's Pissoff. Welcome to earth Pissoff. And where do you
come from?'

'Screw you.'

'From Screwyou; and which constellation is that?'

'Your arsehole.'

'Yourarsehole? No, never heard of it. Could you point it out
for us?'

'If I was an alien in disguise, you'd be the first to know it believe me.'

'Why what would you do to us?' Asked Roger expectantly.

'You know what I would do to you.'

'I don't, that's why I'm asking you; you're the alien.'

'I'd reduce you to the size of a subuteo player and keep you in a box.'

'I know what I'd do.'

'What?'

'Turn you into a donkey and get you to carry fat people up to the Acropolis.'

Roger was so pleased by this he started laughing, heartily.

'Fuck you.'

'Anybody want another beer?' I asked.

A Very Public Romance...

The three of us were hungry and a gyros wasn't going to hack it, so we found a restaurant along the drag and ordered three steaks. Which sadly were a bit chewy and obviously out of the freezer; an end of the season job. They offered us the roof terrace but for some reason beyond our thinking we turned it down, who wants to go up on the roof?. Intending to go straight to 404 we diverted into Antika and bumped into Janet and the girls. Our earlier drinking and chatter had put us in the right frame of mind and we were informal, convivial and funny with them; or at least I was with Janet.

'When is it you're leaving?' She asked me.

'We have to leave thursday.'

'You going to Arches or Qupi's later?'

'I should think so, why?'

'We'll probably be there.'

'I hope so.'

'Really?' She asked.

'Yes really.' I answered.

'Well, see you there then.'

'Why, where you going now?'

'Oh, we're meeting up with some friends in another bar.'

I was about to say we'll come with you but thought better of it, clearly plans had already been made. During this time Mark had spent a large part of it not present and I asked Roger if he knew where he was. 'No.' He blurted, trying not to interrupt his attention from a certain girl he was talking to. Eventually Mark appeared.

'Fuck.' He said.

'Where have you been?'

'I was locked in the damn toilet.'

'All this time?'

'Yes!'

'How?'

'What do you mean how? I closed the door and it wouldn't open when I finished.'

'Well did it have a sliding lock on the door?'

'No, it had one of those knobs that you turn.'

'So how'd you get out?'

'I tried calling Roger's mobile but there was no answer.'

'Rog', Rog'; check your phone.' Reluctantly he did.

'I've got five missed calls from Mark and a message.'

He opened the message, it read: "Help! Stuck in bog. Call 999, Mark."

'999?' I asked.

'That's what you call in an emergency.'

'In Greece?'

'I don't know, do I?'

'Right; so then what?'

'I had to start banging on the door.'

'And did anybody come?'

'Yes, eventually.'

'How long were you banging away for?'

'Fucking ages.'

'Do you want a shot?'

'YES!'

'Hard luck mate. Ah well, it's all over now.'

We both broke into singing, "Because I use to love her, but it's all over now.." And for all of a few seconds became the center of attention in Antika. Mark downed his shot.

'God, that was almost as bad as the other night.'

'The other night?'

'Yes, the last time in here.'

That was another cue for breaking out into a Stones song but we resisted the temptation, coming so soon after the recent outburst.

'Why, what happened then?'

'I took a huge dump in the ladies toilet.'

'The ladies?'

'Gents was busy and I couldn't wait.'

'So? Nothing wrong with that.'

'Yes, but there was a problem. It wouldn't flush after.'

'Hang on, it wouldn't flush or you broke it?'

'I sort of broke it.'

'How?'

'The handle snapped off.'

'How did the handle snap off?'

'I think I pulled too hard on it.'

'Well as long as nobody knew it was you.'

'But they did.'

'Who did?'

'The girls waiting outside the door.'

'Holy shit Mark.'

'Believe me, the smell was holy.'

'So you blocked the ladies toilet up. Broke the flush
mechanism and fouled the air with an horrendous
reek. And now you just broke the lock on the gents?'

'I didn't break the bloody thing, it was already buggered.'

'You know what my advice is?'

'What?'

'Don't use the toilets here.'

'I won't.'

'Imagine it, you could be allowed to drink in here but barred
from using the bog. A new one even for you.'

We moved on to the 404 and sat at the bar chatting to a less than busy
Rob.

'Your sister and the kids make it back to Australia okay?' I asked him.

'Yesterday; yeah their fine thanks. When do you lot leave?'

'Thursday.'

'Make sure you come in tomorrow night and I'll buy
y'er a drink.'

'Thanks we will.'

'You going back to Athens?'

'By way of Syros and Paros first.'

'What island chain is that?'

'Cyclades.'

'Oh yeah, never been me'self, what's it like?'

'Syros is okay but Paros is really nice.'

'Better than Lindos?'

'No, but Paros is an island not a place on its own. If I was to put Lindos on Paros then you'd have a perfect match.'

'You coming back?'

'Next year, already booked it in my head.'

'You blokes got laid since you been in Greece?'

'Not yet.'

'What's keeping y'er?'

'Circumstance.'

'You can't possibly go back to England saying you didn't get laid.'

'Trip's not over yet, we live in hope.'

'Some more than others mate.'

I took out a cigarette, went for my lighter but then had a notion.

'Mark, have you got a light?'

'Somewhere.'

He searched his pockets but without success.

'What's the matter, you lost the lighter I bought you already?'

'No, it's here, I know it is.'

He stood up and did his patting down looking-for-a-lighter exercise, front and back, but still had no joy.

'You've got it haven't you?'

'Absolutely not.'

'I had it. Bollocks.'

'Rob, can we have a shot of Jagermeister. Mark's buying.'

As we walked up towards Sixties bar and Luna I showed Roger that I did indeed have Mark's lighter.

'Did you take it?'

'No, I found it on the floor in Antika.'

'What you going to do with it?'

'Get it back to him without noticing.'

'Why? He'll only lose it.'

We walked in to Sixties bar to be warmly greeted, Mark still a little perplexed by his sudden notoriety. Unfortunately the place was busy and Mark wasn't wasted yet, so any expectant replay of that night before was mistaken. We still got a free shot of Raki out of it though, fame does have it's rewards.

'Oh God, do I have too?' Asked Mark imploringly.

'Yes, we're on tour remember.'

Next stop was Luna and our nightly ogle at Ulla, who every night on first meet was so fresh and inviting; both mind and body. Thus distracted, I managed to place Mark's lighter in his back pocket unnoticed. As we were all giggling about the stag party wig the previous evening, and Mark's recent difficulties in Antika, Mark bawled 'A-HA' And held triumphantly aloft in his upstretched arm the lighter.

'See McCloskey I did have it. You owe me a Jagermeister.'

'What is this?' Asked Ulla intrigued.

I explained the circumstances minus the bit about finding it and placing it back on Mark.

'Where'd you find it?' I asked.

'Back pocket.'

'But you looked there.'

'Not hard enough.'

'Sure you didn't pick one up in Sixties?'

'I would never take another person's lighter, never.'

'No, not knowingly.'

'That's what I mean. Go on then.'

'Go on, what?'

'Get me a Jagermeister.'

'Are you sure?'

'Positive.'

'Would you like one Ulla?'

'Oh yes.' She replied.

So I got five Jagermeisters to include Perri, but not Nikos who was absent. We did the "Yamas" bit and I got invited around to do the brass plate thing. On my first stroke I tried to do a Perri and hit it with all my might, but instead missed it, lost my footing and crashed into the side of the bar, knocking over some bottles and glasses. Suitably chastened by the onlookers hoots of derisive laughter I tried again, and missed yet again. More derision was hurled my way by so called friends.

'You need some glasses mate.' Mark shouted.

'Should have gone to Specsavers.' Said Roger.

"Fuck; I've got to hit this, I look a right tit. How hard can it be?" I said to myself and then pushed the stakes even higher.

'Okay you may laugh, but I'll tell you what I'll hit it while it's moving instead.'

'Go on then, Bullseye.'

'You do it and I'll get another round of shots in.' Said Roger.

So I swung the plate like a pendulum and watched it carefully marking my spot, knowing that if I missed I would draw the biggest humiliating cheer of the night; nay the trip.

'We're waiting; anytime you like.' Shouted a vengeful Mark.

The moment came and, God knows how, I managed to hit the plate smack dab middle as it was moving away and the thing went flying up in the air. So high, that it's chains came off the ceiling hooks and the plate went crashing over onto the dance floor, narrowly missing a couple of customers. Initial reaction was shock and surprise but was quickly followed by hysterical laughter. Perri didn't look too pleased though, going over to rescue the bar's prize possession, like a father seeing to his injured son. But on inspection nothing was broken, it just needed to be hooked up again, which he did; then looked and smiled at me.

'Last time you hit the plate, no more.'

We shook hands and he challenged me to an arm wrestle, which I'm useless at, and he won in easy fashion and was very proud about. Hercules still reigned supreme. Before I left the bar's confines I picked up Ulla in my arms and jokingly said, 'I claim my prize.' And went to walk out with her until putting her down.

From Luna bar we went straight to Qupi's. With all the drinks, especially the shots, we were flying high. Nikos was DJ and spotting us started to play some rock tunes, like bees to honey we were soon up on the dance floor and the bar, dancing away in mad fashion; then Janet appeared with Claire and they got caught up instantly into our whirlwind of energy, fun and laughter. Nikos played The Stones "Brown Sugar" and Mark and I started doing a Mick Jagger impression together, going up and down the room, one arm raised, one arm posed on the hip, neck cocked, and mouth puffed out, strutting for all it's worth. The people in there were clapping and cheering, and upon finishing I collapsed into Janet's arms.

'God that was so much fun.'

'You were great, the both of you.'

'Yeah?'

'Yeah.'

Drawn to each other, we kissed long and hard without a care for our surrounds and upon finishing laughed at the fact. I could hear Mark saying, 'What's McCloskey doing?' And I answered, 'What comes naturally. You should try it sometime, it's good for you.'

Because Roger was getting on with Claire and I was clearly taken with Janet, Mark felt a bit out of it and for the better part of valour decided to leave. Being rat-arsed may have been a reason too.

'I'm going.' He said with everybody ignoring him.

'Okay then, ignore me.' And he trooped off to the door.

'MARK!' I shouted. He turned to look, almost falling over in the process.

'Don't wait up.'

'Good luck, you deserve it mate. She's a nice girl,

treat her well.'

'Where's he going?' Asked a belated Roger.

'Home mate.'

'Ten to one he doesn't make it.'

'He must know the way by now, give him more credit

than that.'

'Should have called the Midnight Donkey.'

'No, he'll make it.'

Forty five minutes later, with the four of us plied with more drink and

a few moves on the dance floor, of which Janet did say about Roger at one

point, 'Does he dance like that on purpose?' I felt obliged to scold Roger

over his prediction.

'See, he made it back, you were wrong. He does know how to

get home.' And just at the moment I said it, I looked up to see Mark

talking to Janet.

'What are you doing here?'

'I'm a little boy lost.' He said convincingly.

'Indeed.' I replied as he sunk into Janet's embrace, eyes closed.

'Ahh.' She said.

'You can cut that out.' I said.

'I need to get home.' He cried.

'Can he not find his way around?' Asked Claire.

'Not at night for some strange reason.'

'Lindos can be like that at times. You can get lost in these

back areas, 'specially when drunk.'

'Shall we walk him home?' Asked Janet.

'Spiffing idea.'

'Spiffing? Are you a toff now then?'

'Yes, toffs in disguise finding out what common people do.

Isn't that right Mark?'

'I don't care, just get me home.'

'Come on then let's go.' I waved.

Janet smacked me playfully on the bottom hard.

'Hey you, careful.'

'Why? What y'er gonna' do?'

'Put you over my knee and spank you hard.'

'You wouldn't dare.'

'Wouldn't I?'

'Being a toff you probably would, they like that sort of thing.'

'Especially with common people.'

'One more word from you and I'll snog your face off.'

'Go on then.'

We stood there kissing until we heard, "Hey come on

you two."

I looked to see the rest of the gang by the door waiting for us.

'Go, we'll catch up.' I said, so they left leaving us chest to chest

staring into each other.

'Hey.' I said.

'Hey.' Janet replied.

'You are lovely.'

'You're not bad yourself.' She smiled.

'Are we going to spend the night together?'

'I'd like too, only problem is I'm sharing a room with Claire.'

'Yeah, I'm sharing with Mark.'

'Kiss me again.' She said.

'Love too.'

So we kissed blissfully, squeezing tight together.

'God, do you always kiss like this?' She asked.

'You make me.' I replied.

'When you swam over today and came out of the water,

I wanted you right there and then.'

'Really?'

'Yes, you got me all hot and bothered.'

'Well I'm glad I swam over.'

'So am I.'

'I've got an idea.'

'What?'

'I'll ask Mark to sleep out on the terrace.'

'You can't do that.'

'Why not? There's nobody else there. Make a bed up for him
outside, he'll be fine.'

So plan devised, we left Qupi's and headed towards the studio, taking
our sweet time getting there because we kept pausing to satisfy our need
for each other, amidst the romantic surrounds of Lindos. After an age we
made it there and found Roger and Claire cuddled up together, watching
the stars above.

'Aye, aye.' I said.

'Where have y'er been?' Asked Claire.

'Making our way here.'

'You'd have been quicker comin' the long way around.'

I went into the room to talk to Mark and found him splayed out atop his bed, dead to the world.

'Mark, hey Mark.' I shook him, shook him again, shook him further still.

'Mark, for Chris'sake wake up.'

It did no good, he was out for the count, Janet came in.

'I can't wake him.'

'Leave him, let's go to the beach. By the way, have you got condoms?'

I certainly did; so we left the studio behind and went down to Pallas beach, kissing and fondling along the way much like before. We went straight to the waters edge and walked in up to our knees.

'Fancy a swim?' I said.

'No, I fancy you instead.'

She took my hand and led me over to the nearest sunbed.

'Let's do it here or over there on the table.'

The table was a distance away by the boardwalk and prominently exposed.

'Here first.' I said with relish and sense.

As we started preliminaries and items of clothing were being loosened two frolicking young couples came charging noisily down the hill.

'Hold on.' I said.

'Come on, who cares?' Janet replied, divulging further a desire to screw in the open and not care who's watching. I wasn't adverse to public sex, having once had intercourse in a busy department store changing room with a girl I'd just met, but I needed a bit more privacy at that moment.

'Wait a minute.'

'Ignore them.' She whispered in my ear before kissing.

But I couldn't; especially as the couples came right by us, unaware of our situation. They ran along the beach shore and on to the jetty, uninhibitedly laughing, shouting and screaming. Followed by the sound of them diving into the water. Janet pulled me towards her.

'I want you, do it now.' She implored erotically.

Upon which Janet and I resumed our love making. We got right down to the point of no return, when of all things a scooter bike came down the hill and parked up behind our row of sunbeds and the rider started talking on the mobile looking in our direction, distracting me.

'Don't stop!' Said Janet ready and willing for insertion.

What had been an idyllic situation had turned into a busy location all of a sudden. What was next I wondered? A night time fishing excursion? A troop of Stargazers? More than bloody likely.

'Hold your horses.' I said and I watched as the rider went behind the building. As he did, one of the couples came out of the water nearby in their underwear and played around on the shore.

'We're not having much luck.' I said.

'God I'm ready to explode.' She said annoyed.

'Sorry babe it's too busy for me.'

She took hold of me and kissed me gently.

'Let's find a bed.' She replied softly.

So we put back what we had removed and walked back up the steep hill towards the studio. As we did, my shorts kept slipping down because I had left my belt behind. In fact, if it hadn't have been for my erection they would have fallen down. Janet thought it quite hilarious, as I did, and she was quite free with her hands when helping me up with them. Eventually grabbing hold of my erection to pull me along.

'Let's bring this banana with us shall we?'

As she was doing so, some guy came walking down the hill towards us, fortunately we didn't know him, and he walked on by, pretending not to notice a grinning man being pulled by his penis, as his shorts were slipping down. While the girl doing the pulling was laughing her head off.

Back at the studio, Roger and Claire were inside his room with the door closed. Janet knocked lightly on the door and it opened ajar and she talked in whispers with Claire before the door closed again.

'We can go to our place.'

I should be honest here and say that I had taken a viagra earlier in the night when it looked like things were going to happen. I had never taken one before but was curious what it's effect would be. I was also wary of the not-being-able-to-perform-on-the-night syndrome which happens to a lot of men over a certain age, so before going to the beach I took it, with some reservation I add. Given how big a turn on Janet was anyway the potency of the pill was remarkably swift and lasting, hence the banana episode. Getting to her place it wasn't long before we flung our clothes off and made love. With a harder than hard erection putting a condom on was no difficulty at all. The biggest, excuse the unintended pun, problem if I can call it that, was I could not reach a climax no matter how long I went at it; which for poor Janet was a long time. We would take a well earned break and try again, erection undiminished throughout.

By that time we were totally knackered and fell asleep, to be woken some hours later in entwined naked repose by the cleaner, who scarpered quickly in horror. I got up and went to the toilet, the erection had finally wavered but felt like it wouldn't take much to raise itself. Satisfyingly I urinated and then rejoined sleepy head Janet, cuddling up to her, feeling her smooth skin. The window near to the bed was open with the curtain drawn and fluttering in the light wind. I could see out to the bay.

'What are you thinking?' Asked Janet, eyes closed.

'How bloody marvelous it is right now.'

She smiled and I kissed her, the taste of the evening on our breaths. There was a knock on the door.

'No clean today, it's okay.' Shouted Janet.

'Janet, it's Claire. Can I grab my stuff for the beach?'

'Hold on.' Janet got off the bed, draped the sheet over me, found her knickers and put them on before letting Claire in, who quickly changed into her bikini and bagged everything she needed for the beach and left.

'See y'er later.'

Janet went to the toilet, during which I got up and tried finding my scattered clothes.

'Do you need to go to the beach?' I asked, not wishing to overstay my welcome or ruin her plans, lovers though we had been.

'Soon.' She said coming out, then kissing me with enthusiasm. I was up in no time.

'One condom left.' I said.

'Okay, but go easy, I'm a bit sore.'

I peeled off her knickers, applied the condom and eased into her. Minutes later breathing hard, sweating in the mid-day heat, Janet desperate to hurry me along with her, I suddenly felt my testicles tighten and a great wave of intense pleasure run through me, jolting my body into a tremendous orgasm (another effect of viagra was the amount of semen ejected, it was like opening a mains tap). I collapsed on top of her and we laughed.

'Thank goodness.' I said.

Ten minutes later I said goodbye at the door, knowing that there would be no repeat that night. We were simply consenting adults after some enjoyment without any strings attached, and from here would move on from each other. But I did have a tinge of regret because she was fun and we got on well. Who knows what she felt afterwards. The same probably.

All Our Farewells...

It was our last day in Lindos. It's alluring charms had waylaid us and kept us from fulfilling our objective of further exploration; but we had been willing participants and I for one was glad we had stayed. Departure would come soon enough and we had a return to Paros to look forward to, much could happen yet.

I went to the beach and found Roger.

'Mark?'

'Pub.'

'How?'

'I gave him some money.'

'How much?'

'Twenty euro.'

'Ah well.'

'Good night?'

'Fantastic, yourself?'

'Great.'

'Tell you something about Viagra.'

'What?'

'It makes your knob hurt.'

'Be careful.'

'Of what?'

'Popping one unexpectedly.'

'Really?'

'It can do that for hours after.'

I made a mental note not to look at any sex stirring women on the beach while I was down there, just in case I had cause for embarrassment. Given how hung over I was on every level it was hardly going to happen. In fact the next two hours were spent dozing and recuperating. It was only towards the end of the afternoon that Roger and I took a stroll down to the wooden planked jetty at the end of the beach, where a group of people were having fun running full pelt along it and hurling off into the sea. Seeing this we had convinced ourselves we needed to give it a try. The running part wasn't easy hung over but flinging yourself off the end and plunging into the water was magic and quite reviving. What larks.

Funned out, I lay down on the jetty catching the last bit of warm sun before it vanished behind the hill, I lay there entirely content and alert to the magic atmosphere.

'Is that Paul?' I heard a brummie voice say.

'It could be.' I answered. I opened my eyes to see Gin standing there in a lovely teeny-weeny bikini, barely covering the delicate parts of her athletically shaped body. I could feel a stirring in my loins.

'Are you still here?' She asked.

'Last day, sadly. I don't want to leave.'

'Ah, never mind, that's Lindos for you.'

'When do you go back?'

'Saturday.'

Roger's warning of post uncontrollable erections was coming true, I had to sit up quickly and bring my knees to my chest to hide the fact. I was hoping the conversation would be brief and Gin would leave, but she nattered on in the most pleasant way and I could not help but engage with her. Furthermore she was standing quite close to me and looking up from my enforced position meant I had great difficulty in diverting my sun glassed eyes from the natural focal point, her perfectly formed crotch; followed upwards by her sizable well shaped breasts. It took great composure and strength of thought to keep fixed on her face and the conversation, with all that flesh and sex raging at me.

After Gin left I had to stay sat there for a good thirty minutes before daring to move. If someone asked me the pros and cons of Viagra I would say it's the most assured thing for men since James Bond, but watch out, like a jack in the box it could go off at anytime post-coitus.

For our last evening, Mark, Roger and I went for a mixed grill we'd seen advertised at one of the restaurants on the drag. The main dining room was full so we opted for the roof terrace and it was then that we, after more than a week in Lindos, understood it's virtue - alfresco dining with the street below to look down on. The other busy rooftop restaurants scattered at various levels around the village, and, the stupendous silent presence of the Acropolis. Crazy not to dine any other way really. The mixed grill was good but not great like the one in Falaraki, and it was more expensive but we were in a beautiful spot so who cared? There was certainly no rush to leave, quite the opposite. Conversation revolved around our time in Rhodes and what time we had left in Greece to make the most out of and enjoy.

'When we get to Syros we should do something.' Said Roger.

'Like what? We get there at what time?'

'Two in the morning.'

'Hardly ideal.'

'How about a game of hide and seek with Mark?

'Any thoughts on that Mark?'

Just then, the waiter approached with two crepes for the next table and Mark said in a heavy Glaswegian accent,

'That reminds me I must have a crap myself.'

It was the one and only funny moment of the whole evening, as last night blues were setting in and it was a turn around day. We took Rob's offer of a drink on him at the 404 and said our good byes, then went to Luna and chatted with Ulla; by the time we came to say good bye there, I was finding it hard to hide my sadness at leaving. Lindos had captured my heart and so had Ulla; all three of us really. She had a sparkle about her difficult to forget.

'It has been such fun meeting you guys.' She said just to make us feel worse.

'I will miss you.' But not as much as we were going to miss you I thought. We each gave her a warm hug and kiss on the cheek and when it was my turn there was a little tingle that passed between us and I said,

'Ulla, you made our time here so wonderful. You are lovelier than Lindos.'

'Ahh, you cannot say that.'

'I can.'

'You will come back, I know.' She said kissing me softly on the cheek.

We shook hands firmly with Perri and Nikos and left, but not before Ulla made those donkey noises.

Once Upon a Beach...

The morning came quickly, both Roger and I were up with the lark; restored to relative health by a good nights sleep. I made a pot of tea and we relaxed up on the top right terrace taking in the last morning, the sound of Mark snoring interrupting the tranquility every so often. Our focus was switching now the travel buzz was taking over, we'd be gone from here in a couple of hours to explore Rhodes Town, then we'd be making that long sea journey back to Paros, that's where the urge lay now. Another couple of nights in Tree Tops, another scooter ride around the island; Naoussa, the bay; lot's more to enjoy, the holiday wasn't over yet. Besides, there was never a dull day with Mark around.

Around eleven am, packed, ready to roll we took one last look at our prime situation and headed to the square, amidst the mayhem of the first time day trippers. As we passed the donkey station we made the sounds so beloved by Ulla.

We took the free bus up to the main road and caught a bus to Rhodes town for three euros each, passing through Falaraki on the way.

'Should we call in to Jimmys?' Asked Roger half heartedly.

'And tell him how much we liked Lindos?'

Twenty minutes later we unloaded at Rhodes Town and discovered we could leave our bags at the tourist information office, close to the old walled city. We had four hours to wander before the ferry was scheduled to leave and we still had to buy our tickets. We opted to roam the sea front first, walking up to the main beach with it's concrete diving platform out in the sea. I'd never seen that before but it was a great idea. Heading back we surveyed the most interesting buildings, generally stuff the Italians had had constructed between 1913-1943 when they controlled the island, they included some of the governmental departments. There was also an interesting Ottoman era structure near the small boat harbour, that given it's narrow sea wall entrance seemed the most likely spot for the supposed Colossus of Rhodes which bestrode the shipping of the ancient day. Fact is nobody knows where the Colossus stood or if it even truly existed, only that if it did it was very likely destroyed after an earthquake, sold for scrap and taken to Syria to be used for metalworking. Pity, really, it would be some sight to behold. Rhodes needs to build a new one, now what an attraction that would be. It would make all those tourist trinkets seem consequential.

Entering the old town through a gateway in it's thick defensive walls, we toured the six hundred year old streets, marveling at it's layout of well constructed medieval dwellings, palaces, institutions, churches and mosques; the vast majority still in constant daily use as homes, businesses and places of worship. It is the most intact place of it's type on earth, surviving the outcome of wars and earthquakes, but whether it will survive the coming of Starbucks and McDonalds and other American driven monoculture is another matter. Seeing the mosques made me think that Rhodes and Paros had been occupied or controlled by the Ottomans for four hundred years right up to the twentieth century, yet very little of that culture survived or existed in any obvious form. By the odds many Greek Islanders should be praying to Mecca and speaking Turkish, but perhaps it's a testimony to their long defiance that they don't.

Time came to reclaim our bags and walk to the main harbour, buy tickets and board the ferry. I enjoyed our short tour of Rhodes Town, old and new, given the ongoing conflict in the middle east here was a place significant to a former clash of cultures and the age of turmoil that unleashed, only to become when the dust had long settled, a tourist haven. The boat was the same one we had come on but much emptier, it meant we had the pick of lounge seats in the bar area which we quickly nabbed and set up camp. Mark and Roger were in no mood to celebrate this time round and even though we all imbibed alcohol it was far from excessive for a change. After calling at Kos and Samas and experiencing the inverse return law; which categorically states that the journey back is always quicker than the journey there even though the duration is the same, (I don't know, that's how it is) we neared the island of Syros.

By using the on board internet we'd established that the first available ferry to Paros was not until ten am, so we had a good eight hours to wait in Syros and make do. I was all for finding a private boat sailing there earlier and asking to come along as extra ballast. Roger was dubious about the quest, though not about to dismiss it entirely. Mark was, well he didn't care just as long as we were leading him in the right direction. He even knew that Paros was our destination though the stopping at Syros thing threw him slightly.

'This isn't Paris.' He said upon leaving the boat and looking around him. Mind you he still hadn't got the hang of the name.

At two am on a Friday morning in Ermoupoli we felt sure things would be going on. A lively bar or club within the harbour would do; but when we stepped off the boat the only thing we could find remotely open was a coffee shop near to the jetty. By the time the ferry had loaded and deftly departed and the offloaded traffic had removed into the interior of town and island, we looked like the harbour's only inhabitants; the entire population of the place tucked away from view. We wandered from one end of the 'L' shaped harbour side to the next, looking for an elusive departing boat and a place to bunk down until daylight came and things got back to life. The surrounds felt like a huge Italian film set with the production shut down. Adrift, we rested at a vacant pavement cafe.

'Hope it's busier on a weekend, it's dead.' I said.

'End of the season.' Said Roger.

'But it's a big town and there's bugger all.'

'Coffee?' Asked Mark in a rare moment of sense.

We strolled back up to the coffee shop and sat outside there instead. Minutes passed and a taxi pulled up nearby. Seizing the night, Roger went to talk to it's driver.

'Hey, for fifteen euros we can go to the other side of the island to a place called Galissas Beach.' He shouted over.

'What's it like?' I asked.

'Taxi driver say's it's busy there. Fancy it?'

'How long will it take?'

'Twenty minutes.'

'Okay, sounds better than this.'

So we left our coffees behind and occupied the taxi. The driver was once again a woman but there was no obvious sign of religious fervour this time around. In fact, the three of us were quite struck by how damned young and attractive she was. Curious about our destination and her, we asked a lot of questions; prime of which was "Does Galissas beach have any bars? Clubs?" Followed by, "Are you married?" She answered that Galissas Bay was the most popular beach resort on Syros, with a night life to match. She wasn't married but had a boyfriend who worked on the ferries. She was curious about us too, wanting to know about our trip and what we did back in London.

Before you knew it, the fifteen minute ride through the hinterland was over and she pulled up next to a street lamp at road's end, near to the beach; and waved us goodbye with a five euro tip. Because naturally, she had no change for a twenty euro note. We looked around taking in the apparent lifeless atmosphere.

'Is it me or is it incredibly quiet?' I asked.

As the loudest noise for miles around sped back up the hill towards Ermoupolis, there didn't seem to be a single sign of the promised lively locale.

'Are we in the right place?' Asked Mark un-ironically.

As our eyes adjusted, the beach of the small inlet bay was devoid of sun beds and umbrellas; and the modest set back town was distinctly deserted. The rocky natural amphitheater was shrouded in darkness and many of the scattered resort apartments were shuttered up.

'Where's the sodding night life?' I asked.

'Anybody here even?' Said Mark.

The question reminded me of a TV film years past, about three hikers who encounter a desert town in America with no inhabitants; yet everything is set in place. They try to figure out why and they discover belatedly, that it's been built by scientists to study the impact of an atomic explosion upon it. That's what Galissas felt like at that moment, but without the impending bomb.

'Ever had the feeling you've been duped?' I said.

'Ah, it's not that bad; we can sleep on the beach.' Proposed Roger gleefully.

'The beach?'

'What else can we do? Stuck here now.' He said chuckling.

Roger was right, I only hoped there was some means of returning in the morning in time for the ferry.

We located to the beach and took stock of our predicament. Did we have enough cigarettes? Some but not many. How about liquid? Some but not much. Did we have any scoobydoo? Yes, a big bag of crisps and a large bar of chocolate from the ferry. We searched for any stored sun beds along the beach to lie on but they had all been cleared away until next summer. At least the ground was soft.

'So this is Syros's most popular beach resort?' I said, dryly.

'Apparently.' Said Roger.

'Wonder what the other places are like?'

'It's a nice bay at least.' Said Mark.

'Thank fuck for that, at least something here is

not a dead loss.' Me.

We got the bright notion to start a fire to add to the camp experience ('That's what we did on Golden beach.' Added Mark) but gave up the idea when we determined there was nothing to burn. This did not stop Mark trying to tear down a wooden structure, which clearly had some purpose.

'Mark! What are you doing?' I shouted.

'Getting some wood.' He replied innocently.

'But that's somebody's shed.'

'Call that a shed?'

'Yes, it's got things in it.'

'I'll stop then.'

'Do, because no doubt the only person for miles around is
watching right now and about to call the police.'

So there was us, three travelers sat beneath the starry skies by a
darkened bay, in a deserted resort town, slowly running out of smokes on
the wrong side of the island.

'Galissasfuckingbay.'

'Is it better than Golden Beach Mark?' Taunted Roger.

'You know the funny thing is, I've always wanted to be able to
say that I slept on a beach in Greece and entirely
unexpectedly I am.' I announced to the others with considerable
satisfaction.

'Lucky you.' Answered Roger.

'I bet that taxi driver is having a really good chuckle.' Said I, and made
a passable imitation of her voice, "I got twenty euros taking those three
British malakers to Galissas Bay."

'That's what she'll be saying guaranteed.'

'Think staying in Ermoupoli would have been better?'

'No, strangely enough we made a good decision. It's not
quite what I expected is all.'

Two hours later, the romance of sleeping on a beach in Greece staring
at the cosmos, began to wear a bit thin with the increasing cold. I for one

was shivering, even though I had sensibly changed into my jeans and applied three t-shirts, my white shirt, two pairs of socks, my thin zipped jacket, and, folded my arms and assumed the foetal position. I was contemplating digging a pit and covering myself in sand when I recalled that I had a "space" blanket, no bigger than a box of plasters, in the bag. The thin foil package had been in my possession for countless years and now finally I could justify it's kept status. I was overjoyed by my wisdom in packing it, even though it had lain in the bag for eons. I folded the wrap out and covered myself, throwing sand on the edges to stop the mild wind blowing it away. It helped but it's warming properties were vastly overstated.

Roger and Mark had sensibly brought thermal tops with them and appeared cosy in contrast to me, but whereas Roger and I settled down to sleep, Mark stayed sitting up as if on sentry duty. Nipping at a small bottle of ouzo in the shape of the Colossus of Rhodes and endlessly smoking. Sometime later I stirred from my slumber to re-adjust myself.

'Did you hear it?' Said Mark in a state of high alert.

'What?'

'That roaring noise. Didn't you hear it?'

'No; was it animal, mineral or vegetable?'

'Definitely animal. Came from over there.' He pointed at the beach's end.

'Probably a goat.'

'No way.'

'A donkey?'

'Hell no.'

'A dog?'

'Far bigger.'

'A sabre toothed tiger?'

'Yes, something like that.'

'Well I wouldn't worry about it. Wake me if

anything happens.'

'I'd stay awake if I were you, I'm not kidding.'

'Mark relax, there's nothing there.'

'How do you know?'

'Because I haven't read anything that would make me

assume that wild creatures exist on Syros, or any other

part of Greece for that matter. And if they ever did,

they most likely got wiped out with the Romans.'

'The Romans?'

'Yes.' I said without elaborating.

'Well I'm going to keep look out in case.'

'You do that.'

I resumed my patchy sleep only to be roused a time later by Mark

running about near me.

'Mark, what are you doing?'

'I saw it!'

'Saw what?'

'The roaring thing, it went right by me.'

'What's up?' Asked an awakened Roger.

'Mark claims there's a wild beast on the prowl.'

'What did it look like?'

'Black, big and fast.'

'Did it have four legs?'

'Yes.'

'And a tail?'

'I think so, did it? Yes.'

'Sounds like a black panther.'

'That's exactly what it was.'

'Yeah, their well known around here.'

'I knew it.' Mark said directing it at me.

Roger got up and walked towards the trees.

'Where are you going?' Asked Mark.

'To take a piss.'

'Be careful.'

'I'll try.'

'I mean it. If it get's whiff of you.'

'If I'm not back in five minutes you know it's got me.'

Roger made it back safely and Mark resumed his concerned vigil. If it was true and Mark had witnessed a big cat of the sabre toothed kind, then one of us was for the chop. Unless it was vegetarian, chances were it was hungry and there was three pieces of easy meat conveniently placed out in the open. I could see the daily tabloid headline. "Ex-actor eaten by mysterious animal on Greek holiday beach while friends slept nearby." It had a certain tragic ring to it.

Come daylight, any wind had died and a slow warmth replaced the cold. The water in the bay was smooth as glass and the watch read, seven ten am. Roger and Mark were asleep; as yet none of us had been savaged or mauled or eaten. I went for a piss and then looked around for signs of life. Out of the corner of my eye I saw something flash by, I turned to look and it was then I saw the creature. Black, four legs and a tail, parading right in front of me, teeth bared, licking it's claws. It came forward and brushed against my leg and "Meowed".

'Hello pussy cat,' I said. 'Was it you?'

I strolled along the beach with the curious cat following me, before returning to wake the two sleepy heads.

'Beach party's over boys, we need to think about

getting back soon.'

'Seen anyone?' Asked Roger.

'Not yet. Came across a cat though.'

'Did you stroke it?' Asked Roger.

'Anyone want some breakfast?'

I looked for the bag with the crisps and chocolate. I found it near to Mark, empty, except for torn wrappings and a drained Colossus of Rhodes ouzo bottle.

'What happened?'

'I was hungry.

'You greedy bastard.'

'Don't worry, I'll get some more.'

'Great, can't wait.'

'Got a cigarette?'

'No, we're out.'

'You finished all the ciggies?'

'Yes.'

'You sadistic bastard.'

At the sound of a car, our heads were turned towards the road into town. It came down the hill, rounded a bend and parked outside the facing block of shuttered shops and restaurants. A man got out and went to one of the shutters and unlocked the fastener and raised it. Hallelujah, it was a small market shop.

We decamped and waited outside the shop until it was open for business. We stocked up on liquids, snacks and cigarettes and enquired about getting back to Ermoupoli. There was a bus but it wasn't due 'till nine thirty am; our only option was to call for a taxi from a nearby town, so we got a number and called for one and waited. Roger asked the owner if a black panther stalked these parts but he was rather perplexed by the question.

'If it does, maybe that's why no one is here.' I said.

The taxi came and our big adventure to Galissas beach was over. Soon we were back in Ermoupoli amongst the living and getting truly excited about leaving for Paros.

'I can't wait to get there.' I said to Roger

'I'm looking forward to Tree Tops tonight.'

'Me too.'

Like two confident teenagers pre-empting the good times.

The ferry was already there in harbour; a tall golden vessel ready to carry us home. Not really, it looked more like an aging tub ready for it's engines to break down half way across. Thankfully they didn't on this trip, in fact it was a wonderful crossing; calm sea, low winds, beautiful warm day, relaxed and carefree. Sitting on the deck in our shorts, shirts off, drinking beer to celebrate our return to magical Paros, conversing to two Canadian girls just setting off on their Greek island adventure; still a little unsure of everything and everybody, and hauling along two monster backpacks. If there was a blissful time on the trip it was that short hop to Paros. It, we, everything, felt good. There was an abundance of smiles.

'Cause it's a Fantastic Dayeeya...

Arriving in Parakia we got fished quickly and were taken to Billy's Studios further down from before. We had the ground floor to ourselves, Mark and I back to single rooms. First thing on the agenda for me was to rent a scooter again. I went to see my lady.

'You come back. You are late no?'

'Too much fun.'

'Rhodes, you like?'

'Lindos I like very much.'

'Ah Lindos. Same bike, before?'

'Yes, you have?'

'I have same bike but not the same.'

'Oh really?' I said sort of knowing what she meant.

'Three days after you, the bike is gone. Accident.'

'Kaput?'

'Yes, kaput. You see.'

'The rider okay?'

'Yes, fine, but bike finished.'

I got given a red one this time, older, tattier, but plenty of power; if anything it was better to ride. I went straight to Naoussa, stopped for a drink and came straight back fast as I dared go, which was flat out. I met the boys at the beach and remarked to Mark that other than the previous night's accommodation he hadn't been with us at the sandy shores for days.

'Yes I have.'

'When was the last time?'

'In Lindos.'

'Yeah, the first day; you only came that one time.'

'Are you sure?'

'Positive.'

'What was I doing then?'

'Going to the Sunburnt Arms.'

'Was I?'

'Don't you remember?'

'Not really.'

'Anyway, nice of you to join us.'

'My pleasure.'

'You planning on getting an all round tan before you go back to England?'

'Maybe.'

'Well start by getting in the sun.'

'What's so great about getting brown?' He complained.

'Use my sunscreen, it'll help.' I threw it to him.

'Factor eight?'

'It will give you some colour. Use it.'

'If I get fucking sunburnt.' He said while applying it.

'You won't.'

'No, but if I do.'

'You'll what?'

'I wont like it is all.'

Roger had bought a frisbee and before long we decided to get in the water and play with it. The game devised involved one person throwing to the other two; who fought for control of it and thence became the thrower. Silly but effective. We created such an illusion of fun that two precocious english boys of twelve or so age, asked if they could join in.

'Cane wie playe too?'

"No, Piss off." We said, or rather we didn't and said they could; but soon we had to devise another game, as Mark was as super competitive in fighting for the frisbee with a twelve year old as he was with us. One thing about the boys was their posh voices, they were incredibly upper-class; mater and pater and all that. An oddity in this day and age, a throwback to another England almost.

'Where do you live?' Asked Roger.

'Wie lieve hon thate bote ovar thare.'

'What, all the time?'

'Yas.'

The boat indicated was a big luxurious yacht with a white ensign displayed. Somewhere inside it was a small prep school, with wood panelled walls, tuck boxes, a prominent latin inscription, and a large dose of elocution before assembly and choir practice.

Afterwards we sat at the beach bar and relaxed in the late afternoon sun drinking a cold greek lager or two. A little feral kitten approached us looking for food but all it got was love and affection which it didn't mind. Feral cats were prominent in Lindos and Paros, they form part of the everyday scenery. It's hard to understand why there is such indifference to them amongst the locals, but they do not feel the same gooey attachment that we demonstrate in northern Europe. The average feral cat there is skeletal, scarred, eye infected and wary. Most will not survive beyond a couple of years. The pickings are good in the summer but come autumn, winter and spring only the meanest, strongest and luckiest will survive. Sadly, a harsh attitude prevails. One thing you don't encounter though is feral dogs or dogs in general. Culturally speaking, pets are not a big thing. So for our little playful fellow it was survival of the fittest and chances were, without the milk of human kindness he or she wasn't going to make it.

The boys wanted to watch the sunset at the tennis club bar, so in the time it took them to walk there I went for a quick blast on the bike; heading south of Parakia for about five miles and then returning. As ever no helmet, such irresponsible freedom. When I got to the bar, the owner was telling us that England were playing Macedonia in the group stages of the european championship that night, but having sidelined football for two weeks in favour of fun in Greece, it didn't fill us with the same enthusiasm as he was evidently showing. Nevertheless we made a promise to come and watch it later.

'England are playing who?' Asked Mark.

'Macedonia.'

'Never heard of 'em.'

'Former Yugoslavia, northern border with Greece.'

'He'll be supporting them then.'

'No, the Greeks are upset with them.'

'How?'

'Macedonia is a province of Greece, famous for Philip

and Alexander the Great, but this Macedonia has nothing
to do with that region. They've upset Greece
by assuming the name.'

'How come you know all this shit McCloskey?'

'I read the papers.'

'So do I.'

'When?' Asked Roger.

'Last time we were here.'

'A day old Daily Mail printed in Greece, that you found
in the bin.'

'So?'

'Doesn't count.'

'Why?'

'Because it doesn't.'

'It does.'

'It doesn't.'

'Does.'

'Doesn't.'

'Chris'sake, shut up you two; like squawking parrots.'

'So Mark.' Said Roger.

'Yes?'

'When we get back home are you going to get a job?'

'I might.'

'When was the last time you worked anyway?'

'Not that long ago.'

'What did you do?'

'I drove a van.'

'Courier?'

'Delivery van for an antique shop.'

'Sounded important.'

'It was, I had a lot to look after and none of the
stuff was cheap.'

'How long did that last?'

'About three months, then they had to let me go.'

'How come?'

'Not enough business.'

'Bullshit, Mark you are such a fucking liar.' I said.

'No I'm not.'

'First of all, that job was three years ago. It wasn't an antique
shop but knocked out pine furniture; and furthermore
you told me you stuck it for two weeks before they
fired you for not showing up. Almost as bad as
the cheese shop fiasco.'

'Cheese shop?' Asked an inquisitive Roger.

'You don't know about the cheese shop?'

'No, what happened there?'

'Mark get's a pretty good job running this cheese shop. He
get's it all organized, works hard; is popular with the
customers and becomes quite the authority on cheeses.
Everything's going really well except there's one
small problem.'

'What was that?'

'If it got quiet in the afternoon, Mark would sneak across to
the bar facing the shop and have a drink, while keeping
an eye out for customers.'
'Not every day.' Injected Mark, plea like.
'This all works fine until one fateful day, he walks in to the
bar around three o'clock and bumps into an old pal. And
of course one drink leads to another and before you know
it the bar is closing and Mark is smashed, and the shop
has been left unlocked.'
'So he got fired.'
'Yes, but only because the owner of the shop had to be
there at six the next morning to accept a delivery, and
he finds the door open. Amazingly nothing was
taken, including the till and it's receipts.'
'Is this true?'
'Could be.'
'Wanker.'
'Why do you think he got the nick name Cheesy Mark?'
'Anyway that's the last proper job he had.'
'I worked in the pub for awhile.'
'For how long?'
'A month.'
'What has this to do with anything?'
'Plenty, you're not paying the mortgage Mark.'
'I am.'
'Are you fuck. The rent doesn't cover it so where's the money

coming from?'

'I have my sources.'

'Bollocks.'

'It's not my fault I can't pay the mortgage.'

'Of course it is. You've become a lazy alcoholic git. Instead of fighting for what you have, you've just given up.'

'So what am I supposed to do then?'

'Become a functioning alcoholic like Roger and get a job.'

'You make it sound easy.'

'Well it is once you stop wallowing in the mire.'

'That's from a Doors song isn't it?'

'Don't change the subject.'

'You two are ganging up on me here, I thought we were on holiday?'

'We are, you just need to start seeing the light mate or you are going to be in deep shit soon.'

'I know!'

'So what other jobs did you fuck up on? Any as good as the cheese shop? Tell me.' Asked an unforgiving Roger.

Around eight pm we met up at the pool hall and had a few games before going to the Katerina restaurant close by. Established in the seventies it's essentially a large open air space with a covered roof. Roger had recommended it and he suggested the lamb chops, three orders were duly made. Grilled, they were deliciously charred and the popular place was very warm and welcoming; naturally we shared a Greek salad and two liters of house white. After settling the bill the owner/waiter delivered three shots of raki to the table in our honour and we "Yamased" his hospitality and thanked him for the fare.

We made a beeline for the tennis club bar to watch the football, the owner was pleased to see us and switched from satellite tennis to find the game. It took him awhile, so long in fact, we were sure he'd got us there under false pretences or at the very least had got the date wrong. Finding it, even he wasn't sure on it's source or the language of the commentary.

'Is okay?' He asked.

'It's great, thank you.'

'Maybe I can find on another channel.'

'No, no, it's fine, we're happy with this.'

'You sure?'

'Very sure.'

'Good; you think England will win?'

What sort of question was that we thought; of course they'll win, who the hell are Macedonia anyway?

'England will win two nil.' I said.

Thirty minutes later and the owner was falling about laughing his head off, as little Macedonia were running rings around a very poor performing England; leading two nil and looking very close to scoring a third. While we were squirming in our chairs, fuming at another woeful defeat and wondering how unfair it was that we were not born German, if only for football reasons.

Suitably chastened, we hit a few of the bars along the front before ending up in Tree Tops, where we were instantly recognized and feted by the staff, and the DJ played some tunes once again in our honour; or at least that's how it seemed. Quite what we had done to deserve all this was anybody's guess, other than this is what Greece is about. Once liked, you are never forgotten. There's a generosity of spirit there, that has yet to be overtaken completely by the cynical sophistication of capitalistic society.

We had a great night, just drinking and talking to a large number of people. In particular, I talked to a young Greek couple, both architects, who were desperate to live in Paros all year round but were unable to, due to the lack of work. It was one of those informative chats outside on the steps landing; drinking, smoking, watching the majestic ferries come in and out. Lovely warm lanquid air, moon in the sky, venus to the right of it and rising. Our differences in nationality and age making no difference to the comfort of our conversation.

Grab Me by the Neck Why Don't You?...

Saturday, and the last full day to enjoy ourselves; and what a day it would turn out to be. I did two bike rides, one again around the island and one to Lefkes, a pretty hill town roughly in the center of Paros. Bright eyed and bushy tailed I joined Roger and Mark on the beach. There was no fun and games this time, instead we lounged in the sun drinking beer, with Mark finally getting the idea of factor eight and making the rest of his body match the colour of his head, neck, arms and feet. He left it too late to succeed but at least he reduced the contrast ratio. Meanwhile Roger was brown as a berry and I was several shades of dark pink.

On leaving the beach we played pool and had another beer, and another, and another. The sun had set when we left and headed to the rooms. Mark was well gone. I wasn't far behind, and Roger wanted to keep going.

'No way, I've got to crash for two hours.' I said.

'What time you want to go out then?'

'Ten.'

'Ten?'

'Take it or leave it.'

'I might go eat first.'

'Do.'

'Knock on my door when you're ready.'

'How about you Mark?' Too late, he was already crashed.

I knocked on Roger's door at ten and he was ready to go.

'Did you eat?'

'Yeah.'

'Where?'

'Katarinas.'

'What you have?'

'Lamb chops.'

'Again?'

'Best thing on the menu. They were delicious.'

'Bastard.'

We walked past Mark's door and out the building.

'What about Mark?' Roger asked.

'He won't want to come out, not in the state he was in.'

'Are you sure? It is the last night.'

I wasn't and thought about what I'd said.

'Maybe your right. I'll go check with him.'

I went back and knocked his door, there was no answer; I opened it.

'Mark, hey Mark.'

He didn't stir so I shook him.

'Wake up matey.'

Waking, he sat up.

'Wa's de tym?'

'Ten o'clock.'

'Listen Roger and I are going into town now.'

'You are?'

'Do you want to come?'

'Right now?'

'Yes.'

'I'll meet you, tell me where.'

'You know the windmill?'

'Windmill, okay.'

'We'll be sitting outside in one of the bars along from there.

The same bars from last night remember?'

'Yeah, okay, I'll meet you.'

'The bars along from the windmill, got it?'

'Got it.'

'If we're not there, Tree Tops.'

'Right.'

Roger and I left him to it.

'Think he'll come?' Asked Roger.

'Doubt it, he's pretty walloped.'

'For the best then.'

'I think so.'

We visited three or four of the bars along the front, keeping an eye out for Mark in case he did turn up, but by about eleven thirty we had given up on him.

'Well Mark didn't make it.'

'Didn't think he would.'

'Tree Tops?'

'Tree Tops, but first I've got to grab a gyros.'

There were two options for us to take on the sunday return to Athens and onwards to London. Our easy jet flight was a late one, ten thirty at night. So we could catch the eleven am ferry to Piraeus and get there at three thirty pm; or we could catch the one thirty pm ferry and arrive at five thirty. If we caught the earlier ferry we could have time to see a bit of Athens. Given the day so far, both of us felt it would be wise to have a couple more drinks, say our good byes to the good folk at Tree Tops and take the early ferry and see Athens. The decision was made easier by the fact that the night was fairly flat in terms of social liveliness. So we did exactly that, departing from our favourite bar at around one am, slow walking the deserted shore road back to the rooms.

Turning up the street to the abode, we got around halfway there, when Mark emerged from the shadows a few meters ahead.

'There's Mark.' Said Roger.

'Bloody hell, your right.'

Then in the most angered of states shouted for all to hear.

'YOU CUNTS! YOU FUCKING CUNTS!'

It was difficult to say what was more surprising, Mark's appearance, his active condition or his upset exclamations. My initial reaction was bemusement.

'What?' I said with a jocular air.

'YOU FUCKERS LEFT ME THERE!'

He turned and stormed towards the rooms.

'Hang on, what are you talking about? Mark!'

'FUCK OFF!'

'Jesus Christ. Mark come back, talk to me.'

'CUNTS!'

I ran after him and grabbed him by the arm, he stopped and stood away.

'What the fuck is going on?'

'I WAITED THERE FOR AN HOUR!'

'Waited where?'

'THE WINDMILL!'

'The windmill?' I laughed a bit, realizing his mistake.

'YOU SAID TO MEET YOU AT THE WINDMILL!'

'Mark, calm down. That's not what I said. I said to meet us at one of the bars past the windmill. We were there waiting for you.'

'YOU'RE A FUCKING LIAR!'

Unfortunately that made me laugh too, the misunderstanding seemed humourous. By this time Roger had caught up to us.

'RIGHT I WANT THE REST OF MY MONEY NOW!'

I was pricked by this effrontery.

'What money? Your budget ran out two days ago, you haven't got any money. In fact we've been carrying your fucking arse most of the holiday you wanker!'

'MOVE YOUR FUCKING CARAVAN OUT OF MY PLACE NOW!'

'You're out of order Mark, it's not our fault. It's yours. Why didn't you go to Tree Tops?'

'I HAD NO MONEY DID I? YOU CUNT!'

It was then in a blinding flash that I lost it, a total and utter red reaction.

'Why you fucking arsehole!'

With lightening speed, I grabbed hold of his shirt near the neck and lifted him off the ground and pulled back my right arm, ready to punch his lights out. Mark's tanned face went white and Roger was deeply concerned I'd end Mark's existence.

'Paul, don't!'

The words had good effect, but also Mark's scared pathetic face. I held back the punch and just held him by the neck for awhile longer, before letting go. We were all a bit stunned, then Mark ran towards the room exclaiming,

'That's it, no more, that's it!'

I was a bit shaken myself, it had been a long time since I had been so provoked.

'Fuck I shouldn't have done that but he made me.'

'It's not your fault.'

'Yeah but it's Mark isn't it? Come what may he's a mate.'

'Maybe he deserved it?'

'Nah that wasn't good, he's a fuck up we know that.

Fuck, what is it about first night and last night

with him?'

'What do we do now?'

'I've got to go talk to him, apologize and convince him to

come out for a drink.'

'If you do I'll come.'

'You sure?'

'Last night, why not?'

'Thanks mate.'

I knocked on Mark's door.

'Mark, it's Paul. Look I apologize, I didn't mean for that to
happen. What I did was wrong. Can I come in and chat?
He didn't answer.

'Come on mate I know you're upset but I want to talk to you.'

Without answering, he opened the door and sat down on the end of his
bed all shook up. I sat down next to him.

'Mate, what happened was bad, really bad and there's
no excuse for what I did.'

'You scared me.'

'Mate, I scared myself. I really wanted to hit you, I was
that mad.'

'I thought you were going to.'

'What you said was out of order.'

'You said the windmill.'

'I should have made a better arrangement to meet up.
It was my fault. How long did you wait there?'

'Fucking ages.'

'Sorry mate I fucked up.'

'I thought you two didn't want me around.'

'Absolutely not, whatever gave you that idea?'

'I don't want this to ruin our friendship.'

'Me either.'

'What say we go in to town and have a drink?'

'What now?'

'Yeah now, the three of us.'

'I don't know if I could.'

'Since when did you turn down a drink?'

'Will they still be open?'

'Yeah of course, it's early still.'

'You don't mind?'

'Mark, why would I mind? Let's go out and forget this ever happened, okay?

'Okay.'

I went to Roger's room.

'How'd it go?' He asked

'We're catching the later ferry.'

So the three of us walked back to Tree Tops keeping the mood light and jokey, without a note of provocation other than fun ribbing. When we got there lo and behold, the place was transformed. With people filling the outside terrace and the bar, quite different from when Roger and I left. The bar staff were surprised by our return but glad to see us. The dreadful incident had energized me, possibly Roger too; certainly Mark. The drinks were going down easy and soon we were dancing to the rhythm of the night. It was a great atmosphere. An hour had passed when Mark visited the little boys room and didn't return. Concerned, I went in search and found him outside on the terrace bench talking to some drunk American lady in her early forties. They looked to be getting on like a house on fire.

'There you are.' I said interrupting their laughter.

'Paul! This is the guy I was telling you about, my mate.'

With a big pearly white smile and strong eye contact she put out her hand to shake mine.

'Cassie, nice to meet you. Mark is such a gas, he's been telling me all about your trip.'

'Not the last part I hope.'

'Where were you in America?' Asked Mark.

'California.'

'That's where Cassie's from, isn't it?'

'Born and raised.'

'Oh yeah, whereabouts?'

'Santa Ynez, heard of it?'

'Lived nearby in Santa Barbara.'

'Wow, small world.'

I went and got Roger and we joined them. Cassie was quite good entertainment and picked up on our humour straightaway, but she was flying high; demonstrative, loud, and a bit loopy. Roger got personal.

'So you live here now?'

'Most of the year. Hell, you don't want to live here in the winter, it's dead.'

'Where else do you go?'

'Switzerland, the States, depends.'

'You rent a place here?'

'No, no, we got a house here. Outside Parakia. I married a Greek guy. You wanna' come back?

I got some grass, we can get high if you want?'

'Maybe, we'll see.'

'What about your husband?' Asked Mark all concerned.

'He's away at the moment. Shit he won't mind. I can
take you back. Hell, I'll take all three of you on if you
want, I don't care.'

The offer was firmly on the table, question was should we take her up
on it? Being reticent, no, and anyway Roger and I were thinking along the
same lines; "Mark can get off with her and get laid. What a way to make
his holiday." We skillfully parried the intriguing proposal by being
terribly English and carried on socializing, until she asked.

'Have you guys been to a real Greek place?'

'Isn't this?'

'Oh hell no; I can take you to a real locals bar.'

'Now?' Asked Mark.

'Sure.'

'How far is it?'

'Five minute walk, how about it?'

Well why not? Unlike her last offer, this was one we didn't wish to
refuse. We said farewell to Tree Tops for a second and last time;
promising to return the following year and followed our swinging
American woman to the promised land. Taking a side alley off the shore
road into the old town, we came to a set of wall doors and entered into a
courtyard. First impression was we had invaded someone's private home
but then the door to the house opened and loud greek music could be

heard, along with a noisy crowd. Cassie went and spoke to a guy at the door and then waved to us.

'There's a private wedding party going on but we've

been invited in.'

We walked in to a scene out of a wild new years eve party. There was a mass of people all dressed for the occasion, well lubricated by hours of celebrating. The ground was piled in white napkins and some people were throwing thick handfuls of them into the air. There were no chairs only tables, and we stuck out like a foreskin at a jewish sauna and, truth be told, treated like one. Not that that affected our fun time hostess.

'Follow me there's a table.'

The table she had in mind was smack in the middle of everything. As soon as we reached it, Mark got straight into the swing of things by dancing along with the crowd. I thought I'd better go to the bar and get a round.

'Cassie what do you want to drink?' I asked.

'Save your money, it's on the house. We'll order from

the waitress.' Roger and I were seriously impressed by that bit of good news. Cassie signaled for a pretty girl to come over.

'Paul, Roger, this is Erin, she's American too.'

'Not another god damn yank?' I said playfully.

'Hi, great to meet you.' She purred. 'What can I get you?'

'Your'e the waitress?'

'Yeah.'

'Don't you have to speak greek in here?'

'I do.'

'Wish I did. But I've learnt the most important word.'

'What's that?'

'Yamas.'

She gave a big beam of a smile and returned five minutes later with our ordered drinks, plus two unordered shots each, herself included. Grabbing Mark's person, we stood around the table and did the shots with a loud "Yamas" each time. Ten seconds later and Erin produced two big packs of white napkins. Like kids on a xmas morning we tore at the packaging, then like seasoned Greeks we picked up handfuls and threw them in the air. And so it went.

Six shots and assorted drinks later, I dropped a pen on the floor and bent over to pick it up, as I did I felt a hand goose my balls. I looked back to see Roger and Mark laughing wondering which one was responsible, when Cassie's face peered into view.

'It was meee!' She happily confessed.

Out of earshot I talked to Mark.

'Mate she's hot to trot, here's your big chance.'

'But she's married.'

'You could have fooled me.'

'Think I could?'

'Too bloody right you could.'

'I don't know.'

'Chris'sake she's ready and willing, get stuck in.'

'You're right.'

Roger and I watched as they danced together.

'Think he will?'

'Probably not.'

'Why?'

'Because he's agonizing over her marital status.'

'What?'

'Precisely.'

'Maybe we should leave them to it.'

'Sneak away you mean?'

'Yes.'

'Good idea, let's go.'

In deploying so, we hoped it would force the issue and she would take Mark home. The only concern was, would Mark remember to get back in time for the one thirty pm ferry? Getting back to the rooms Roger and I said good night, and he like me, no doubt secretly prayed that Mark was getting his end away this night. The chances were good at least. "Please God, please let him get laid." I silently pleaded .

Rousing six hours later around ten fifteen am, I was desperate to discover if Mark had succeeded. If he was in his room then no, but if not, then hallelujah. I knocked on his door.

'Mark?'

On hearing me Roger opened his door, open book in hand.

'Morning squire.'

'Morning; is he there?'

I knocked again.

'Mark?' No answer.

'Looks like he did it. Well done boy.'

As I walked back to my room we heard the dread sound of his door being unlocked and opening. He stepped out in his creased boxer shorts, eyes like a glinting chinaman.

'Whatssup?'

There being a slim chance he could have bought her back with him, I looked into his room but there was no sign of Cassie.

'Don't tell me you didn't do the business.'

'What business?'

'Cassie.'

'Who?'

'The American woman.'

'She had to go home.'

'You blew it.'

'I guess I did.'

'We set you up perfectly and everything.'

'I know.'

'You couldn't fail.'

'Does it matter?'

'No, but it would have been nice if you had come strolling back here this morning with a spring in your step, whistling zippitty-doo-dah. Don't you think?'

'Well I didn't.'

'Did you have a good time?'

'Yes.'

'Then that's all that counts. Hey Rog'?'

'Mark?'

'Yes?'

'You utter tit.'

All Over Bar the Return...

Sitting in the sun on the ferry back to Piraeus, it hardly seemed possible we were at an end with the holiday, but reality bites and the lovely island of Paros was slipping from view. Mark became fully engaged with a group of french people on the table next to us. His rusty francais no barrier to discourse across the cultures, and they were delighted by him, his fun personality shining bright. They were worldly farmers from Brittany, and little did they know I had been ready to kill him earlier that day for his truculence. I was fascinated by the undoubted rapport but understood little of what was spoken, as their english was like my french, non-existent. Mark did alarm and amuse them greatly a few times by his use of the wrong term, La chat for Le chat being one.

Reaching Piraeus we decided to hang out there at one of the bars in the port and waste two hours before catching the bus to the airport. Mark and Roger got into one of their battle of the wills, Roger teasing Mark mercilessly. Bored by it all I went for a walk; as I turned the corner of the complex and went a few meters I became suddenly aware of loud whistles and cheers, as if directed my way. I wasn't far wrong. The pavement bar to my left was full of men frantically waving to me. Either, I had stumbled upon Piraeus's welcoming committee for lonely tourists or I had found the headquarters of the local male prostitutes union. I suddenly knew what it was like to be a sexually attractive women passing by a group of spirited lads. Though I was flattering myself, after all, chances were they had services to sell and were advertising them in the best way they knew how.

Roger and Mark appeared a little dubious of my encounter; so Mark went to check it out for himself and came running back with a nervous look over his shoulder.

'What did I tell you?' I said.

'There's loads of them.'

'Did you find out how much they charge?' Asked Roger.

'No, I was going to leave that to you.'

'But you're so much better at it Mark.'

'Isn't it time we got going?' I intervened.

Sitting in the bar at the airport waiting for the call to depart, it struck me that Mark had been flashing the cash since we had left Paros and was currently in duty free, stocking up on two months worth of fags.

'Where's Mark been getting his money today?' I asked Roger.

'I advanced him two weeks rent.'

'You did?'

'What could I do, he kept on about it.'

'What's he going to live on the next four weeks?'

'Six you mean.'

'Six?'

'Yeah I'd already given him four weeks advance.'

'When?'

'Last week.'

'So did I.'

'He's got Greg's money I guess.'

'How long will that last and how's the gas and electric

to be paid?'

Roger put his hands up in the air and smirked. Suddenly, Mark

plonked four bags packed with cigarette cartons on the table.

'Who want's a beer?'

'Me.' Said Roger.

'Paul?'

'Go on then.'

He went to the counter and opened his wallet, checking and looking in

it for awhile, then came back to us.

'Can somebody lend me some money?'

Going through security, Mark's bag once again drew a red flag and he

was taken aside and searched. What could he possibly have packed this

time? That ornamental Greek dagger he'd been playing with in Lindos?

Or was it that large shiny steel cross he'd wanted in old Rhodes Town?.

No, it had to be the 9mm replica handgun that he had been coveting in

Paros. Logically, if it didn't fire real bullets then it was no use as a

hijacking tool was it? Oh, if only; no it was a souvenir from Paros. A

bottle opener ...with a built in corkscrew and knife.

'But it's for opening wine.'

The End (of the tail)